THE BEST OF
Sunset

Light & Healthy
Cook Book

By the Editors of Sunset Books and Sunset Magazine

Pepper, Pasta & Orange Salad (recipe on page 74)

Sunset Publishing Corporation ▪ Menlo Park, California

Research & Text
Tori Ritchie Bunting

Special Consultant
Patricia Kearney, R.D.
Clinical Dietitian,
Stanford University Hospital,
Stanford, California

Coordinating Editor
Deborah Thomas Kramer

Design
Joe di Chiarro

Illustrations
Guy Porfirio

Calligraphy
Sherry Bringham

Photo Styling
Susan Massey-Weil

Additional photo styling: Karen
Hazarian: 187, 194; JoAnn Masaoka
Van Atta: 42.

Photography
Kevin Sanchez

Additional photography: Victor Budnik:
187, 194; Peter Christiansen: 1, 111;
Darrow M. Watt: 70, 115; Tom Wyatt:
91, 99, 126, 170; Nikolay Zurek: 42, 46,
51, 78, 107, 151.

About the Recipes

All of the recipes in this book were
tested and developed in the *Sunset*
test kitchens.

Food & Entertaining Editor,
Sunset Magazine
Jerry Anne Di Vecchio

Front cover: Elegance and good nutrition
combine beautifully when you offer
Halibut with Tomatoes & Dill (recipe on
page 114), along with lightly steamed
potatoes, summer squash, and sugar snap
peas. Design by Susan Bryant. Photography by Kevin Sanchez. Photo styling by
Susan Massey-Weil. Food styling by Tori
Ritchie Bunting. Background by Lori
Hunter.

Back cover: Relax on a warm day with a
nutritious picnic—Tuscan Bean Salad
(recipe on page 73), Summer Sandwich
(recipe on page 53), fresh fruit, and lemonade. Photography by Kevin Sanchez.

Editor, Sunset Books: Elizabeth L. Hogan

Second printing November 1990

Foreword THE BASICS OF GREAT EATING

Good news! Light and healthy cooking is easier than ever before. You don't have to follow a rigorous regimen, nor do you have to give up your favorite foods. Just choose from a wide variety of fresh, wholesome ingredients, prepare them with a light touch, and then reap the rewards of great taste and good nutrition.

To begin, turn to the introduction, where you'll learn the basics of good nutrition, guidelines for building a balanced diet, and techniques for cooking light. Next, delve into our recipe section—you'll discover more than 220 dishes made with nutrient-dense ingredients, minimal fat and cholesterol, and increased fiber. From appetizers to desserts, there's something for every palate, plus great ideas for guilt-free snacks, wholesome sandwiches, seafood made in the microwave, and much more.

Since exercise is so important for physical fitness, we've devoted an entire chapter to ways in which you can incorporate both exercise and good nutrition into your everyday life. And for those special times when you need to prepare dinner ahead of time or you're entertaining family or friends, you'll discover a wealth of menu ideas sure to please the most discriminating guests. Finally, browse through the appendix—it's chock-full of nutritional information and guidelines designed to help you eat smarter than ever.

Whether you're shopping for food, preparing meals, or planning menus for the family, let this book guide you on a delicious new adventure in eating healthy, cooking light, and feeling great.

For our recipes we provide a nutritional analysis (see page 23) prepared by Hill Nutrition Associates, Inc., of Florida. We are grateful to Lynne Hill, R.D., for her advice and expertise.

We thank Fran Feldman for her skillful and careful editing of the text and Barbara Szerlip for her help with the manuscript. We also thank Dr. Frank I. Katch and Jim Mobley for sharing their expertise on exercise, Laurin Lynch and Christopher Coughlin for their valuable assistance with the photographs, and Cookin', Marmot Mountain Works, Fillamento, and Beaver Bros. Antiques for sharing props used in our photographs.

Contents

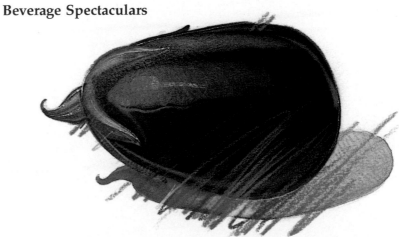

Eating Light & Healthy

Confused about what you should and should not be eating today? Baffled by all the information about diet and nutrition? Rest easy. Eating right isn't as complicated as it seems; what's important is getting back to basics. In this section, you'll learn the fundamentals of good nutrition, the facts on fiber and cholesterol, and the importance of exercise for a healthy lifestyle. Included are guidelines for planning healthy menus, for cooking with a light touch, and for choosing lowfat foods. Then you can turn to the hundreds of delicious, nutrient-rich recipes that follow. So start eating light and healthy today, and feel great about it!

For balanced nutrition in one easy recipe, try
Chicken-on-a-Stick with Couscous (recipe on page 101).
It combines lean poultry, a filling starch, and a lowfat yogurt
sauce for a deliciously healthy and captivating main course.
Cilantro leaves garnish the platter.

■ THE ABC'S OF NUTRITION

Why are we concerned about what we eat? An obvious answer is because it affects the way we look and feel. But more importantly, it's because food provides the nutrients we need to survive. Without the right balance of those nutrients, we may cause great harm to our bodies. Research has shown that a host of diseases and ailments, including obesity, heart disease, hypertension, diabetes, anemia, osteoporosis, and even cancer, can be affected by too much or too little of the right nutrients.

Below we discuss the life-giving nutrients—both caloric and noncaloric—and identify the foods in which they can be found.

Caloric Nutrients

Three nutrients in food—protein, carbohydrates, and fat—provide us with the energy we need to live. This energy is usually measured in calories (technically, kilocalories, or kcals). Whatever energy in foods we don't use right away is stored, usually in the form of body fat, for use later on.

Protein and carbohydrates each contain 4 calories per gram; fat contains more than twice as much—9 calories per gram. All three are considered vital because they promote the growth, maintenance, and repair of body cells.

■

Three vital nutrients provide calories: protein, carbohydrates, and fat. Protein and carbohydrates each have 4 calories per gram; fat contains 9 calories per gram.

■

Protein. Muscles, both our own and those of animals, are composed of protein. Ask anyone to name a high-protein food and the answer will probably be beef.

But protein doesn't come exclusively from animal flesh, nor is it used just to build muscles. In addition to building new tissue and repairing damaged tissue, the body utilizes protein to maintain proper fluid balance, to fight infection, to clot blood, to help transport other nutrients, and to develop bones, teeth, hair, and nails.

Chemically, protein is composed of a string of amino acids. Twenty-two amino acids are vital to human nutrition; of those, nine are essential, meaning that the human body doesn't manufacture or synthesize them on its own, so the only way to get them is from food.

Proteins from animal sources (meat, poultry, fish, dairy products, and eggs) contain all nine essential amino acids and are considered complete proteins. Proteins from such plant sources as grains, legumes, nuts and seeds, and vegetables, however, contain incomplete amounts of one or more of the essential amino acids; to form complete proteins, they should be eaten in complementary combinations.

One of the most common misconceptions about protein is that we need to eat a lot of it. Many people, in fact, eat far more protein than they need, usually in the form of fatty meats that are also high in calories, saturated fat, and cholesterol. Some aspiring athletes believe that the more protein they consume, the greater their muscle bulk will be. But protein isn't just deposited into muscles, and excess protein is converted into fat. Also, overconsumption of protein can strain the kidneys and interfere with the body's absorption of certain minerals, including calcium.

Many health professionals recommend that protein compose about 15% of total caloric intake. To determine just how much protein you need to consume, consult the Recommended Dietary Allowances (RDA) on page 222. Then choose your protein sources carefully, remembering that lean meat or nonmeat protein will reduce the amount of cholesterol and fat in your diet. Also, strive for variation; with the diverse protein sources available, the culinary possibilities are many.

Carbohydrates. In many ways, carbohydrates, the main source of energy in our diet, are the easiest of the nutrients to understand and identify. Most of us can readily name foods that contain them: breads, pasta, and potatoes come quickly to mind. But carbohydrates are also found in grains, legumes, fruits, vegetables, and milk products (the only animal source).

What is less well known is that there are two classes of carbohydrates: sugars, or *simple carbohydrates*, and starches, or *complex carbohydrates*. Both are found naturally in foods; the difference is in their molecular structure. Sugars, such as sucrose, lactose, and fructose, are composed of one or two sugar molecules; starches are many sugars linked together. The two are digested differently; because complex carbohydrates must be broken down into simple sugars, they take longer to be absorbed into the bloodstream than simple carbohydrates. As a result, sugars are quickly converted to energy, while starches sustain energy and leave you feeling sated longer.

Complex carbohydrates are very nutritious. They're found in foods that generally contain lots of water (corn, a very high carbohydrate food, is 74% water), as well as vitamins, minerals, some protein, and only a trace of fat. Most importantly, complex carbohydrates are a good source of dietary fiber. (The subject of much recent attention, fiber is discussed in detail on page 13.)

Refined sugar has been maligned over the years as being "bad for you." However, most of the accusations leveled at sugar are largely unfounded; its main sin is that it contributes calories without any nutrients, and excess calories—no matter what the source—can cause weight gain. The only proven health threat from sugar is tooth decay. All refined sugars (white, brown, honey, or otherwise) are equally at fault.

Another myth worth dispelling is that carbohydrates are fattening. Actually, per gram they contain less than half the calories of fat. However, eating an excess of foods containing processed or refined sugars and starches depleted of most of their nutritional value can result in unnecessary weight gain.

Dietitians and health organizations recommend that about 55% of our total caloric intake come from carbohydrates. Complex carbohydrates, in all their varied and delicious forms, should compose a far greater portion of this intake than sugars, which should comprise no more than 10% of total calories (we currently consume about twice as much refined sugar as we should). This shift will result in better nutrition, more lasting energy, and added fiber.

Fat. It seems that the more we know about fat and its role in our diet, the more we fear it. Excessive consumption of fat has been linked to obesity, heart disease, and cancer. While it's true that we need to be selective about the type of fat we consume and limit the total amount, it's also true that fat is vital to our health: it helps maintain cell viability and transports fat-soluble vitamins (discussed on page 10). And from a culinary standpoint, fat gives many foods their enticing flavor and aroma.

Fat is either *saturated* or *unsaturated*. Unsaturated fat is further classified as *monounsaturated* or *polyunsaturated*. Depending on the kind of fat present in largest proportion, a food fat, such as margarine or oil, will be labeled saturated, monounsaturated, or polyunsaturated.

Saturated fats are usually solid at room temperature; the higher the saturation, the harder they get. They're found in highest concentration in such animal products as whole milk, cream, butter, whole milk cheeses, ice cream, lard, and red meat. Poultry and seafood also contain saturated fat, but in lesser amounts.

Saturated fats, which elevate blood cholesterol levels even more than dietary cholesterol does, should comprise no more than a third of total fat calories.

Some vegetable fats, the so-called tropical oils—coconut oil, palm kernel oil, palm oil, and cocoa butter—are also highly saturated. And when hydrogen is added to vegetable oils to make them solid or semisolid at room temperature, such as with margarine and shortening (a process called hydrogenation), they become even more saturated.

Monounsaturated and polyunsaturated fats are mostly of plant origin and are generally liquid at room temperature. Monounsaturated fats include olive, canola (rapeseed), peanut, and avocado oils. Corn, safflower, sunflower, sesame, and cottonseed oils are polyunsaturated.

From a dietary standpoint, saturated fats have been shown to elevate blood cholesterol levels; unsaturated fats seem to lower them. Polyunsaturates may lower both high-density lipoproteins (HDL), or "good cholesterol," and low-density lipoproteins (LDL), the "bad cholesterol." Monounsaturates may lower only LDL.

Recently, attention has focused on polyunsaturated omega-3 fatty acids, which have been shown to be beneficial in reducing the risk of high blood pressure and blood clots. Found in highest concentration in such fatty fish as mackerel, sardines, salmon, and tuna, omega-3s are also present in other fish and shellfish, canola oil, and the green vegetable purslane. By substituting fish for meat in your diet a few times a week, you'll reap the benefits of omega-3s and, at the same time, reduce your intake of cholesterol and cholesterol-raising fat. Note that fish oil supplements are not a substitute for consuming these valuable fats from their natural sources.

Another important dietary reason to limit fat intake is weight gain. Simply put, fat is more "fattening" than protein or carbohydrates: it contains 9 calories per gram compared with 4 calories per gram for protein and carbohydrates. Also, dietary fat is converted more easily than carbohydrates into body fat.

Health experts recommend that total fat intake be limited to no more than 30% of total calories and that saturated fat intake should be limited to no more than a third of total fat calories. By reducing fat intake and compensating for this calorie deficit by eating more fruits, vegetables, and grains, you'll be increasing your intake of valuable vitamins, minerals, and fiber, too. You can actually eat greater quantities of carbohydrates and still maintain your weight. If you're trying to lose weight, limiting fat cuts down on the most concentrated source of calories in your diet. (For tips on cutting fat from your diet, turn to page 27.)

Noncaloric Nutrients

The other nutrients essential for survival are vitamins, minerals, and water. Because they don't contain calories—and thus don't add energy—they're called noncaloric. Of all the nutrients, both caloric and noncaloric, water is the one we need in the greatest amounts. On the other hand, the body requires only small amounts of vitamins and minerals.

Vitamins. The word "vitamin" comes from *vita*, which means life, and *amine*, which means nitrogen-containing. Each of the 13 vitamins plays a different role in nutrition.

Vitamins are categorized as either *water soluble* or *fat soluble*. This classification helps explain the kinds of foods that contain them and how the body absorbs, transports, and gets rid of them. The individual RDA for vitamins are listed on page 222.

■ *Water-soluble vitamins.* Found in the watery parts of food, the water-soluble vitamins, B and C, are carried in the body's bloodstream. Because they're quickly depleted, they must be replenished every day.

When initially discovered, *vitamin B* was thought to be one substance. Since then, eight B vitamins have been identified: thiamin, riboflavin, B6, niacin, folacin, B12, biotin, and pantothenic acid. Each one plays an important role in metabolizing food. Though rare, deficiencies in any of the B vitamins can lead to health complications, the best

known being beriberi (caused by a deficiency of thiamin). Any deficiency can be corrected by consuming foods rich in the necessary B vitamin.

Because the B vitamins are found in varying amounts in almost all foods—vegetables, whole grains, legumes, meats, poultry, fish, eggs, dairy products, and brewer's yeast—eating a balanced diet is the best defense against any deficiency.

Vitamin C played an historic role in eliminating scurvy among sailors in the 18th century. Since vitamins were not then understood, the substance was called antiscorbic (literally, "against scurvy"), later shortened to ascorbic acid.

Vitamins, minerals, and water don't contain calories, but they're still considered nutrients because they're vital for human nutrition.

Besides protecting against disease, vitamin C helps form the protein collagen, acts as an antioxidant (it defends other substances in the body from oxygen destruction), and may even help prevent cancer in cigarette smokers. It also aids in the absorption of iron and calcium.

To ensure that you're getting an adequate amount of vitamin C, include fresh fruits and vegetables on the menu daily. Good sources of vitamin C are bell peppers, strawberries, tomatoes, citrus, parsley, broccoli, and asparagus.

■ *Fat-soluble vitamins.* Unlike vitamins B and C, the fat-soluble vitamins—A, D, E, and K—are stored longer in the body and aren't flushed out daily. In foods, they're carried with the fats and may be whisked away when the fat is removed. That's the reason that nonfat milk, for example, has to be fortified (vitamins A and D are put back in).

Vitamin A is known primarily for promoting good vision. It's also essential for healthy skin, bones, and teeth, and for a variety of nerve, cell, and blood functions. Much of the vitamin A we eat comes in the form of beta-carotene in fruits and vegetables; our body then converts it to vitamin A. It's also found in a retinol compound in foods from animal sources.

The nutritional term used to measure amounts of vitamin A is retinol equivalent, or RE. Thus, the U.S. RDA for vitamin A is expressed as 1,000 RE per day. (Some listings still use the older term of international unit, or IU. IU figures for vitamin A are roughly 5 times greater than RE; this would make the U. S. RDA equivalent to about 5,000 IU.)

The best sources of vitamin A are dark, leafy greens and deep yellow or orange vegetables. Milk, eggs, liver, apricots, cantaloupe, mangoes, and papayas also contribute significant amounts.

Vitamin D works in conjunction with calcium (a mineral) to build strong bones. It's unique among the nutrients because it can be synthesized from sunlight; however, most people don't get enough sun to meet their needs. A deficiency of vitamin D can cause rickets, or soft bones, in children.

Eggs, liver, and some fish supply vitamin D, but our primary source is milk, fortified with extra vitamin D to ensure that we consume a sufficient amount of this crucial nutrient.

Like vitamin C, *vitamin E* is an antioxidant, protecting lipids (fats in the body) and certain cells from oxygen damage. Most of the vitamin E in our diet comes from vegetable oils and margarines, but small amounts are also present in many fresh foods.

Lesser-known *vitamin K* is crucial for blood coagulation; a deficiency may cause hemorrhaging. It also works with vitamin D to regulate blood calcium. Liver, leafy green vegetables, cabbage, egg yolks, and milk all contain vitamin K.

Minerals. The foods we eat contain numerous minerals, all of which contribute to good nutrition. Three of the most common ones—calcium, iron, and sodium—are discussed here. Both calcium and iron have RDA designations. Although there's no RDA for it, sodium is an important—though controversial—mineral in its own right.

■ *Calcium.* Most people know that calcium, important for building strong bones and teeth, is derived chiefly from milk and other dairy products. What is less well known is how difficult it is to meet our daily calcium requirement. As a result, calcium deficiencies are widespread. If you know an elderly woman who has recently broken her hip, chances are she didn't get enough calcium in her younger years. The message is clear: We need to eat sufficient amounts of calcium-rich foods at an early age and all through adulthood to prevent serious bone deterioration. (Exercise can also be helpful in preventing osteoporosis, or brittle bones.)

Drinking a few glasses of milk every day is an excellent way to meet your body's calcium needs; opt for lowfat or nonfat varieties for fewer calories, less saturated fat, and slightly more calcium per serving than whole milk. Cheese, buttermilk, yogurt, canned sardines and salmon with bones, oysters, broccoli, spinach, collards, and mustard greens also contain appreciable amounts of calcium.

■ *Iron.* Considered a trace mineral, iron is present in minute quantities in the human body, yet no substitute will perform its vital functions. Even though it's needed only in small amounts, iron deficiencies are common, especially in women. The number one problem resulting from insufficient iron is anemia, a loss of hemoglobin in red blood cells.

With some careful choices in your diet, you can absorb enough iron from the foods you eat to stay healthy. Meat, liver, fish, and poultry are superior sources of iron. Other sources include spinach, lima beans, dried apricots, oysters, split peas, blackstrap molasses, and prune juice. Vitamin C greatly enhances the body's absorption of iron.

■ *Sodium.* Sodium works with potassium, another mineral, to maintain the right balance of bodily fluids; this, in turn, impacts blood pressure and kidney functions. Although mainly associated with salt, sodium occurs naturally in many foods. Often, it's added to processed foods, with the result that many people consume far more sodium than they actually need.

While a certain amount of sodium in the diet is crucial, an excess can cause hypertension or high blood pressure in sodium-sensitive people. Health professionals recommend different daily intakes of sodium. About 3,000 milligrams a day is considered a safe range for people not sensitive to salt.

Water. What's a discussion of water doing in a book about food? Because 60% of our body weight is composed of water, we need more of this nutrient than any other—2,000 to 3,000 grams (about 2 to 3 quarts) a day, compared to only about 50 grams of protein. Also remember that

> ■———————————————————
> # W
> ater is as important to good health as a balanced diet.
> ———————————————————■

water is constantly being lost through perspiration and excretion; therefore, we need to replenish the supply regularly.

Although most of our water needs are met by the food and beverages we consume, drinking 6 to 8 glasses of cool, clear water each day will greatly enhance health, keep waste systems running, and prevent dehydration and its many complications. *In fact, drinking lots of water is as important to good health as adhering to a balanced diet.*

Take your pick! A light and healthy diet includes an array of fresh fruits and vegetables, a variety of high-carbohydrate grains, legumes, breads, and pastas, and a selection of lean meats, poultry, seafood, and lowfat dairy products. There's variety enough to please every palate.

■ THE FACTS ON FIBER & CHOLESTEROL

Both fiber and cholesterol are in the forefront of nutritional concern because of studies showing that they have a significant impact on our health.

Fiber. Friend or fantasy? With so many overstated claims about fiber, it's easy to get confused. But dietary fiber—plant material that passes undigested through the human intestine—is believed to offer some very real health benefits. These include preventing constipation, protecting against certain cancers, lowering blood cholesterol, and improving the control of blood sugar levels in diabetics.

Although the list of claims is very impressive, bear in mind that fiber cannot achieve miracle cures. Moreover, it's beneficial only when eaten as part of a prudent, balanced diet. Also, excessive fiber can cause severe gastrointestinal side effects and can interfere with the body's absorption of iron and other nutrients.

The different kinds of fiber—all of which are found only in plant foods—are divided into two groups: *soluble* and *insoluble*. Many foods contain both kinds, but one usually predominates.

Soluble fiber has been found to lower blood cholesterol levels. The best sources of this type of fiber are oats, legumes, barley, apples, carrots, and citrus. Insoluble fiber, found in wheat bran, whole wheat, other whole grains, fruits, and vegetables, has no effect on blood cholesterol, but it contributes bulk ("roughage") and is very effective in preventing and relieving constipation. It may also play a role in preventing colorectal cancers.

Although the full benefits of fiber are still not known, health experts recommend that the average person consume 25 to 35 grams of fiber (both soluble and insoluble) a day. If you're like most people, you're probably not getting enough fiber in your diet. Eating more whole grains, breads, cereals, fresh fruits, vegetables, and legumes, and fewer processed foods, will help increase your fiber intake.

Cholesterol. Cholesterol is a waxy, fatlike substance used, among other things, for the synthesis of vitamins and hormones and the formation of nerve sheaths and cell membranes. The body (specifically, the liver) can manufacture enough cholesterol to meet its needs; there's no need to consume any at all. However, every time we eat foods of animal origin—meat, fish, poultry, eggs, and dairy products—we're consuming what's called dietary cholesterol. (Plant foods contain *no* cholesterol.)

As the body metabolizes cholesterol, it enters the bloodstream. The higher a person's blood cholesterol level, the greater the chances are of developing heart disease. (Of course, other factors also increase the risk of heart attack, including high blood pressure, smoking, obesity, diabetes, vascular disease, a family history of heart disease, and simply being male.)

Cholesterol is carried through the blood in protein packages called lipoproteins. Low-density lipoproteins (LDL) carry the cholesterol that's deposited in the arteries; thus, they're often labeled "bad cholesterol." High-density lipoproteins (HDL), the so-called "good cholesterol," help sweep cholesterol away from artery walls and deliver it to the liver for elimination.

■

The body can survive on the cholesterol it makes; no cholesterol from food is required.

■

In general, the lower the level of total blood cholesterol and LDL and the higher the level of HDL, the better. Most health experts consider a total blood cholesterol reading of 240 milligrams or more per deciliter of blood to be high, 200 to 239 borderline-high, and less than 200 desirable. (If you're concerned about your cholesterol level, have your blood tested by a physician. Although high cholesterol can be dangerous for people of all ages, risk factors vary from person to person.)

There's no RDA for dietary cholesterol. However, the National Cholesterol Education Program, the American Heart Association, and numerous federal health agencies recommend a daily intake of no more than 300 milligrams. Equally important is your intake of saturated fats, which contribute to raising blood cholesterol levels even more than dietary cholesterol does.

Many foods high in cholesterol (red meat and whole milk dairy products, for example) are also high in saturated fats. But note that some cholesterol-free foods, such as tropical oils (coconut oil, palm oil, palm kernel oil, and cocoa butter) and hydrogenated fats, are also highly saturated.

To limit your intake of cholesterol, plan your menus around lowfat, high-carbohydrate recipes, such as the ones in this book, and choose lean meats, poultry, and seafood (see the charts on pages 84, 100, and 116 for detailed cholesterol breakdowns). Also, become familiar with the American Heart Association diet plan (see pages 224–225).

■ BUILDING A BALANCED DIET

It may be age-old advice, but it's still the best: eat a balanced diet. The hard part is knowing what "balanced" means. The nutrients required by the body are discussed on pages 8–11. In this section, you'll learn how to build a diet that guarantees you'll get sufficient amounts of those essential nutrients. (For a week of menus that reflect the correct balance of nutrients, turn to pages 16–19.)

The only way to achieve a balanced diet is to eat a variety of foods in moderation. By following the four food groups plan, which helps you select the right combination of foods, and the Dietary Guidelines, which provide a framework for moderate consumption, you can meet your RDA for vital nutrients and maintain good health.

The four food groups. Whether you first learned about them in elementary school or noticed a food chart on your pediatrician's wall, the food groups have been around long enough for many people to have grown up with them. The chart shown on the facing page divides foods into four groups—milk and milk products, meat and meat alternatives, fruits and vegetables, and grains, breads, and cereals. Each group has been assigned a recommended number of servings per day.

The variety of foods and the exchange potential within each food group allow for a lot of flexibility, including building a healthy nonmeat diet. Use the food groups as a planning tool for designing balanced daily menus.

The Dietary Guidelines. The food groups plan ensures that your diet will contain adequate nutrients. The Dietary Guidelines, issued by the U. S. Departments of Agriculture and Health and Human Services, help you avoid consuming *too much* of certain things: they stress moderation. Because the number one diet problem in this country is excess, not deprivation, these guidelines are especially important:

- Eat a variety of foods.
- Maintain desirable weight.
- Avoid too much fat, saturated fat, and cholesterol.
- Eat foods with adequate starch and fiber.
- Avoid too much sugar.
- Avoid too much sodium.
- If you drink alcoholic beverages, do so in moderation.

■ *Eat a variety of foods.* Because no single food can supply all the nutrients your body needs, the key to a balanced diet is to choose a healthy variety of foods. That goal is ensured by the four food groups plan. Variety also makes planning menus more interesting and mealtimes more enjoyable.

■ *Maintain desirable weight.* Although weight maintenance is not the focus of this book, it's very important for good health. Most people gain weight in only one way—from eating more calories than they expend. Substituting high-carbohydrate foods for high-fat foods is a good way to reduce total calories. Adopting a safe exercise program (see pages 20–22) is also crucial to weight maintenance.

■ *Avoid too much fat, saturated fat, and cholesterol.* The importance of adhering to this guideline cannot be overstated. An excess of fat, especially saturated fat, in the diet is a major cause of heart disease. Experts recommend limiting total fat intake to 30% or less of total calories, and saturated fat to a third or less of total fat calories. (Currently, it's believed that Americans consume from 36% to 42% of their total calories in fat.)

Too much dietary cholesterol can result in elevated levels of blood cholesterol, which is linked to heart disease (for more on cholesterol, see page 13). Health professionals recommend limiting cholesterol intake to no more than 300 milligrams a day.

For help in reducing the amount of fat and cholesterol in your diet, see page 27.

■ *Eat foods with adequate starch and fiber.* To increase your intake of starch and fiber, you'll need to eat more complex carbohydrates (grains, legumes, breads, and cereals), vegetables, and fruits. Ideally, carbohydrates should compose about 55% of total calories. Complex carbohydrates provide concentrated energy, leave you feeling fuller, and are low in fat, relatively low in calories (4 per gram), and high in vitamins and minerals.

Both soluble and insoluble fiber offer health benefits. The average person should consume 25 to 35 grams a day. For more on fiber, see page 13.

■ *Avoid too much sugar.* Sugar, a simple carbohydrate, causes tooth decay, adds calories without any nutrients, and often plays a major role in weight gain. Limit sugar intake to 10% of your total calories by replacing sugary foods with nutrient-dense foods, such as fresh fruit and whole grain breads and cereals. When purchasing processed food, read the label carefully to determine the amount of sugar the food contains (for help, see page 223).

■ *Avoid too much sodium.* While some sodium in the diet is essential, an excess may contribute to high blood pressure in certain people. Even if you're not salt-sensitive, it's wise to limit your sodium intake to about 3,000 milligrams a day.

As with sugar, pay attention to food labels: many processed foods contain very high levels of sodium. When possible, buy low-sodium products.

■ *If you drink alcoholic beverages, do so in moderation.* Like sugar, alcohol adds no nutrients to your diet; its calories (7 per gram) are often referred to as empty calories. For this reason, it can throw off a balanced diet.

Alcohol has other health implications. Consumed in excess, it can cause fatal damage to the liver (the only organ that can process it), as well as the disruption of other physical and mental functions. Nutritionally, it's important to be aware of alcohol's contribution to your daily caloric intake and use it only in moderation.

■ The Four Food Groups

In this table of the basic food groups, the number of recommended servings is based on the needs of normal adults; children, teenagers, and pregnant and nursing women have specific dietary needs that should be addressed by a dietitian or physician. Fats are not included here; for information on how much fat to eat each day, see the Dietary Guidelines on the facing page.

MILK & MILK PRODUCTS*

2 servings per day

Milk (1 cup)
Cheese, hard (1¼ oz.)
Cottage cheese (2 cups)
Yogurt, plain (1 cup)
Buttermilk (1 cup)

*To cut back on fat intake, choose lowfat or nonfat varieties when possible.

MEAT & MEAT ALTERNATIVES

2 servings per day

Meat, lean (2 to 3 cooked oz.)
Poultry (2 to 3 cooked oz.)
Fish (2 to 3 cooked oz.)
Eggs (2)*
Cheese, hard (2 oz.)
Cottage cheese (½ cup)
Dried peas or beans (1 cup cooked)
Peanut butter (4 tablespoons)
Nuts and seeds (½ cup)
Tofu (1 cup)

*The American Heart Association recommends limiting your intake to 4 eggs per week.

FRUITS & VEGETABLES*

4 servings per day

Apple, banana, orange, pear, tomato (1 medium-size)
Grapefruit (½ medium-size)
Melon (½ medium-size)
Potato, sweet potato (1 medium-size)
Vegetables, cut up (½ cup)
Fruits, cut up (½ cup)
Salad greens (1 cup)
Vegetable/fruit juices (½ cup)

*Category includes fresh, frozen, and canned.

GRAINS, BREADS & CEREALS*

4 servings per day

Bread (1 slice)
Bagel (½ of 3-inch diameter)
Cooked cereal (½ to ¾ cup)
Dry cereal (1 oz.)
Pasta (½ to ¾ cup cooked)
Rice (½ to ¾ cup cooked)
Pita bread (½ of 6-inch diameter)
Dinner roll (1 oz.)
Tortilla (7-inch diameter)

*To obtain adequate fiber, choose whole grain varieties when possible.

Eating a balanced diet doesn't mean adhering to a grueling regimen of lackluster foods. In this section, we've put together suggestions for a week's worth of menus to prove that you can eat a varied, normal diet and still achieve good nutrition.

The suggestions in these menus include single servings of recipes from this book, dishes that don't require a recipe to prepare, and purchased prepared food. Daily consumption averages about 1,800 calories over a week's time. (For help in calculating what your own daily caloric intake should be, see pages 226–227.)

If you need to increase daily calories to meet your personal needs, turn to the charts on pages 228–235; they'll help you select recipes that add the necessary calories and nutrients. To reduce calories, follow the suggestions given with each menu. You can also choose lowfat (1%) or nonfat milk.

On average, total calories are distributed as follows: about 15% from protein, about 55% from carbohydrates (about 10% from simple sugars), and 30% or less from fat (no more than a third of those from saturated fat). Daily consumption includes no more than 300 milligrams of cholesterol, no more than 3,000 milligrams of sodium, and at least 25 to 35 grams of dietary fiber. (Those are the amounts recommended by various health organizations for normal, healthy adults.)

Saturday represents a splurge day: although the fat, calorie, and cholesterol totals for the day exceed the limits, they balance out over the whole week. It's important to remember that this is only an occasional indulgence.

In addition to the suggested beverages, be sure to drink a lot of water every day. Coffee or tea is optional; opt for decaffeinated blends, if possible, and use lowfat or nonfat milk instead of cream.

Finally, in keeping with your goal to pursue a light and healthy lifestyle, try to burn at least 300 calories a day in some form of physical activity. (For information on exercising to keep fit, see page 20.)

Start your day—and the week—with a nutritious breakfast. For lunch, an easy meatless sandwich and salad add vital nutrients. Lean lamb chops are the centerpiece of a home-cooked dinner; serve them with crusty whole wheat bread to add fiber. To reduce total calories, eliminate the bacon for breakfast and the dessert at dinner.

BREAKFAST

Banana-Oatmeal Pancakes with Warm Applesauce (page 34)

1 large orange

1 slice Canadian bacon, cooked with no oil

Tea or coffee (optional)

LUNCH

Eggplant, Radish & Cucumber Sandwiches (page 53)

1 cup cold cooked broccoli sprinkled with 1 teaspoon *each* reduced-sodium soy sauce and sesame oil

1 medium-size apricot

1 cup lowfat (2%) milk

SNACK

1 medium-size banana

DINNER

Lamb Chops with Papaya Chutney (page 92)

½ cup *each* steamed zucchini and red bell pepper seasoned with 1 teaspoon lemon juice

2 slices whole wheat Italian bread with 2 teaspoons margarine

1 cup lowfat (2%) milk

Minted Poached Pears (page 186)

Sparkling mineral water with lemon slice

■ *Totals for day: 15% protein, 60% carbohydrates, 25% total fat; 1,813 calories, 72 g protein, 286 g carbohydrates, 51 g total fat (14 g saturated fat), 152 mg cholesterol, 35 g dietary fiber, 1,791 mg sodium*

Monday

It's back to work and a quick breakfast is the choice for convenience. Bring the sandwich from home; or purchase a Greek salad (made with minimal feta cheese and 1 tablespoon of dressing) and eat whole wheat pita bread alongside. At the end of the day, return home to a delicious chicken dinner. Omit the dessert if you want to cut down on total calories.

BREAKFAST

Fruit Muesli (page 30) topped with
½ cup *each* plain lowfat yogurt and
sliced fresh strawberries

1 cup freshly squeezed orange juice

Tea or coffee (optional)

LUNCH

Greek Salad Pockets (page 53)

1 medium-size apple

Sparkling mineral water or low-calorie
beverage

SNACK

2 high-fiber crispbreads

1 cup lowfat (2%) milk

DINNER

Oven-fried Chicken (page 98)

Spiced Bulgur with Apple (page 156)

1 cup cooked sliced carrots seasoned
with 1 tablespoon margarine and dry
tarragon leaves

Crazy Cocoa Cake (page 193)

Sparkling mineral water with lemon slice

■ *Totals for day:* 17% protein, 58% carbohydrates, 25% total fat; 1,710 calories, 76 g protein, 253 g carbohydrates, 49 g total fat (12 g saturated fat), 125 mg cholesterol, 26 g dietary fiber, 1,770 mg sodium

Tuesday

A simple breakfast gets the day off to a relaxed start. Lunch is easy to fix at home; or purchase a comparable substitute. For dinner, offer an iron-rich seafood entrée. For fewer total calories, omit the soup at dinner.

BREAKFAST

½ pink grapefruit

Homestead Bran Muffin (page 32)

1 cup unsweetened apple juice

Tea or coffee (optional)

LUNCH

Quesadillas made with 2 six-inch corn
tortillas topped with 3 tablespoons *total*
shredded Cheddar cheese and cooked in 2
teaspoons margarine; served with ½ cup
shredded looseleaf lettuce and ¼ cup salsa

1 medium-size pear

1 cup lowfat (2%) milk

SNACK

4 rice cakes with 2 teaspoons unsalted
peanut butter

DINNER

Caribbean Corn Chowder (page 57).

Oyster Jambalaya (page 127)

½ cup cooked fresh spinach seasoned with
1 teaspoon olive oil

1 cup sliced fresh peaches with ¼ cup
vanilla lowfat yogurt and 1 tablespoon
sliced almonds

Sparkling mineral water with lemon slice

■ *Totals for day:* 13% protein, 60% carbohydrates, 27% total fat; 1,857 calories, 65 g protein, 288 g carbohydrates, 59 g total fat (15 g saturated fat), 129 mg cholesterol, 28 g dietary fiber, 1,892 mg sodium

Wednesday

Breakfast today consists of a bowl of hot oatmeal, followed by a substantial meatless lunch. For dinner, offer a delicious beef dish and lots of leafy greens. To reduce calories, omit the sandwich at lunchtime.

BREAKFAST

⅔ cup cooked oatmeal with ½ cup lowfat (2%) milk, ¼ cup raisins, and 1 medium-size banana, sliced

1 cup unsweetened grapefruit juice

Tea or coffee (optional)

LUNCH

Winter Minestrone (page 58) or purchased low-sodium minestrone soup

Vegetarian sandwich made with ½ medium-size avocado, sliced; 2 slices (1 oz.) tomato; 1 romaine lettuce leaf; and 2 teaspoons reduced-calorie mayonnaise on 2 slices whole wheat bread

3 dried apricot halves

1 cup lowfat (2%) milk

DINNER

Chile Beef Stir-fry on Mixed Greens (page 82)

½ cup cooked brown rice

Lemon-Garlic Swiss Chard (page 172)

½ cantaloupe filled with ½ cup fresh raspberries

Sparkling mineral water with lime slice

■ *Totals for day: 16% protein, 58% carbohydrates, 26% total fat; 1,712 calories, 70 g protein, 262 g carbohydrates, 51 g total fat (14 g saturated fat), 102 mg cholesterol, 29 g dietary fiber, 1,406 mg sodium*

Thursday

Wake up to a delicious high-fiber scone, sweetened with a little margarine and low-sugar jam. Calcium-rich canned salmon is featured for lunch. A meatless dinner based on high-protein alternatives is a good way to reduce your intake of fat and cholesterol. If you're concerned about total calories, skip the almonds at lunch and the dessert at dinner.

BREAKFAST

Apricot–Oat Bran Scone (page 182) with 1 teaspoon margarine and 1 tablespoon reduced-calorie jam

1 cup stewed fruit, such as prunes, Kadota figs, or plums, seasoned with cinnamon

1 cup lowfat (2%) milk

Tea or coffee (optional)

LUNCH

Dilly Salmon on Dark Rye (page 54)

1 ounce unsalted whole almonds

1 large orange

Sparkling mineral water or low-calorie beverage

SNACK

1 cup cut-up raw vegetables, such as carrots, celery, jicama, and cucumbers

¼ cup Curried Spinach Dip (page 41)

DINNER

Spinach & Tofu Manicotti (page 142)

Red & Yellow Pepper Salad (page 69)

Bulgur Wheat Roll (page 178) with 1 teaspoon margarine

Angel Food Cake (page 192)

Sparkling mineral water with lime slice

■ *Totals for day: 16% protein, 59% carbohydrates, 25% total fat; 1,769 calories, 74 g protein, 269 g carbohydrates, 52 g total fat (12 g saturated fat), 99 mg cholesterol, 29 g dietary fiber, 2,119 mg sodium*

Friday

Today's menu features fewer calories and less cholesterol than any of the other menus. Begin on a high-fiber, high-calcium note with a filling breakfast of cereal along with cottage cheese on toast. Pasta salad made at home is a light lunch choice. Dinner is special enough for guests.

BREAKFAST

½ cup 100% bran cereal with ½ cup lowfat (2%) milk

Cottage Cheese & Tomato Breakfast Stack (page 52)

1 cup low-calorie cranberry juice

Tea or coffee (optional)

LUNCH

Pepper, Pasta & Orange Salad (page 74)

1 cup fresh cherries or grapes

1 cup lowfat (2%) milk

DINNER

Dilled Roughy in Parchment (page 123)

½ cup steamed Chinese pea pods seasoned with 1 teaspoon sesame oil

¼ pound steamed small red thin-skinned potatoes with 1 teaspoon margarine

Papaya Snow (page 189)

Sparkling mineral water with lime slice

■ *Totals for day: 17% protein, 56% carbohydrates, 27% total fat; 1,408 calories, 66 g protein, 210 g carbohydrates, 45 g total fat (9 g saturated fat), 63 mg cholesterol, 29 g dietary fiber, 1,097 mg sodium*

Saturday

Dinner tonight is a splurge, representing what you might eat once in a while, especially if dining out. Although the totals exceed the goals for fat, cholesterol, and calories, moderate consumption on other days of the week compensates for the higher figures. Just don't indulge like this very often!

BREAKFAST

1 poached egg on a toasted whole wheat English muffin

⅔ cup cooked shredded potatoes

1 cup orange juice from concentrate

Tea or coffee (optional)

LUNCH

Vegetable Taco Roll-ups (page 54)

1 cup fresh fruit salad, such as cubed melon, sliced strawberries, grapes, and chopped, unpeeled apple

Sparkling mineral water or low-calorie beverage

DINNER

½ cup shredded butterhead lettuce with 3 tablespoons Roquefort dressing and 2 tablespoons croutons

Broiled 4-ounce sirloin steak

Baked potato topped with 1 tablespoon sour cream and 1 teaspoon chopped chives

¾ cup steamed mixed vegetables

2 slices garlic bread

1 slice apple pie

4-ounce glass red wine

■ *Totals for day: 15% protein, 54% carbohydrates, 31% total fat; 2,203 calories, 83 g protein, 293 g carbohydrates, 73 g total fat (26 g saturated fat), 378 mg cholesterol, 26 g dietary fiber, 2,622 mg sodium*

■ EXERCISE: THE KEY TO FITNESS

Keeping fit involves more than just what you put into your body. The energy you put out directly affects your health, too. That's why regular exercise is so important. Of course, any activity at any level burns calories; but to become truly fit, you need to work at your endurance level, or target heart rate, on a regular basis.

Why be fit? Study after study has shown that physically active people have more stamina and manage their weight better than sedentary people. Other proven health benefits include increased HDL ("good cholesterol"), decreased heart disease, reduced blood pressure, and buildup of bone mass (helpful in minimizing the debilitating effects of osteoporosis).

Harder to prove, but widely recognized, is the fact that exercise makes you feel good; people who exercise regularly report that it relieves stress, helps them relax and sleep better, and even boosts their self-esteem.

The best news is that you don't have to be a serious athlete to reap the health rewards of exercise. In fact, scientific evidence shows that people who move just one level up from sedentary—by taking a brisk walk for just 30 to 60 minutes a day—make substantial gains on the road to fitness. To start, all you need to do is get moving; then keep it up, gently pushing yourself to higher levels of exertion.

It's easy to be fit. Various health organizations recommend that every person burn *at least 300 calories a day* in some form of physical activity. Fortunately, this doesn't mean that you have to race around a track, cycle up a mountain road, or swim a couple of miles every day. While all those activities are wonderful for people who are in shape for them, the truth is that it's easy and painless to burn 300 calories a day. An average (150-lb.) adult walking at a brisk pace (3 to 3.5 miles per hour) for an hour will burn about 300 calories. So will a person who does a half hour of vigorous aerobic dancing or an hour of mowing, weeding, and raking in the yard.

What can you do if you don't have an hour to devote to exercise every day? Look for creative ways to incorporate activity into your regular schedule: walk up stairs instead of using elevators; take a walk during lunch instead of sitting down to a meal; do calisthenics while watching the evening news. The chart on page 209 lists caloric expenditures per hour for a wide variety of physical activities; use it to help you find as many ways as you can to keep moving!

How do you know when you're fit? Standard signs of fitness include improved cardiovascular capacity, muscle strength and endurance, flexibility, and a favorable balance of lean and fat body composition. Remember, though, that individual differences mean that each person feels fit at a different level. Whatever that point is for you, exercise is one of the best ways to get there.

The most important component of physical fitness is *improved cardiovascular capacity*, or the ability to engage in a vigorous activity over an extended period of time. This type of conditioning is gained through regular, vigorous aerobic exercise, that is, exercise that extends over a period of more than a few minutes and stresses the cardiovascular system to increase oxygen delivery to the muscles. Such exercise includes brisk walking, jogging, skiing, and lap swimming.

Being fit means enjoying better health, achieving greater stamina, and having more control over your weight.

To build *muscular strength*, the force exerted by a muscle group, many people turn to weight lifting, which expends energy in short, anaerobic bursts. Repeated muscular contractions, such as push-ups, gradually build *muscular endurance*, the ability to perform stop-and-start activities over and over.

Flexibility is the ability of joints to move through their full range of motion; it's built through gentle, static stretching of muscle groups. *Proper body composition* is achieved through a balance of exercise and a lowfat, high-carbohydrate diet consumed in amounts geared to your body frame (to find out how many calories you should eat in a day, see pages 226–227).

Determining your target heart rate. To gain the optimum benefits from aerobic exercise, you need to work at endurance level. This means that

A regular exercise program is just as important to your health as a good diet. After a workout alone or with friends, whirl up a batch of Fruit Smoothies (recipe on page 197) as a quick pick-me-up.

you must work out at your target heart rate sustained for at least 20 minutes a minimum of three times a week.

The simplest way to calculate target heart rate is to subtract your age from 220 and then multiply by both 60% and 80%; your target heart rate per minute should fall between the two numbers.

Here's an example of the calculation for a 45-year-old person:

$$220 - 45 = 175$$

$$60\% \text{ of } 175 = 105 \ (.6 \times 175)$$

$$80\% \text{ of } 175 = 140 \ (.8 \times 175)$$

In this case, the target heart rate should be between 105 and 140 beats per minute.

Target heart rates for some other ages are as follows:

Age 20: 120 to 160 beats per minute

Age 25: 117 to 156 beats per minute

Age 30: 114 to 152 beats per minute

Age 35: 111 to 148 beats per minute

Age 40: 108 to 144 beats per minute

Age 50: 102 to 136 beats per minute

Age 55: 99 to 132 beats per minute

Age 60: 96 to 128 beats per minute

Age 65: 93 to 124 beats per minute

To find out if you're reaching your target heart rate, work out for at least 10 minutes. Then stop and count your pulse (place your middle fingers on your wrist, alongside the tendon that lies directly down from your thumb). Begin at zero and count for 10 seconds; then multiply this number by 6 to calculate your heart rate per minute. If this number is less than your target heart rate, increase your workout pace; if it's above your target heart rate, slacken your pace. Once you have a feel for your correct rate, you probably won't need to take your pulse every time you exercise; you'll just know when you've hit that level.

When you're beginning an exercise program, work at the lower target heart rate figure. As you get in better shape, gradually work up to the higher level to maximize the benefits from your fitness program. Each time you work out, be sure to warm up first for a few minutes by jogging in place or doing your planned exercise at a slower pace. Then gradually increase the intensity until you reach endurance level.

After exercising, when your muscles are warmed and flexible, do some gentle stretching to cool down; don't bounce while stretching. Never come to a complete stop right after finishing a vigorous exercise; always taper off slowly.

Make exercise fun. If your excuse for not exercising is that it's boring, think again. There are lots of different—and fun—ways to exercise. Starting on page 200, you'll find a whole chapter of ideas for getting friends and family together to share in physical activities and nutritious meals.

Another way to make exercise more enjoyable is to employ the "buddy system." Ask a friend to work out with you; that way, you'll keep each other going and make the time more convivial. It's also a good idea to vary your selection of activities, walking one day, cycling the next, and so on.

Exercise more, eat more. As you burn calories through exercise, you can take in more calories. This translates to eating more and, if you're choosing a healthy diet, to extra nutritional benefits. When you eat more, you take in nutrients in greater quantities, which helps you meet your daily requirements.

For example, an average inactive 45-year-old woman who needs 800 milligrams of calcium and 15 milligrams of iron daily may not be meeting those requirements with her current caloric intake. However, if this same woman were to start exercising enough to burn 300 calories per day, she could add 300 more calories of calcium- and iron-rich foods to her diet and not gain weight.

Go do it! Knowing how good exercise is for you is the best reason to do it. If you'd like to lose weight, you'll probably find it easier to increase your caloric expenditure by exercising than to decrease your caloric intake. Moreover, you'll feel a lot better.

Most importantly, for any exercise program to work it has to be fun and adapted to your needs and lifestyle. Don't decide on a form of exercise that's too costly for you, that's inconvenient, or that's easily called off because of other circumstances. Choose something you enjoy doing and that you can do on a regular basis. If exercise is a hassle, it won't get done. And if it doesn't get done, you won't reap all the benefits of being fit.

A word of warning: If you're just starting an exercise program, begin slowly. Select the proper exercise for your capacity and use common sense. If something you're doing hurts, back off. Always consult your physician before beginning any exercise regimen.

■ COOKING LIGHT & HEALTHY

Changing your diet to one that's light and healthy isn't complicated. Basically, it means eating a variety of foods, cutting back on cholesterol and fat, consuming salt, sugar, and alcohol in moderation, and increasing your intake of fiber. (The basics of good nutrition are discussed on pages 8–15.) Adding daily exercise to the equation will make you feel even more fit.

But how can you apply your knowledge about nutrition to cooking meals for yourself and your family? One answer is to look to the more than 220 recipes in this book. Designed with healthy eating in mind, they're made with a variety of nutrient-dense foods and prepared with minimal added fat. Cholesterol is kept low by controlling portion size. High-fiber ingredients are used when possible, and low-sodium products are substituted for the high-sodium originals. Sugar is used with discretion in desserts and baked goods.

What if you're not using one of our recipes? It's easy to make your own dishes light and healthy, too. One way is to choose foods that contain less fat and cholesterol (for help, see page 27). Other ideas appear on pages 24–26, where we show you how to transform traditional recipes into versions that have a lighter profile.

Tips for cooking light and healthy. Here are some techniques used in this book that you can adopt at home for healthier cooking:

■ *Drain and thoroughly rinse* canned beans, olives, and capers to remove excess salt. Or, for a salt-free alternative, cook beans from scratch (see "Basic Legume Cookery" on page 160).

■ *Use low-sodium canned broth,* no-salt-added tomato sauce, and reduced-sodium soy sauce, all widely available in supermarkets. If you can't find a low-sodium broth you like, make your own un-salted broth.

■ *Keep a variety of fresh and dry herbs and spices* on hand to use as tasty alternatives to salt.

■ *Use only small amounts of bacon* as a flavoring agent in recipes, rather than serving several whole bacon strips. Or use Canadian bacon.

■ *When you're sautéing or browning food,* choose polyunsaturated oil (safflower, sunflower, or corn) or monounsaturated oil (canola, olive, or peanut). Use margarine instead of butter for spreading and baking.

■ *Use a nonstick frying pan* to cook with little or no added fat. Or coat pans with nonstick cooking spray.

■ *When sautéing foods in less oil than usual,* stir more often to keep ingredients from sticking.

■ *Trim meat of all visible fat before cooking.* For the leanest ground meat, buy lean cuts, such as beef round or lamb sirloin, and have them trimmed and freshly ground by your butcher.

■ *Cut up fruits and vegetables at the last minute* to prevent vitamin depletion. Steaming vegetables, rather than boiling them, preserves their heat-sensitive and water-soluble vitamins.

■ *Use plain yogurt as a lowfat topping;* blend it until smooth to give it a creamier texture.

■ *For safest handling,* let hot foods (except baked goods) cool briefly; then refrigerate as soon as possible. To cool large amounts of food more quickly, spoon into smaller containers.

Using the nutritional data. The nutritional analysis accompanying each recipe lists the calories and amounts of protein, carbohydrates, total fat, saturated fat, cholesterol, and sodium per serving. The figures are based on the most recent data available and are intended to be used as guidelines.

An extended nutritional analysis for each recipe, which includes grams of dietary fiber, milligrams of calcium and iron, IUs (International Units) of vitamin A, and milligrams of vitamin C, begins on page 228. Use this chart to build menus specifically geared to your needs and the needs of your family. (For help determining those needs, see the RDA chart on page 222 and the personal profile information beginning on page 226.)

About Our Nutritional Data

For our recipes, we provide a nutritional analysis stating calorie count; grams of protein, carbohydrates, total fat, and saturated fat; and milligrams of cholesterol and sodium. Generally, the analysis applies to a single serving, based on the number of servings given for each recipe and the amount of each ingredient. If a range is given for the number of servings and/or the amount of an ingredient, the analysis is based on an average of the figures given.

The nutritional analysis does not include optional ingredients or those for which no specific amount is stated. If an ingredient is listed with a substitution, the information was calculated using the first choice.

■ LIGHTENED-UP RECIPES

Unwilling to give up your traditional favorites, even though the recipes don't meet today's nutritional standards? Here's an example of how you can modify two classics so they fit into a light and healthy diet, with no sacrifice of flavor.

New Pot Roast (recipe at right) is lower in calories, fat, cholesterol, and sodium than Old-fashioned Pot Roast (recipe below). What are the differences? The revised recipe uses a leaner cut of beef (bottom round instead of chuck), trimmed of all visible fat; the meat is "steam-stewed" rather than browned in oil. Low-sodium beef broth reduces the salt content; additional seasonings, red wine, and tomato paste boost flavor and make a naturally richer sauce that needs no flour thickening. Carrots and potatoes add fiber and fill you up so you're satisfied with less meat per serving (thus reducing your intake of cholesterol).

Can cheesecake actually be lightened up? One bite of our creamy, rich-tasting Lowfat Cheesecake (recipe on page 26) and you'll know the answer is yes. This version uses lowfat dairy products, less fat in the crust, and less sugar, and replaces two of the whole eggs with egg whites to create a lean, low-calorie, high-calcium dessert that's just as satisfying as Classic Cheesecake (recipe on page 26). Serve the lowfat version with fresh fruit to add extra fiber and vitamins.

Compare the old and new versions for a quick lesson in how to modify recipes for healthier results; then apply what you've learned to lighten up some of your favorite recipes. For other suggestions on reducing fat and cholesterol, see page 27.

Old-fashioned Pot Roast

> 1   boneless beef chuck roast (about 5 lbs.)
> 4   tablespoons all-purpose flour
> 2   tablespoons salad oil
> 5   tablespoons butter
> 1   bay leaf
> 1   teaspoon pepper
> 1½   teaspoons dry thyme leaves
> 1   can (14½ oz.) regular-strength beef broth
> 2   cups water

Coat roast with 1 tablespoon of the flour. Heat oil and 2 tablespoons of the butter in a 5-quart pan

over medium-high heat. Add meat and cook, turning, until well browned on all sides. Add bay leaf, pepper, thyme, beef broth, and water; bring to a boil over high heat. Reduce heat, cover, and simmer until meat is tender when pierced (2 to 2¼ hours).

Transfer meat to a platter and keep warm. Skim fat from pan juices. Remove and measure juices; add enough water to make 2 cups total.

Melt remaining butter in pan over medium heat; add remaining flour and cook, stirring, until bubbling. Remove from heat and pour in reserved juices, whisking until smooth. Return to heat and cook, stirring, until thickened. Offer with meat. Makes 10 servings.

Per serving: 686 calories, 42 g protein, 3 g carbohydrates, 55 g total fat (24 g saturated fat), 172 mg cholesterol, 340 mg sodium

Pictured on facing page

New Pot Roast

> ⅓   cup boiling water (optional)
> ⅓   ounce (about ¼ cup) dried porcini mushrooms (optional)
> 1   boneless beef bottom round or rump roast (3½ lbs.), fat trimmed
> 2   tablespoons Worcestershire
>   About ½ cup water
> 1   large onion, chopped
> 2   cloves garlic, minced or pressed
> 2   cups low-sodium beef broth
> 1   cup dry red wine
> 1   can (6 oz.) tomato paste
> 1½   pounds small red thin-skinned potatoes
> 1½   pounds carrots, cut into ½-inch-thick sticks

In a small bowl, pour the ⅓ cup boiling water over mushrooms, if desired; let soak until softened (about 20 minutes). Pour mushrooms and liquid through a cheesecloth-lined strainer, reserving liquid, and squeeze mushrooms to extract any remaining liquid. Finely chop mushrooms. Set mushrooms and liquid aside.

Meanwhile, combine meat, Worcestershire, and ½ cup of the water in a 5-quart pan. Cover and bring to a boil over high heat; reduce heat to medi-

*Two family favorites, pot roast and cheesecake, take
on healthy new profiles when lightened up to reduce fat,
calories, and cholesterol. New Pot Roast (recipe on facing
page), steamed broccoli, Lowfat Cheesecake (recipe on page
26), and a glass of milk make good nutrition easy.*

um and cook for 30 minutes. Uncover, increase heat to high, and cook, turning meat to brown evenly, until liquid has almost evaporated (if drippings begin to burn, add 2 to 3 tablespoons water to pan). Skim off and discard any fat.

Add onion, garlic, and about 2 more tablespoons water to pan. Reduce heat to medium-high and cook, stirring, until vegetables are glazed with pan drippings (about 5 minutes).

Add beef broth, wine, tomato paste, and, if used, reserved mushrooms and liquid; reduce heat, cover, and simmer for 2 hours, turning meat once or twice. Tuck potatoes around meat and continue cooking for 20 more minutes. Add carrots and continue cooking until meat and vegetables are tender (about 20 more minutes).

With a slotted spoon, remove vegetables and meat. Skim and discard fat from pan juices. Slice meat and arrange on individual plates with vegetables. Moisten with sauce. Makes 10 servings.

Per serving: 351 calories, 38 g protein, 25 g carbohydrates, 11 g total fat (4 g saturated fat), 94 mg cholesterol, 290 mg sodium

Classic Cheesecake

> 1½ cups graham cracker crumbs
> ⅓ cup butter, melted
> 1¼ cups plus 2 tablespoons sugar
> 3 large packages (8 oz. *each*) cream cheese, at room temperature
> ½ teaspoon salt
> 1 tablespoon vanilla
> 4 eggs
> 2 cups sour cream

Stir together graham cracker crumbs, butter, and ¼ cup of the sugar until well combined. Press firmly over bottom and partway up sides of an 8-inch spring-form pan. Bake in a 350° oven for 10 minutes. Let cool on a rack.

In a large bowl, beat cream cheese, salt, and vanilla until soft and creamy. Add eggs, one at a time, beating well after each addition. Gradually beat in 1 more cup of the sugar.

Pour filling into crust and bake until center jiggles only slightly when pan is gently shaken (30 to 35 minutes). Let stand for 10 minutes. Increase oven temperature to 450°.

In a small bowl, blend sour cream and remaining 2 tablespoons sugar; spread over top of cake. Return to oven and bake until top is set (about 5 minutes). Let cool completely on a rack. Wrap airtight and refrigerate until next day. Makes 10 servings.

Per serving: 602 calories, 10 g protein, 45 g carbohydrates, 43 g total fat (25 g saturated fat), 196 mg cholesterol, 530 mg sodium

Pictured on page 25

Lowfat Cheesecake

> 1½ cups graham cracker crumbs
> 3 tablespoons margarine, melted
> 1 cup lowfat (1% or 2%) cottage cheese
> 2 cups plain nonfat yogurt
> ½ cup sugar
> 1 tablespoon all-purpose flour
> 1 egg
> 2 egg whites
> 2 teaspoons vanilla
> 2 cups fresh raspberries or other sliced fresh fruit

Stir together graham cracker crumbs and margarine until well combined. Press firmly over bottom and partway up sides of an 8-inch spring-form pan. Bake in a 350° oven for 7 minutes. Let cool on a rack. Reduce oven temperature to 300°.

In a blender, whirl cottage cheese and yogurt until smooth and glossy (at least 1 minute). Add sugar, flour, egg, egg whites, and vanilla; whirl until smooth.

Pour filling into crust and bake until top feels dry when lightly touched and center jiggles only slightly when pan is gently shaken (about 55 minutes). Let cool completely on a rack. Wrap airtight and refrigerate for at least 8 hours or until next day.

Slice cheesecake, arrange on individual plates, and top each portion with some of the raspberries. Makes 10 servings.

Per serving: 211 calories, 8 g protein, 31 g carbohydrates, 6 g total fat (0.9 g saturated fat), 23 mg cholesterol, 292 mg sodium

■ Substitutions for Reducing Fat & Cholesterol

INSTEAD OF	CHOOSE
Bacon	Canadian bacon
Butter	Polyunsaturated margarine, with liquid oil listed as first ingredient
Cheese	Lowfat (1% or 2%) cottage cheese, part-skim mozzarella, or part-skim ricotta
Cheesecake	Lowfat Cheesecake (facing page)
Chicken leg with skin	Skinned chicken leg or breast
Chocolate, unsweetened	3 tablespoons unsweetened cocoa plus 1 tablespoon salad oil per ounce chocolate
Corn chips	Water-crisped Tortilla Chips (page 40)
Cream sauce	Tomato sauce or puréed vegetable sauce
Croissant	Homestead Bran Muffin (page 32) or whole wheat bagel
Devil's food cake	Crazy Cocoa Cake (page 193)
Doughnut	Angel Food Cake (page 192)
Eggs	1 egg plus 2 egg whites for every 2 whole eggs
French fries	Potato & Carrot Oven-fries (page 175) or baked potato
Ground beef, regular	Extra-lean ground beef, ground turkey, or half of each
Guacamole	Texas Caviar (page 38)
Ice cream	Frozen nonfat or lowfat yogurt, or sorbet
Mayonnaise	Light mayonnaise, or half mayonnaise and half plain nonfat yogurt
Milk, whole	Lowfat (1% or 2%) or nonfat milk
Nondairy creamer	Lowfat (1% or 2%) or nonfat milk
Peanuts, roasted	Roasted chestnuts or pretzels
Popcorn, buttered	Garlic-Herb Popcorn (page 40) or air-popped popcorn, plain
Potato chips	Dry-roasted Potato Chips (page 40) or pretzels
Salad dressing	Lowfat dressing (choices on page 77) or purchased lowfat dressing
Sour cream	Plain nonfat or lowfat yogurt, or lowfat (1% or 2%) cottage cheese, blended until smooth
Sour cream–vegetable dip	Curried Spinach Dip (page 41)
Tuna packed in oil	Light tuna packed in water
Whipped cream	Plain nonfat or lowfat yogurt, or sweetened part-skim ricotta cheese, blended until smooth

Breakfasts

Fruit Muesli ■ Couscous in Cantaloupe ■

Blueberry Muffins ■ Homestead Bran Muffins

■ Joe's Morning Special ■ Tropical Ham

Plate with Basil Honey ■ Orange-Yogurt Waffles

■ Banana-Oatmeal Pancakes with

Warm Applesauce

Rise and shine! Want to start the day off right? Make this commitment to yourself: I will eat a nutritious breakfast. It's a decision that will make you feel good all day. Why is breakfast so important? After a night's rest, your blood sugar is down. This means a groggy body, a foggy mind, and slow reactions. Your body needs the boost of energy-rich complex carbohydrates from nonsugary cereals and whole grain toast or pancakes, vitamins from fresh fruit and juices, and calcium and protein from lowfat dairy products and eggs (perhaps one or two a couple of days a week). In this chapter you'll find breakfast recipes for both relaxed weekends and on-the-go weekdays. Other good choices for rushed mornings include Ginger-Peach Smoothies (page 203) and Cottage Cheese & Tomato Breakfast Stack (page 52). Or you may want to consider the non-traditional— spaghetti, soups, or even leftover pizza. Whatever path you take, just be sure to eat a good breakfast every day. You'll feel better for it.

FRUIT MUESLI

Per serving: 127 calories, 3 g protein, 28 g carbohydrates, 1 g total fat (0.2 g saturated fat), 0 mg cholesterol, 2 mg sodium

Preparation time: About 10 minutes
Chilling time: At least 8 hours

This moist, homemade muesli is rich in fiber and wholesome ingredients. It keeps for up to a week in the refrigerator; add your favorite healthful toppings.

2 medium-size Golden Delicious apples (about ½ lb. *total*)
1 cup pitted prunes
1¾ cups water
2 cups regular rolled oats
2 tablespoons *each* honey and lemon juice
½ teaspoon ground cinnamon
Lowfat (2%) milk or yogurt
Toppings (suggestions follow), optional

Core apples and cut into chunks. In a blender or food processor, whirl apples, prunes, and water, scraping container sides often, until fruit is finely chopped. Pour into a bowl; stir in oats, honey, lemon juice, and cinnamon. Cover and refrigerate for at least 8 hours or up to 1 week.

Spoon muesli into bowls and add milk. Offer toppings, if desired. Makes about 10 servings (½ cup *each*).

Toppings. Offer chopped **nuts,** such as almonds, pecans, walnuts, and peanuts; or sliced or whole **fruit,** such as banana, pineapple, oranges, and berries.

Pictured on facing page

COUSCOUS IN CANTALOUPE

Per serving: 302 calories, 12 g protein, 49 g carbohydrates, 8 g total fat (2 g saturated fat), 3 mg cholesterol, 80 mg sodium

Preparation time: About 25 minutes

When the day dawns hot, greet morning with this refreshingly cool combination of fruit and starch. It gives you the energy you need without weighing you down.

1⅓ cups low-sodium chicken broth
¾ teaspoon ground coriander
½ cup couscous
1 large cantaloupe (about 3½ lbs.)
1 cup plain lowfat yogurt
⅓ cup chopped dry-roasted peanuts
¼ cup golden raisins
2 tablespoons minced fresh mint leaves
Mint sprigs (optional)

In a 1½- to 2-quart pan, bring chicken broth and coriander to a boil over high heat. Stir in couscous. Cover, remove from heat, and let stand until broth is absorbed (about 5 minutes). Transfer couscous to a bowl and let cool. Meanwhile, cut cantaloupe lengthwise into quarters; scoop out and discard seeds. Arrange on individual plates.

Add yogurt, peanuts, raisins, and minced mint to couscous; mix well. Spoon into cavity of each cantaloupe wedge. Garnish with mint sprigs, if desired. Makes 4 servings.

Cool off on a hot morning with refreshing Couscous in Cantaloupe (recipe on facing page). Offered with Wheat Toast Points (recipe on page 38) and ice-cold juice, it's a balanced way to start the day.

■ *Pictured on page 202*

BLUEBERRY MUFFINS

Per muffin: 265 calories, 6 g protein, 48 g carbohydrates, 6 g total fat (1 g saturated fat), 37 mg cholesterol, 331 mg sodium

Preparation time: About 15 minutes
Baking time: About 35 minutes

Is there anything more comforting than fresh-baked muffins? Probably not. And when made with whole wheat flour and a minimum of fat, they add extra goodness to your morning.

- 1½ **cups** *each* **whole wheat flour and all-purpose flour**
- 1 **cup plus 2 tablespoons firmly packed light brown sugar**
- 2 **teaspoons baking soda**
- 4 **teaspoons baking powder**
- 1 **tablespoon ground cinnamon**
- ¼ **teaspoon salt (optional)**
- 2 **eggs**
- 1½ **cups lowfat buttermilk**
- ¼ **cup salad oil**
- 2 **cups fresh or unsweetened frozen thawed blueberries**

In a large bowl, mix whole wheat flour, all-purpose flour, 1 cup of the sugar, baking soda, baking powder, cinnamon, and, if desired, salt. In another bowl, beat eggs, buttermilk, and oil. Stir into flour mixture just until moistened. Add blueberries, stirring briefly and gently to mix through batter.

Spoon batter into 12 paper-lined or greased 2½-inch muffin cups (cups will be very full). Sprinkle with remaining 2 tablespoons sugar. Bake in a 375° oven until well browned (about 35 minutes). Remove from pan.

If made ahead, cool, wrap airtight, and store at room temperature until next day; freeze for longer storage (thaw wrapped). To reheat, place in a baking pan, cover with foil, and heat in a 350° oven until warm (15 to 18 minutes). Makes 12 muffins.

HOMESTEAD BRAN MUFFINS

Per muffin: 213 calories, 5 g protein, 37 g carbohydrates, 7 g total fat (0.9 g saturated fat), 19 mg cholesterol, 211 mg sodium

Preparation time: About 15 minutes
Baking time: About 30 minutes

Bran muffin recipes abound, but we're sure you'll agree that this is one of the best. As an added bonus, the batter keeps for up to 2 weeks in the refrigerator, so you can bake fresh, hot muffins anytime you like.

- 3 **cups bran cereal (not flakes)**
- ¾ **cup boiling water**
- 3 **tablespoons frozen orange juice concentrate, thawed**
- ½ **cup salad oil**
- 2 **eggs**
- 2 **cups lowfat buttermilk**
- 2½ **cups all-purpose flour**
- 1½ **cups sugar**
- 2½ **teaspoons baking soda**
- 1 **cup dried currants**
- ½ **cup finely chopped walnuts**

In a large bowl, mix 1 cup of the cereal, water, juice concentrate, and oil. Add eggs and buttermilk, mixing well. In a small bowl, mix remaining 2 cups cereal, flour, sugar, baking soda, and currants. Add to egg mixture, stirring until evenly moistened. (At this point, you may cover and refrigerate for up to 2 weeks; stir well before using.)

Spoon batter into 24 paper-lined or greased 2½-inch muffin cups; sprinkle with nuts. Bake in a 350° oven until well browned (about 30 minutes). Remove from pan. (To store, see directions for Blueberry Muffins, above.) Makes 24 muffins.

JOE'S MORNING SPECIAL

Per serving: 151 calories, 12 g protein, 14 g carbohydrates, 6 g total fat (1 g saturated fat), 54 mg cholesterol, 187 mg sodium

Preparation time: About 10 minutes
Cooking time: About 20 minutes

If you're looking for a low-cholesterol breakfast scramble, this bountiful mix of vegetables, eggs, and cheese will fit the bill.

- 1 tablespoon salad oil
- 1 large onion, sliced
- 2 large green bell peppers (about 1 lb. *total*), stemmed, seeded, and thinly sliced
- ½ pound mushrooms, thinly sliced
- 1 package (10 oz.) frozen chopped spinach, thawed and squeezed dry
- 1 egg
- 6 egg whites
- 1 teaspoon ground oregano
  Freshly ground pepper
- 4 teaspoons grated Parmesan cheese

Heat oil in a wide frying pan over medium-high heat. Add onion and bell peppers and cook, stirring, until tender-crisp (about 3 minutes). Add mushrooms and cook, stirring, until liquid has evaporated and mushrooms are browned (about 10 minutes).

Add spinach to pan and cook, stirring, until hot (about 3 minutes). In a bowl, lightly beat whole egg, egg whites, and oregano. Pour into pan and cook, stirring, until eggs are scrambled (about 3 minutes). Season to taste with pepper. Divide eggs among individual plates. Sprinkle each serving with 1 teaspoon of the Parmesan. Makes 4 servings.

■ *Pictured on page 202*

TROPICAL HAM PLATE WITH BASIL HONEY

Per serving: 303 calories, 11 g protein, 53 g carbohydrates, 8 g total fat (1 g saturated fat), 21 mg cholesterol, 608 mg sodium

Preparation time: About 15 minutes
Cooking time: About 3 minutes

Sparkling tropical fruits, lean Canadian bacon, and a refreshing honey dressing combine for an easy morning meal.

- 1 tablespoon salad oil
- 6 ounces thinly sliced Canadian bacon
- ¼ cup lime juice
- 2 tablespoons honey
- 1 tablespoon minced fresh basil leaves or 1½ teaspoons dry basil leaves
- 1 peeled and cored pineapple (about 2½ lbs.)
- 2 kiwi fruit (about ½ lb. *total*)
  Basil sprigs (optional)

Heat oil in a wide frying pan over medium-high heat. Add bacon and cook, turning once, until lightly browned (about 3 minutes). Meanwhile, mix lime juice, honey, and minced basil; set aside.

Slice pineapple crosswise about ⅓ inch thick. Peel kiwi fruit and slice crosswise about ¼ inch thick. Arrange pineapple, kiwis, and bacon on individual plates. Drizzle with honey mixture. Garnish with basil sprigs, if desired. Makes 4 servings.

■ *Pictured on facing page*

ORANGE-YOGURT WAFFLES

■

Per serving: 264 calories, 12 g protein, 38 g carbohydrates, 7 g total fat (2 g saturated fat), 76 mg cholesterol, 488 mg sodium

Preparation time: About 20 minutes
Cooking time: About 15 minutes

On leisurely mornings, these crisp waffles, bursting with orange flavor, are a sure winner. Using whole wheat flour in the batter gives a chewier texture and added fiber.

2 eggs, separated
2 egg whites
2 cups plain lowfat yogurt
¼ cup nonfat milk
1 tablespoon grated orange peel
¼ cup orange juice
2 tablespoons sugar
¼ teaspoon ground nutmeg
2 tablespoons margarine, melted
1 cup all-purpose flour
¾ cup whole wheat flour
1 teaspoon baking powder
2 teaspoons baking soda

Place egg yolks in a large bowl; place whites in a small bowl and set aside. Beat yolks with yogurt, milk, orange peel, orange juice, sugar, nutmeg, and margarine until smooth.

In another bowl, mix all-purpose flour, whole wheat flour, baking powder, and baking soda. Stir flour mixture into yolk mixture just until moistened (do not overmix).

Beat egg whites until stiff, moist peaks form; fold into batter. Cook in a preheated waffle iron according to manufacturer's directions. Makes 6 servings (6 large or 12 small waffles).

■

BANANA-OATMEAL PANCAKES WITH WARM APPLESAUCE

■

Per serving: 252 calories, 8 g protein, 39 g carbohydrates, 8 g total fat (2 g saturated fat), 45 mg cholesterol, 247 mg sodium

Preparation time: About 10 minutes
Cooking time: About 10 minutes

Thick and fluffy, these pancakes, topped with warm applesauce, provide ample energy to start the day. For thinner pancakes, add more buttermilk. To cook without added fat, use a nonstick pan.

¾ cup quick-cooking rolled oats
⅔ cup whole wheat flour
1 teaspoon baking powder
½ teaspoon baking soda
1 tablespoon sugar
¼ teaspoon salt (optional)
1 medium-size ripe banana (about 6 oz.)
1 egg
 About 1¼ cups lowfat buttermilk
2 tablespoons salad oil
 Nonstick cooking spray or salad oil (optional)
1 jar (14 oz.) unsweetened applesauce
 Ground cinnamon

Mix oats, flour, baking powder, baking soda, sugar, and, if desired, salt. Set aside.

In a blender or food processor, whirl banana until smooth. Add egg, 1¼ cups of the buttermilk, and oil; whirl until smooth. Stir banana mixture into dry ingredients, blending well. (If batter is too thick, add more buttermilk, a tablespoon at a time.)

Place a wide nonstick frying pan over medium-high heat (or lightly coat a regular frying pan or griddle with cooking spray). For each pancake, spoon 3 tablespoons of the batter into pan; cook until tops are bubbling and bottoms are golden brown (about 2 minutes). Flip pancakes and cook for about 1½ more minutes. Meanwhile, warm applesauce in a small pan over medium heat.

Arrange pancakes on individual plates. Spoon about 2 tablespoons of the applesauce over each pancake; sprinkle with cinnamon. Makes 5 servings (2 pancakes *each*).

Pamper your sweetheart with a nourishing breakfast in bed. Made in a heart-shaped waffle iron, tender Orange-Yogurt Waffles (recipe on facing page) are strewn with ruby red fresh berries and offered with maple syrup.

Appetizers

Texas Caviar ■ Mushroom Pâté with Wheat
Toast Points ■ Crostini with Fresh Tomatoes ■
Jicama & Fresh Fruit Platter ■ Hummus with
Pita Crisps ■ Turkey-Broccoli Bundles ■ Chili
Chicken Chunks with Blender Salsa ■ Lamb
Shish Kebabs ■ Crabby Potatoes ■ Shrimp with
Tart Dipping Sauce

Company's coming and you want to serve something delicious that's also good for you and your guests. Treat them to a dazzling array of crunchy vegetables, sparkling fresh fruits, and succulent meats and seafood. Offer dips prepared with a light hand and chips that are baked instead of fried. Because they're high in nutrition, these before-meal nibbles satisfy empty stomachs without adding empty calories. For some people, appetizers can be a healthy way to curb hunger so they consume less at the main meal. Even be-tween-meal snacking can be a healthy habit as long as you choose wisely. Entertaining is also an opportunity to showcase wholesome foods from other cultures, such as Crostini with Fresh Tomatoes from Italy or Hummus with Pita Crisps from the Middle East. Closer to home we find goodness in such recipes as high-fiber Texas Caviar or crispy Chili Chicken Chunks with Blender Salsa, a lean twist on deep-fried chicken nuggets. And don't wait just for special occasions to serve these nourishing noshes; our appetizers can add variety and fun to the menu anytime.

■ *Pictured on facing page*

TEXAS CAVIAR

■

Per serving: 104 calories, 7 g protein, 19 g carbohydrates, 0.4 g total fat (0.1 g saturated fat), 0 mg cholesterol, 130 mg sodium

Preparation time: About 30 minutes
Cooking time: About 50 minutes

From the state that knows how to entertain come these zesty tomato- and chile-flavored black-eyed peas. They're thought to bring good luck when eaten on New Year's Day, but this high-fiber party favorite is a good choice anytime.

Water-crisped Tortilla Chips (recipe on page 40) or packaged tortilla chips
1½ cups dried black-eyed peas
2 large tomatoes (about 1 lb. *total*), seeded and chopped
½ cup chopped cilantro (coriander)
1 or 2 jalapeño or other small hot chiles, stemmed and seeded
2 tablespoons white wine vinegar
Salt
Cilantro (coriander) sprigs (optional)

Prepare Water-crisped Tortilla Chips and set aside.

In a 2- to 3-quart pan, bring 1 quart water to a boil. Add peas; reduce heat, cover, and simmer until tender (about 50 minutes). Drain, rinse well with cold water, and drain again. Transfer to a bowl and set aside.

In a blender or food processor, combine tomatoes, chopped cilantro, and chiles. Whirl until finely chopped; stir in vinegar. Add mixture to peas and stir well; season to taste with salt. Garnish with cilantro sprigs, if desired, and offer with tortilla chips. Makes 8 to 10 servings.

MUSHROOM PÂTÉ WITH WHEAT TOAST POINTS

■

Per serving: 99 calories, 4 g protein, 16 g carbohydrates, 3 g total fat (2 g saturated fat), 7 mg cholesterol, 149 mg sodium

Preparation time: About 10 minutes
Cooking time: 10 to 15 minutes

The flavor of a delicate pâté is a special treat; yet pâtés traditionally made with meat are high in fat and cholesterol. Mushrooms make a lean and savory substitute; a touch of butter adds richness, but you can opt for margarine if you prefer.

Wheat Toast Points (directions follow)
2 tablespoons butter or margarine
1 pound mushrooms, chopped
¾ cup chopped shallots
1 small carrot (about 3 oz.), chopped
1 clove garlic, minced or pressed
Ground white pepper
Chopped parsley

Prepare Wheat Toast Points.

Meanwhile, melt butter in a wide frying pan over medium-high heat. Add mushrooms, shallots, carrot, and garlic. Cook, stirring often, until liquid has evaporated and mushrooms are browned (10 to 15 minutes). Transfer mixture to a blender or food processor and whirl until puréed. Season to taste with pepper. Mound on a plate and sprinkle with parsley. Serve warm or at room temperature, surrounded by toast points. Makes 10 servings (2 appetizers *each*).

Wheat Toast Points. Stack 10 slices **whole wheat bread** (about 10 oz. *total*) and trim crusts. Cut bread in half diagonally. Place triangles on a baking sheet and broil about 5 inches below heat, turning once, until browned on both sides (2 to 3 minutes *total*). Makes 20 pieces.

Greet guests down-home style with Texas Caviar
(recipe on facing page), scooped up with Water-crisped
Tortilla Chips (recipe on page 40). It's lively enough to
arouse taste buds without bogging down appetites.
Sparkling mineral water with lime tames the heat.

It's that time of day again. You're hungry for something crunchy, salty, or creamy, and all around you temptation looms. You know that junk food is out, but carrot sticks don't hit the spot either. What should you reach for?

Don't despair. With a little nutritionally conscious preparation, you can still enjoy many of your favorite munchies. Below we present a selection of creamy dips, chunky salsas, and tangy spreads. Pair them up with our crunchy lowfat potato chips or tortilla chips made without frying. Or choose good old popcorn, seasoned with herbs, garlic, and a touch of margarine. Your taste buds won't feel deprived.

Dry-roasted Potato Chips

These double-cooked chips achieve true crispness without added fat; salt is added to taste. The chips take 2 to 2½ hours to bake, so plan ahead.

> 1   **pound white thin-skinned potatoes**
>   **Nonstick cooking spray**
>   **Salt**

With narrow blade of a food slicer (mandolin) or food processor, cut potatoes into very thin slices. In a 3- to 4-quart pan, bring 2 quarts water to a boil. Cook potatoes, about a third at a time, until slightly translucent (about 1½ minutes). Lift out with a slotted spoon; let drain.

Place wire racks on large baking sheets (you'll need about 4 sheets, or use them in sequence). Lightly coat racks with cooking spray.

Arrange potato slices on racks in a single layer. Season to taste with salt. Bake in a 200° oven until chips are crisped (2 to 2½ hours). Serve hot or at room temperature. If made ahead, let cool; store airtight at room temperature for up to 1 week. Makes about 1 quart.

Per cup: 91 calories, 2 g protein, 20 g carbohydrates, 0.3 g total fat (0 g saturated fat), 0 mg cholesterol, 7 mg sodium

Pictured on page 39
Water-crisped Tortilla Chips

For dipping into either of the fresh salsas on the facing page, try these baked tortilla chips. A quick dunking in water before cooking adds crispness.

> 12   **corn or flour tortillas (6- or 7-inch diameter)**
>   **Salt**

Dip tortillas, one at a time, in water; let drain briefly. Season to taste with salt. Stack and cut into 6 or 8 wedges.

Arrange wedges in a single layer on large baking sheets (you'll need about 3 sheets, or use them in sequence). Bake in a 500° oven for 4 minutes. Turn and continue baking until browned and crisped (about 2 more minutes). If made ahead, let cool; store airtight at room temperature for up to 1 week. Makes 2 quarts.

Per cup corn tortilla chips: 100 calories, 3 g protein, 19 g carbohydrates, 2 g total fat (0 g saturated fat), 0 mg cholesterol, 80 mg sodium

Garlic-Herb Popcorn

Popcorn *is* a healthy snack—it's the butter you add to it that can hurt. Instead, douse your popcorn with herbs, garlic, and just a little margarine.

> **Garlic-Herb Sprinkle (recipe follows)**
> ½   **cup popcorn kernels**
> 1   **tablespoon margarine, melted**

Prepare Garlic-Herb Sprinkle and set aside.

Pop corn in a hot-air popper according to manufacturer's directions. Pour into a bowl; add margarine and stir well. Toss with herb mixture. Makes 3 quarts.

Garlic-Herb Sprinkle. Mix 2 teaspoons *each* **dry oregano leaves, dry basil leaves,** and **dry thyme leaves.** Add 1 teaspoon *each* **garlic powder** and **onion powder;** stir well.

Per cup: 43 calories, 1 g protein, 7 g carbohydrates, 1 g total fat (0.2 g saturated fat), 0 mg cholesterol, 12 mg sodium

Curried Spinach Dip

Based on a lowfat blend of cottage cheese and skim milk instead of sour cream, this emerald green dip goes beautifully with spears of red bell peppers, white jicama, or yellow squash; or stuff the mixture inside hollowed cherry tomatoes.

- 2 cups lowfat (2%) cottage cheese
- ¼ cup nonfat milk
- 2 tablespoons lemon juice
- 1 package (10 oz.) frozen chopped spinach, thawed and squeezed dry
- 3 green onions (including tops), sliced
- 2 teaspoons curry powder

In a blender or food processor, combine cottage cheese, milk, and lemon juice. Whirl on high speed until smooth and glossy (at least 2 minutes). Add spinach, onions, and curry; whirl on high speed until blended. Pour into a bowl; cover and refrigerate for at least 2 hours or until next day. Makes about 2¾ cups.

Per tablespoon: 12 calories, 2 g protein, 1 g carbohydrates, 0.2 g total fat (0.1 g saturated fat), 0.8 mg cholesterol, 47 mg sodium

Sweet & Sour Onion Spread

Spoon this tangy-sweet mixture onto triangles of toasted pumpernickel, or scoop up with crisp celery sticks or Dry-roasted Potato Chips (recipe on facing page).

- 2 tablespoons salad oil
- 3 large onions, chopped
- 1 cup plain nonfat yogurt
- 1 tablespoon unseasoned rice vinegar or cider vinegar
  Freshly ground pepper

Heat oil in a wide frying pan over medium-high heat. Add onions and cook, stirring often, until limp (10 to 15 minutes). Reduce heat and continue cooking, stirring occasionally, until onions are golden and sweet-tasting (about 20 more minutes). Let cool.

Stir in yogurt and vinegar. Spoon mixture into a serving bowl and sprinkle generously with pepper. Makes 2 cups.

Per tablespoon: 19 calories, 0.7 g protein, 2 g carbohydrates, 0.9 g total fat (0.1 g saturated fat), 0.1 mg cholesterol, 6 mg sodium

Salsa Fresca

Enjoy vibrant color and flavor with this homemade fresh vegetable salsa.

- 2 cloves garlic
- ½ medium-size onion, quartered
- 1 or 2 jalapeño or other small hot chiles, stemmed and seeded
- ¼ cup packed cilantro (coriander)
- 1 pound firm-ripe tomatoes, seeded
- 2 tablespoons salad oil
  Juice of 1 lime

In a blender or food processor, combine garlic, onion, chiles, cilantro, and tomatoes; whirl briefly until coarsely chopped. Add oil and lime juice; whirl until mixture is finely chopped.

If made ahead, cover and refrigerate for up to 2 days. Makes 2 cups.

Per tablespoon: 11 calories, 0.1 g protein, 0.8 g carbohydrates, 0.9 g total fat (0.1 g saturated fat), 0 mg cholesterol, 1 mg sodium

Salsa Verde

Fresh tomatillos are the special ingredient in this tart green salsa; look for them in produce markets and in well-stocked supermarkets.

- 1¼ pounds tomatillos, husks removed
- ⅓ cup chopped cilantro (coriander)
- 1 jalapeño or other small hot chile, stemmed and seeded
- ¾ cup low-sodium chicken broth
- ⅓ cup lime juice

Rinse tomatillos to remove sticky film; arrange in a single layer on a baking sheet and roast in a 500° oven until slightly singed (about 15 minutes). Let cool. Place in a blender or food processor with cilantro and chile; whirl until puréed. Stir in chicken broth and lime juice.

If made ahead, cover and refrigerate for up to 2 days. Makes 3 cups.

Per tablespoon: 4 calories, 0.2 g protein, 0.6 g carbohydrates, 0.1 g total fat (0 g saturated fat), 0 mg cholesterol, 1 mg sodium

Sparkling under a shower of palate-tingling chili powder, a mosaic of fresh, crunchy morsels announces Jicama & Fresh Fruit Platter (recipe on facing page), a popular Mexican hors d'oeuvre.

CROSTINI WITH FRESH TOMATOES

Preparation time: About 15 minutes
Broiling time: About 4 minutes

It's common practice to start a meal in Italy with little appetizers known as *crostini*. Pieces of grilled bread are spread with fresh toppings, such as the tomato, basil, and onion mixture used here.

- 1 **pound very ripe pear-shaped tomatoes, seeded and chopped**
- ⅓ **cup chopped red onion**
- 2 **tablespoons chopped fresh basil leaves or 1 tablespoon dry basil leaves**
- 2 **tablespoons olive oil**
- 6 **slices (about 3½ by 5 inches and about ½ inch thick *each*) crusty Italian or French bread**
  Freshly ground pepper

Per serving: 188 calories, 5 g protein, 31 g carbohydrates, 5 g total fat (0.6 g saturated fat), 0.5 mg cholesterol, 282 mg sodium

Place about two-thirds of the tomatoes in a clean towel or cheesecloth. Wring tightly to remove juice. Set crushed tomatoes aside. Mix remaining tomatoes with onion, basil, and oil; set aside.

Place bread in a single layer on a baking sheet. Broil about 5 inches below heat, turning once, until golden on both sides (about 4 minutes *total*).

Spread slices with crushed tomatoes. Mound onion mixture on top. Season to taste with pepper. Makes 6 servings.

Pictured on facing page

JICAMA & FRESH FRUIT PLATTER

Preparation time: 30 minutes

Fruit and spice contrast deliciously in this eye-catching hors d'oeuvre. Jicama, a Mexican root vegetable available in most supermarkets, adds definitive crunch. We've recommended a few of our favorite fruits; other good choices are mangoes, kiwis, and green apples.

- 1 **small jicama (about 1 lb.), peeled and rinsed**
  Fresh Fruit (directions follow)
- ⅔ **cup lime juice**
- ½ **teaspoon salt**
- 1 **tablespoon chili powder**

Cut jicama in half lengthwise; then slice each half thinly.

Prepare Fresh Fruit. Coat jicama and fruit with lime juice; arrange separately on a platter. If made

Per serving: 88 calories, 2 g protein, 21 g carbohydrates, 0.6 g total fat (0 g saturated fat), 0 mg cholesterol, 155 mg sodium

ahead, cover and refrigerate for up to 2 hours.

In a small bowl, combine salt and chili powder; sprinkle over jicama and fruit. Makes 8 servings.

Fresh Fruit. Remove rinds from 1 large slice **watermelon** and ½ small **honeydew melon;** then cut fruit into chunks. Peel, seed, and slice 1 large (about ¾ lb.) **papaya.** Peel 3 medium-size **oranges** (about 1¼ lbs. *total*), remove white membrane, and separate into sections.

HUMMUS WITH PITA CRISPS

Per serving: 175 calories, 6 g protein, 32 g carbohydrates, 3 g total fat (0.3 g saturated fat), 0 mg cholesterol, 354 mg sodium

Preparation time: About 10 minutes
Baking time: 12 to 15 minutes

Long a nutritional mainstay in the Middle East, the garbanzo bean earns raves when whipped into the delicious blend known as hummus. This version is made without added oil, resulting in a lighter, fluffier dip. Sesame tahini can be found in health food stores and many supermarkets.

  Pita Crisps (directions follow)
1 can (about 15½ oz.) garbanzo beans
2 tablespoons sesame tahini
2 cloves garlic
3 tablespoons lemon juice
⅛ teaspoon ground red pepper (cayenne)
½ small onion
2 tablespoons minced parsley

Prepare Pita Crisps and set aside.

Meanwhile, drain beans, reserving liquid. Rinse beans well and place in a blender or food processor with tahini, garlic, lemon juice, red pepper, onion, and 3 tablespoons of the reserved bean liquid. Whirl until smooth. With motor running, add more of the bean liquid, a little at a time, until mixture is smooth and thick.

Transfer to a shallow bowl and sprinkle with parsley. Offer with pita triangles. Makes 8 to 10 servings.

Pita Crisps. Cut 6 **whole wheat pita breads** (6-inch diameter) in half crosswise. Peel halves apart; stack and cut into 3 wedges. Place in a single layer on baking sheets and bake in a 350° oven until browned and crisped (12 to 15 minutes). Makes 72 pieces.

TURKEY-BROCCOLI BUNDLES

Per serving: 88 calories, 12 g protein, 4 g carbohydrates, 3 g total fat (1 g saturated fat), 27 mg cholesterol, 62 mg sodium

Preparation time: About 15 minutes
Cooking time: About 3 minutes

Wrap turkey slices around crunchy broccoli stalks and dunk into a peppery horseradish dip for an appetizer that's long on nutrition and short on calories.

1 pound broccoli
10 thin slices (⅔ lb. *total*) cooked skinless turkey breast
¾ cup part-skim ricotta cheese
⅓ cup plain lowfat yogurt
¼ cup prepared horseradish
1 teaspoon pepper

Trim broccoli, leaving about 2 inches of stalk below flowerets; peel stalks, if desired. Cut broccoli length-wise into 20 spears. Place spears on a rack in a pan above 1 inch boiling water; cover and steam over high heat until tender-crisp (about 3 minutes). Lift out and immerse in ice water until cool. Drain and set aside.

Cut turkey slices in half lengthwise. Wrap each spear of broccoli with a piece of turkey, leaving top of floweret exposed. In a small bowl, beat ricotta, yogurt, horseradish, and pepper.

Arrange bundles on a platter. Offer with yogurt mixture. Makes 10 servings (2 appetizers *each*).

CHILI CHICKEN CHUNKS WITH BLENDER SALSA

Preparation time: About 15 minutes
Baking time: About 15 minutes

Treat company to these spicy, crispy nuggets of chicken; they're baked instead of fried to keep them lean. A super-easy salsa goes alongside for dipping.

Blender Salsa (recipe follows)
¾ cup soft whole wheat bread crumbs
¼ cup yellow cornmeal
2 teaspoons chili powder
½ teaspoon *each* paprika, ground cumin, and dry oregano leaves
Nonstick cooking spray or salad oil
2 whole chicken breasts (about 1 lb. *each*), skinned, boned, and split
2 egg whites

Prepare Blender Salsa and set aside.

Spread bread crumbs in a pie pan and bake in a 350° oven, stirring once, until lightly browned

Per serving: 128 calories, 19 g protein, 9 g carbohydrates, 1 g total fat (0.3 g saturated fat), 43 mg cholesterol, 116 mg sodium

(about 5 minutes). Add cornmeal, chili powder, paprika, cumin, and oregano; stir well. Set aside.

Lightly coat a baking sheet with cooking spray. Cut each breast half into 8 pieces. Place egg whites in a small bowl and beat lightly with a fork. Dip chicken pieces into egg whites; lift out, letting excess egg drain off. Then roll in bread crumb mixture to coat and place on baking sheet.

Bake chicken until meat in center is no longer pink; cut to test (about 15 minutes). Offer with salsa. Makes 8 servings (4 appetizers *each*).

Blender Salsa. In a blender or food processor, combine ¾ pound **tomatoes,** cut into chunks; ½ small **onion;** 3 tablespoons **canned diced green chiles;** 4 teaspoons **white vinegar;** and 1 tablespoon chopped **cilantro** (coriander). Whirl until smooth.

LAMB SHISH KEBABS

Preparation time: About 45 minutes
Marinating time: At least 4 hours
Grilling time: About 8 minutes

Soak water chestnuts and lean lamb cubes in a blackberry-soy marinade and alternate them on skewers for a succulent hors d'oeuvre offering.

½ cup blackberry syrup
¼ cup red wine vinegar
2 tablespoons *each* reduced-sodium soy sauce and chopped fresh mint leaves
2 cloves garlic, minced or pressed
½ teaspoon pepper
2 cans (about 8 oz. *each*) whole water chestnuts, drained
1½ pounds lean boneless lamb (leg or shoulder), fat trimmed, cut into 1-inch cubes

Per serving: 238 calories, 25 g protein, 19 g carbohydrates, 7 g total fat (2 g saturated fat), 76 mg cholesterol, 164 mg sodium

Mix syrup, vinegar, soy sauce, mint, garlic, and pepper. Add water chestnuts and lamb, stirring to coat. Cover and refrigerate for at least 4 hours or until next day, stirring several times.

Soak 12 bamboo skewers in hot water to cover for 30 minutes. Drain meat and water chestnuts and thread alternately on skewers (to avoid splitting water chestnuts, rotate skewer as you pierce them).

Place skewers on a lightly greased grill 4 to 6 inches above a solid bed of medium coals. (Or place on a rack in a broiler pan and broil about 4 inches below heat.) Cook, turning occasionally, until meat is browned but still pink in center; cut to test (about 8 minutes). Makes 6 servings (2 skewers *each*).

Who can resist nibbling on plump, tender
Shrimp with Tart Dipping Sauce (recipe on facing page)?
Fetchingly tied with chive sashes and dipped into a
piquant, fat-free sauce, they'll disappear as quickly as
you'll garner compliments.

CRABBY POTATOES

Per serving: 83 calories, 4 g protein, 11 g carbohydrates, 3 g total fat (0.6 g saturated fat), 12 mg cholesterol, 69 mg sodium

Preparation time: About 20 minutes
Cooking time: About 32 minutes

Bursting with the flavors of crab, chives, and cheese, these one-bite tidbits are irresistible. For best results, look for very small red potatoes, sometimes labeled creamers.

- 12 **small red thin-skinned potatoes (about 1½ lbs. *total*)**
- 1 **teaspoon olive oil**
- ¼ **pound flaked crabmeat**
- 2 **tablespoons *each* plain lowfat yogurt and mayonnaise**
- 2 **tablespoons minced chives or green onion tops**
- 2 **teaspoons lemon juice**
- 1 **tablespoon chopped parsley**
- 3 **tablespoons grated Parmesan cheese Freshly ground pepper**

Place potatoes in a baking pan just large enough to hold them in a single layer. Add oil, turning to coat. Bake in a 350° oven until tender when pierced (about 30 minutes). Let cool.

Cut potatoes in half crosswise and scoop out centers with a small melon baller, leaving about a ¼-inch shell. Reserve centers for other uses.

In a small bowl, stir together crab, yogurt, mayonnaise, chives, lemon juice, parsley, and Parmesan; season to taste with pepper. Spoon mixture into potato shells. Broil about 4 inches below heat until golden (about 2 minutes). Makes 12 servings (2 appetizers *each*).

■ *Pictured on facing page*

SHRIMP WITH TART DIPPING SAUCE

Per serving: 57 calories, 10 g protein, 1 g carbohydrates, 0.8 g total fat (0.2 g saturated fat), 70 mg cholesterol, 69 mg sodium

Preparation time: About 25 minutes
Cooking time: 3 to 4 minutes

A favorite on any hors d'oeuvre table, these shrimp are accompanied by a lean, assertive sauce of wine, vinegar, and two kinds of onions. For added elegance, each shrimp is tied with a chive sash.

- 35 **medium-size shrimp (about 1 lb. *total*), shelled and deveined**
- 35 **whole chives (about 7 inches long *each*)**
- ¼ **cup *each* dry white wine and white wine vinegar**
- 1 **tablespoon *each* minced shallots and minced chives**
- ½ **teaspoon pepper**

In a 4- to 6-quart pan, bring about 1 quart water to a boil over high heat. Add shrimp; reduce heat, cover, and simmer until opaque in center; cut to test (3 to 4 minutes). Lift out and immerse in ice water until cool. Drain and set aside.

Drop whole chives into pan and cook just until wilted (about 5 seconds). Remove immediately with tongs. Tie a chive around center of each shrimp.

In a small bowl, stir together wine, vinegar, shallots, minced chives, and pepper. Arrange shrimp on a platter and offer with sauce. Makes 8 servings (about 4 appetizers *each*).

Soups

Cold Cucumber & Dill Bisque ■ Cool Scallop
Soup ■ White Gazpacho ■ Green & Gold
Melon Soup ■ Roasted Eggplant Soup
■ Caribbean Corn Chowder ■ Sweet Potato &
Carrot Soup ■ Winter Minestrone ■ Jamaican
Black Bean & Rice Soup ■ Creamy Garbanzo
Soup with Barley ■ Lemony Lentil Soup
■ Mexican Albondigas Soup ■ Tortellini &
Chicken Soup ■ Shrimp & Rice Chowder

Throughout the ages, soup ladled from steaming kettles has nourished civilizations around the world. Often a mélange of whatever is on hand, soup allows the cook to make a few ingredients go a long way. Even the most humble pot of soup is rich in alchemy, transforming scrubby vegetables, knobby bones, and indigestible raw grains and legumes into nutritional gold. The transfer of vitamins and minerals from the simmered foods into the broth gives soup its goodness; long, slow cooking develops incomparable flavor. Of course, soup doesn't always have to be cooked. Cool purées of raw vegetables or fruits in clear or creamy broths are also nutritious and satisfying. The whole gamut is explored on the following pages, where you'll find enough variety for every palate. As a base for most of our soups, we call for low-sodium broth. You can either make it yourself or purchase canned broth (look for a brand that's low in salt and rich in flavor). Then choose a soup—whether hot or cold, as first course or main dish—to suit the occasion.

COLD CUCUMBER & DILL BISQUE

Preparation time: About 15 minutes

Per serving: 132 calories, 17 g protein, 12 g carbohydrates, 2 g total fat (0.8 g saturated fat), 114 mg cholesterol, 196 mg sodium

Crisp cucumbers and delicate pink shrimp contrast in this creamy, no-cook soup. It's a snap to prepare, yet elegant enough for company.

 2 large English cucumbers (about 2 lbs. *total*), peeled
 1 cup low-sodium chicken broth
 1 cup plain lowfat yogurt
 ¼ cup lightly packed chopped fresh dill
 3 tablespoons lime juice
 ½ pound small cooked shrimp
 Dill sprigs (optional)

Cut cucumbers into 1½-inch chunks. Place in a blender or food processor with chicken broth; whirl until puréed. Add yogurt, chopped dill, and lime juice; whirl until blended. (For a smoother texture, rub bisque through a fine sieve.)

Ladle into bowls and top with shrimp. Garnish with dill sprigs, if desired. Makes 4 servings.

Pictured on facing page

COOL SCALLOP SOUP

Preparation time: About 20 minutes
Chilling time: At least 4 hours

Per serving: 178 calories, 24 g protein, 17 g carbohydrates, 2 g total fat (0.7 g saturated fat), 41 mg cholesterol, 240 mg sodium

Part soup and part salad, this frosty main-dish offering stars marinated scallops atop a creamy purée of vegetables. Chopped tomatoes and sliced cucumbers add crunch.

 1 pound bay or sea scallops, rinsed and drained
 ⅔ cup lemon juice
 3 medium-size cucumbers (about 1¾ lbs. *total*)
 ⅓ cup firmly packed watercress sprigs
 ⅓ cup thinly sliced green onions (including tops)
 1 cup plain lowfat yogurt
 Salt
 2 medium-size pear-shaped tomatoes (about 6 oz. *total*), seeded and diced

Cut sea scallops, if used, into ½-inch pieces. Place scallops in a nonmetal bowl with lemon juice; mix. Cover and refrigerate, stirring occasionally, for at least 4 hours or until next day. With a slotted spoon, lift out scallops, reserving lemon juice. Cover scallops and return to refrigerator.

Cut off a third of one of the cucumbers; score its skin lengthwise with a fork; then thinly slice. Set slices aside along with 4 of the watercress sprigs.

Coarsely chop remaining cucumbers. Place in a blender or food processor with reserved lemon juice, remaining watercress, onions, and yogurt; whirl until smooth. Season to taste with salt.

Drain scallops, reserving any liquid, and stir liquid into cucumber mixture. Pour into bowls; add scallops, tomatoes, and cucumber slices to each serving. Garnish with watercress. Makes 4 servings.

On a steamy day, cool off with a cold soup.
Succulent bay scallops float in a frosty cucumber and
watercress purée in Cool Scallop Soup (recipe on facing
page). Iced tea and sunny corn muffins are all the
accompaniments you'll need.

Portable, packable, quick-to-fix, a meal-in-one—these are some of the reasons we love sandwiches. Nutritionally, they're wonderful, too. All the essentials can be incorporated into one hand-held package: carbohydrates and fiber from bread and vegetables; protein from meats, cheeses, fish, or beans; and fats from spreads and oils (be sparing). Season with a little creativity and the possibilities are endless.

Start by choosing different wrappers—sliced bread, pita, buns, tortillas, or hollowed whole loaves. Vary fillings from the exotic to the familiar; serve some hot and some cold. Then offer them for lunch, a light supper, or even breakfast.

Cottage Cheese & Tomato Breakfast Stack

Here's a balanced way to start the day. Serve this breakfast sandwich with a glass of orange juice; the vitamin C helps your body absorb the calcium in the cottage cheese.

- 1 slice whole wheat bread
- ¼ cup lowfat (2%) cottage cheese
- 1 small pear-shaped tomato (about 2 oz.), sliced
   Ground allspice and freshly ground pepper

Toast bread. While still warm, spread with cottage cheese. Arrange tomato in an overlapping pattern atop cheese; season to taste with allspice and pepper. Makes 1 serving.

Per serving: 118 calories, 11 g protein, 16 g carbohydrates, 2 g total fat (0.8 g saturated fat), 5 mg cholesterol, 355 mg sodium

Pictured on page 205
Spiced Lentil Pockets

The piquancy of red chile is balanced with a minty yogurt sauce in this excellent picnic choice. You can prepare the filling ahead and then assemble the sandwiches on site.

- 1 cup lentils
- 1 bay leaf
- 1 small dried hot red chile
- 1 teaspoon cumin seeds
- ¼ cup olive oil
- 3 tablespoons wine vinegar
- 1 clove garlic, minced or pressed
   Yogurt Sauce (recipe follows)
- ½ cup thinly sliced green onions (including tops)
- 1 cup chopped celery
- 4 whole wheat pita breads (6-inch diameter), cut in half

Rinse lentils and sort through, discarding any debris; drain. Place in a 3- to 4-quart pan with 1 quart water, bay leaf, chile, and cumin. Bring to a boil; reduce heat, cover, and simmer until lentils are tender (about 40 minutes). Drain and let cool; discard chile.

In a large bowl, combine oil, vinegar, and garlic; add lentils and gently mix. Prepare Yogurt Sauce. (At this point, you may cover and refrigerate lentils and sauce separately until next day.)

Up to 3 hours before serving, add onions and celery to lentil mixture; stir well. Scoop into pita halves and top with sauce. Makes 4 servings.

Yogurt Sauce. Combine 1 cup **plain nonfat yogurt**, 2 tablespoons chopped **fresh mint leaves**, and 2 tablespoons **golden raisins**.

Per serving: 488 calories, 23 g protein, 69 g carbohydrates, 15 g total fat (2 g saturated fat), 1 mg cholesterol, 397 mg sodium

Eggplant, Radish & Cucumber Sandwiches

Based on the creamy Middle Eastern eggplant spread known as *baba ganoush,* this sandwich is an adventurous change of pace from meat.

- 1 medium-size eggplant (about 1 lb.), pierced in several places with a fork
- 1 or 2 cloves garlic
  About ¼ cup lemon juice
- 1 tablespoon *each* olive oil and sesame tahini
- 4 large slices (about 5½ by 4 inches *each*) whole wheat bread
- 10 radishes, thinly sliced
- 1 small cucumber (about 6 oz.), peeled and thinly sliced
  Chopped cilantro (coriander) or parsley (optional)

Place eggplant in a baking pan and roast in a 350° oven until very soft when pressed (about 45 minutes). When cool enough to handle, peel and cut into large chunks. Place in a food processor or blender with garlic, ¼ cup of the lemon juice, oil, and tahini; whirl until smooth. If necessary, add more lemon juice. Let cool.

Toast bread. Spread with eggplant mixture. Top with radishes and cucumber arranged in rows; sprinkle with cilantro, if desired. Makes 4 servings.

Per serving: 194 calories, 7 g protein, 30 g carbohydrates, 7 g total fat (1 g saturated fat), 1 mg cholesterol, 244 mg sodium

Pictured on page 55

Summer Sandwich

For dramatic picnic fare, present this hollow bread shell filled with summer's seasonal favorites— tomatoes, basil, and red bell peppers.

- 3 medium-size red bell peppers (about 1¼ lbs. *total*), stemmed, seeded, and quartered
- 1 round loaf (about 1 lb.) French bread
- 2 cups firmly packed fresh basil leaves
- 2 cloves garlic
- 3 tablespoons olive oil
- ¼ pound thinly sliced Black Forest ham
- 1 medium-size tomato (about 6 oz.), sliced
- 4 red leaf lettuce leaves, rinsed and crisped

Place bell peppers, skin sides up, on a foil-lined baking sheet and broil 3 inches below heat until charred (about 7 minutes). Let cool slightly; then peel off skins under cool running water and discard. Pat peppers dry and cut into 1-inch-wide strips; set aside.

Cut a wide circle in top of bread loaf, about 1 inch in from edge; carefully lift off lid. Pull out bread from lid and bottom, leaving a ½-inch-thick shell. Reserve crumbs for other uses.

In a food processor or blender, whirl basil and garlic until finely chopped. With motor running, pour in oil; whirl until thickened. Spread basil mixture inside bread shell and on underside of lid. Arrange half the bell pepper strips in shell. Layer with ham, tomato, and remaining bell pepper; top with lettuce. Replace lid and press down lightly. If made ahead, wrap in foil and refrigerate until next day. To serve, cut into wedges. Makes 6 servings.

Per serving: 277 calories, 10 g protein, 36 g carbohydrates, 11 g total fat (2 g saturated fat), 13 mg cholesterol, 591 mg sodium

Greek Salad Pockets

You can prepare this salad ahead; dress it just before stuffing into pita bread. Rinsing the olives removes excess salt.

- 2½ cups shredded romaine lettuce
- 2 medium-size tomatoes (about 12 oz. *total*), seeded and chopped
- ½ small red onion, halved and thinly sliced crosswise
- 12 large ripe olives, rinsed and chopped
- 2 ounces (about ½ cup) crumbled feta cheese
- ⅓ cup lemon juice
- 2 teaspoons dry oregano leaves
- 1 tablespoon olive oil
- 4 whole wheat pita breads (6-inch diameter), cut in half

Combine lettuce, tomatoes, onion, olives, and feta. (At this point, you may cover and refrigerate for up to 4 hours.)

In a small bowl, stir together lemon juice, oregano, and oil. Pour over lettuce mixture and toss well. Gently pack into pita halves. Makes 4 servings.

Per serving: 262 calories, 9 g protein, 38 g carbohydrates, 10 g total fat (3 g saturated fat), 13 mg cholesterol, 571 mg sodium

(Continued on next page)

Vegetable Taco Roll-ups

Rolling vegetables and condiments into a warm tortilla is a welcome sandwich surprise. It's also a good way to feature two important cruciferous vegetables—broccoli and cauliflower.

- ¾ **pound** *each* **broccoli and cauliflower**
- 1 **large red or green bell pepper (about ½ lb.), stemmed, seeded, and chopped**
- 1 **large can (7 oz.) diced green chiles**
- 12 **flour tortillas (7- to 9-inch diameter)**
  Condiments (suggestions follow)
- ¾ **cup (about 3 oz.) grated Cheddar or jack cheese**

Peel broccoli stalks. Slice broccoli and cauliflower lengthwise into thin pieces. Place on a rack in a pan above 1 inch boiling water. Add bell pepper and chiles. Cover and steam over high heat until tender-crisp (about 10 minutes).

Meanwhile, stack tortillas, wrap in foil, and place in a 350° oven until hot (about 10 minutes). Also prepare Condiments. Spoon vegetables onto tortillas; top with Cheddar and condiments. Roll up. Makes 6 servings.

Per serving without condiments: 329 calories, 13 g protein, 57 g carbohydrates, 6 g total fat (3 g saturated fat), 15 mg cholesterol, 731 mg sodium

Condiments. In small bowls, place 1 cup **plain lowfat yogurt**, ½ cup sliced **green onions** (including tops), and ½ cup **Salsa Fresca** (page 41) or bottled salsa.

Dilly Salmon on Dark Rye

Here's a tuna sandwich variation that might become a new favorite. Serve open-faced, or top with bread for portability.

- 1 **can (about 6½ oz.) salmon packed in water, drained**
- 1½ **teaspoons dry dill weed**
- 2 **tablespoons** *each* **lemon juice and plain lowfat yogurt**
- 2 **or 4 slices dark rye or pumpernickel bread**
  Dill sprigs and paper-thin lemon slices (optional)

Stir together salmon, dill weed, lemon juice, and yogurt. To serve open-faced, toast 2 slices of the bread; spread each with salmon mixture and gar-

nish, if desired, with dill sprigs and lemon slices. To serve closed-faced, use 2 slices untoasted bread per sandwich and do not garnish. Makes 2 servings.

Per serving (open-faced): 183 calories, 20 g protein, 15 g carbohydrates, 5 g total fat (2 g saturated fat), 31 mg cholesterol, 527 mg sodium

Pictured on page 59

Chinese Chicken Sandwiches

This fragrantly spiced offering is sophisticated enough for company, or try it as a novel family dinner. Marinate the chicken for a day before you cook it.

- 1 **tablespoon Chinese five spice; or ½ teaspoon** *each* **ground allspice, crushed anise seeds, ground cinnamon, ground cloves, and ground ginger**
- 1 **teaspoon** *each* **salt and sugar**
- ½ **teaspoon pepper**
- 2 **pounds boneless and skinless chicken breasts**
- 1 **tablespoon salad oil**
  Shredded iceberg lettuce
  Cilantro (coriander) sprigs (optional)
  Condiments (suggestions follow)
- 16 **soft dinner rolls (preferably whole wheat), split in half**

In a bowl, stir together Chinese five spice, salt, sugar, and pepper; add chicken, turning to coat. Cover and refrigerate until next day.

Place chicken in a single layer in a 10- by 15-inch baking pan and brush lightly with oil. Bake in a 350° oven until meat in center is no longer pink; cut to test (about 20 minutes). Refrigerate until cool. Slice crosswise into ¼-inch-thick pieces.

Line a platter with lettuce and top with chicken. Garnish with cilantro, if desired. Prepare Condiments and offer with chicken. Serve rolls alongside. Makes 8 servings.

Per sandwich without condiments: 282 calories, 32 g protein, 28 g carbohydrates, 5 g total fat (0.9 g saturated fat), 68 mg cholesterol, 648 mg sodium

Condiments. In small bowls, place about ⅓ cup *each* **hoisin sauce, Dijon mustard**, and thinly sliced **green onions** (including tops). Peel 3 large **oranges**, remove white membrane, and slice crosswise; arrange on platter with chicken.

When you head for the beach, tote along *Summer Sandwich* (recipe on page 53) and *Tuscan Bean Salad* (recipe on page 73) for a carefree picnic. Tuck fresh fruit, lemonade, and ice into your cooler as well, and don't forget a breadboard and knife to cut the sandwich.

WHITE GAZPACHO

Per serving: 111 calories, 8 g protein, 14 g carbohydrates, 3 g total fat (1 g saturated fat), 7 mg cholesterol, 111 mg sodium

Preparation time: About 15 minutes
Chilling time: At least 2 hours

When the weather sizzles, whip up a batch of this cooling soup. It can be made ahead and doesn't require you to stand over a hot stove. The flavors of this gazpacho are tamer than those of its fiery, tomato-based cousins.

- 1 **large English cucumber (about 1 lb.), peeled and coarsely chopped**
- 2 **cups plain lowfat yogurt**
- 2 **tablespoons lemon juice**
- 1 **clove garlic**
- 2 **cups low-sodium chicken broth**
- 1 **cup water**
- 2 **tablespoons minced cilantro (coriander)**
- 2 **tablespoons thinly sliced green onions (including tops)**
- 4 **whole green onions or 4 cucumber spears (4 to 6 inches long *each*)**

Place cucumber in a blender or food processor with yogurt, lemon juice, garlic, and ½ cup of the chicken broth; whirl until coarsely puréed. Pour into a large bowl; stir in remaining chicken broth and water. Cover and refrigerate for at least 2 hours or until next day.

Stir in cilantro and sliced onions. Ladle into bowls and garnish with whole onions. Makes 4 servings.

GREEN & GOLD MELON SOUP

Per serving: 115 calories, 2 g protein, 29 g carbohydrates, 0.5 g total fat (0 g saturated fat), 0 mg cholesterol, 27 mg sodium

Preparation time: About 20 minutes

Cool fruit soups are always a welcome addition to brunches, suppers, and light lunches. For a particularly striking effect, pour the two purées side by side into each soup bowl.

> **Honeydew Melon Soup (recipe follows)**
> **Cantaloupe Soup (recipe follows)**
> **Plain lowfat yogurt (optional)**
> **Mint sprigs (optional)**

Prepare Honeydew Melon Soup and Cantaloupe Soup.

Pour each into a separate small pitcher. With a pitcher in each hand, simultaneously and gently pour soups into wide bowls. Top with a dollop of yogurt and with mint, if desired. Makes 6 to 8 servings.

Honeydew Melon Soup. In a blender or food processor, smoothly purée 5 cups chopped **honeydew melon** and ⅓ cup **lime juice**. Stir in 2 tablespoons **sugar.** (At this point, you may cover and refrigerate until next day.) Stir in 2 teaspoons minced **fresh mint leaves** before serving.

Cantaloupe Soup. In a blender or food processor, smoothly purée 5 cups chopped **cantaloupe** and ⅓ cup **lemon juice.** Stir in 2 tablespoons **sugar.** (At this point, you may cover and refrigerate until next day.) Stir before serving.

ROASTED EGGPLANT SOUP

Per serving: 71 calories, 4 g protein, 13 g carbohydrates, 1 g total fat (0.4 g saturated fat), 0 mg cholesterol, 49 mg sodium

Preparation time: About 15 minutes
Baking time: About 1¼ hours

Rich in minerals (especially potassium), the mild, earthy eggplant takes on sophisticated character in this puréed soup. Serve as a first course with sesame-sprinkled breadsticks.

  1 **large eggplant (about 1½ lbs.), pierced in several places with a fork**
  1 **small onion**
  3 **cups low-sodium chicken broth**
  2 **tablespoons lemon juice**
    Freshly ground pepper
 12 **thin red bell pepper strips**
  4 **teaspoons finely chopped parsley**

Place eggplant and unpeeled onion in a small baking pan. Bake in a 350° oven until vegetables are very soft when squeezed (about 1¼ hours). Let stand until cool enough to handle. (At this point, you may cover and refrigerate for up to 8 hours.)

Peel eggplant and onion. Place in a blender or food processor with ½ cup of the chicken broth; whirl until puréed. Add remaining chicken broth and whirl until blended. Pour into a 2- to 3-quart pan and bring to a boil over high heat. Remove from heat; add lemon juice and season to taste with pepper. Ladle into bowls and top with bell pepper and parsley. Makes 4 servings.

CARIBBEAN CORN CHOWDER

Per serving: 159 calories, 6 g protein, 26 g carbohydrates, 5 g total fat (0.9 g saturated fat), 0 mg cholesterol, 67 mg sodium

Preparation time: About 15 minutes
Cooking time: About 15 minutes

Island flavors—sweet bell peppers, mild chiles, and subtle tarragon—mingle with mellow corn in this unique soup. In tropical fashion, it can be served hot or cool.

  1 **tablespoon salad oil**
  1 **large onion**
  1 **large red bell pepper (about ½ lb.), stemmed, seeded, and chopped**
  3 **fresh green Anaheim or other large mild chiles (about ½ lb. *total*), stemmed, seeded, and chopped**
 5½ **cups low-sodium chicken broth**
  2 **tablespoons minced fresh tarragon leaves or 1 teaspoon dry tarragon leaves**
  ¼ **teaspoon pepper**
  5 **large ears corn (about 3½ lbs. *total*), husks and silk removed**
    Tarragon sprigs (optional)

Heat oil in a 5- to 6-quart pan over medium-high heat. Add onion, bell pepper, and chiles. Cook, stirring, until onion is limp (6 to 8 minutes). Add chicken broth, minced tarragon, and pepper. Cover and bring to a boil.

Meanwhile, cut corn kernels off cobs. Add to broth mixture. Reduce heat, cover, and simmer until corn is hot (about 5 minutes). Serve hot or cool. If made ahead, cover and refrigerate until next day.

Ladle into bowls and garnish with tarragon sprigs, if desired. Makes 6 servings.

■ *Pictured on facing page*

SWEET POTATO & CARROT SOUP

■ *Per serving: 234 calories, 8 g protein, 45 g carbohydrates, 3 g total fat (0.7 g saturated fat), 0 mg cholesterol, 447 mg sodium*

Preparation time: About 15 minutes
Cooking time: About 1 hour

Two blockbuster sources of vitamin A—carrots and sweet potatoes—team up in this family-style soup from China. Fresh ginger and garlic add beguiling flavor; remove them before serving or leave them in for a more authentic presentation.

- 6 cups low-sodium chicken broth
- 6 slices fresh ginger (*each* about the size of a quarter)
- 2 green onions (including tops), thinly sliced
- 2 cloves garlic, cut in half diagonally
- 2 tablespoons reduced-sodium soy sauce
- 2 tablespoons rice wine or dry sherry
- 4 large carrots (about 1½ lbs. *total*), cut into chunks
- 1 large sweet potato (about ¾ lb.), peeled and cut into chunks
- 1 medium-size russet potato (about ½ lb.), peeled and cut into chunks

In a 5- to 6-quart pan, combine chicken broth, ginger, onions, garlic, soy sauce, and wine. Cover and bring to a boil over high heat. Add carrots; reduce heat, cover, and simmer for 15 minutes. Add sweet potato and russet potato; cover and simmer until vegetables are very tender when pierced (35 to 45 more minutes). If desired, remove ginger and garlic with a slotted spoon. Makes 4 servings.

■ WINTER MINESTRONE

■ *Per serving: 241 calories, 9 g protein, 41 g carbohydrates, 5 g total fat (0.8 g saturated fat), 0 mg cholesterol, 314 mg sodium*

Preparation time: About 20 minutes
Cooking time: About 1 hour and 5 minutes

It's no wonder that this soup, chock-full of robust ingredients, is called minestrone, or "big soup." Winter vegetables, grains, beans, potatoes, and cheese guarantee a hearty dose of vitamins, minerals, fiber, and protein in every bowl.

- 2 tablespoons olive oil
- 1 large onion, finely chopped
- 1 large celery stalk, finely chopped
- 2 large cloves garlic, minced or pressed
- 1 teaspoon dry basil leaves
- ½ teaspoon *each* dry rosemary, dry oregano leaves, and dry thyme leaves
- ¼ cup pearl barley
- 2 large thin-skinned potatoes (about 1¼ lbs. *total*), diced
- 3 large carrots (about 1 lb. *total*), diced
- 8 cups low-sodium chicken broth
- 1 large turnip (about ½ lb.), peeled and diced
- 1 can (about 15 oz.) cannellini (white kidney beans) or red kidney beans, drained and rinsed
- ⅔ cup small shell pasta or elbow macaroni
- ¼ cup tomato paste
- 2 cups finely shredded green cabbage Grated Parmesan cheese

Heat oil in a 5- to 6-quart pan over medium-high heat. Add onion, celery, garlic, basil, rosemary, oregano, and thyme. Cook, stirring, until onion is soft (about 5 minutes). Add barley, potatoes, carrots, and chicken broth; bring to a boil over high heat. Reduce heat, cover, and simmer for 20 minutes. Add turnip. Cover and simmer for 20 more minutes.

Stir in beans, pasta, and tomato paste. Bring to a boil over high heat; reduce heat, cover, and simmer until pasta is al dente (about 15 minutes). Add cabbage and simmer, uncovered, until tender-crisp (about 5 more minutes). Ladle into bowls and offer with Parmesan. Makes 8 to 10 servings.

For a casual dinner with family and friends, ladle up
bowlfuls of country-style *Sweet Potato & Carrot Soup*
(recipe on facing page) while guests assemble *Chinese
Chicken Sandwiches* (recipe on page 54) with the
condiments of their choice.

JAMAICAN BLACK BEAN & RICE SOUP

Per serving: 280 calories, 15 g protein, 45 g carbohydrates, 5 g total fat (1 g saturated fat), 2 mg cholesterol, 46 mg sodium

Preparation time: About 15 minutes
Cooking time: About 2¼ hours

Throughout the Caribbean and Latin America, the humble black bean has held body and soul together for many a generation. In this Jamaican soup, beans team up with rice for a complete protein.

- 1 pound (about 2½ cups) dried black beans
- 6 cups water
- 4 cups low-sodium chicken broth
- 2 tablespoons salad oil
- 1 large onion, finely chopped
- 5 cloves garlic, minced or pressed
- 1½ teaspoons *each* ground cumin and dry oregano leaves
- 1½ cups cooked brown rice
- 2 tablespoons red wine vinegar
  Salt
- 1 cup plain lowfat yogurt
- 4 green onions (including tops), thinly sliced
- 6 radishes, thinly sliced
  Lime or lemon wedges

Rinse beans and sort through, discarding any debris; drain well. Place in a 4- to 5-quart pan with water and bring to a boil over high heat. Reduce heat, cover, and simmer until beans swell, absorbing most of the water (about 45 minutes). Add chicken broth. Cover and simmer until beans are tender (about 1½ more hours).

Meanwhile, heat oil in a small frying pan over medium heat. Add chopped onion, garlic, cumin, and oregano and cook, stirring, until onion is limp (about 7 minutes). Set aside.

In a blender or food processor, whirl about 2 cups of the beans and a little of the broth until smooth; return to bean mixture. Stir in onion mixture, rice, and vinegar; season to taste with salt. Cook over medium heat until steaming.

Ladle into bowls and offer with yogurt, green onions, radishes, and lime. Makes 8 to 10 servings.

CREAMY GARBANZO SOUP WITH BARLEY

Per serving: 322 calories, 12 g protein, 46 g carbohydrates, 11 g total fat (1 g saturated fat), 0 mg cholesterol, 485 mg sodium

Preparation time: About 15 minutes
Cooking time: About 45 minutes

Ounce for ounce, beans are a superb nutritional bargain. Combined with grains and seeds, they form a complete protein package in this mouthwatering potage.

- 2 tablespoons salad oil
- 1 medium-size onion, chopped
- ⅓ cup pearl barley
- 1 teaspoon cumin seeds
- 5 cups low-sodium chicken broth
- 2 cans (about 15½ oz. *each*) garbanzo beans, drained and rinsed
- ¼ cup sesame seeds
- 6 green onions (including tops), thinly sliced

Heat 1 tablespoon of the oil in a 5- to 6-quart pan over medium-high heat. Add chopped onion, barley, and cumin. Cook, stirring often, until barley is opaque and onion is soft (about 5 minutes).

Add chicken broth and bring to a boil; reduce heat, cover, and simmer until barley is tender (about 25 minutes). Add beans; cover and simmer until hot (about 10 minutes). Pour half the bean mixture into a blender; whirl until puréed. Return to pan.

Meanwhile, heat remaining oil in a small frying pan over medium-high heat. Add sesame seeds and cook, stirring often, until golden (about 4 minutes). Add green onions and cook, stirring, until bright green (about 1 minute). Ladle soup into bowls and offer with sesame mixture. Makes 6 servings.

LEMONY LENTIL SOUP

Per serving: 295 calories, 19 g protein, 41 g carbohydrates, 7 g total fat (1 g saturated fat), 0 mg cholesterol, 303 mg sodium

Preparation time: About 20 minutes
Cooking time: About 40 minutes

In this meal-in-a-bowl soup, lentils and Swiss chard team up for a winning nutritional ticket. It's a hearty choice for fiber, protein, and vitamin A.

- 1½ cups lentils
- 8 cups low-sodium chicken broth
- 1 large thin-skinned potato (about ½ lb.), cut into ½-inch cubes
- 2 bunches Swiss chard (about 1½ lbs. *total*), sliced crosswise into ½-inch strips
- 2 tablespoons salad oil
- 1 medium-size onion, finely chopped
- 3 cloves garlic, minced or pressed
- ½ cup coarsely chopped cilantro (coriander)
- ¼ teaspoon pepper
- ½ teaspoon ground cumin
- 3 tablespoons lemon juice
  Lemon slices

Rinse lentils and sort through, discarding any debris; drain well. Place in a 6- to 8-quart pan with chicken broth; cover and bring to a boil over medium-high heat.

Add potato; cover and cook for 20 minutes. Add chard; cover and cook until lentils are tender (about 20 more minutes).

Meanwhile, heat oil in a small frying pan over medium heat. Add onion and cook, stirring occasionally, until limp and golden (about 10 minutes). Add garlic and ⅓ cup of the cilantro; cook, stirring, until garlic is soft (1 to 2 minutes).

Add onion mixture to lentil mixture during last 5 minutes of simmering. Stir in pepper, cumin, and lemon juice. Ladle into bowls and top with lemon slices and remaining cilantro. Makes 6 servings.

MEXICAN ALBONDIGAS SOUP

Per serving: 265 calories, 18 g protein, 29 g carbohydrates, 9 g total fat (2 g saturated fat), 33 mg cholesterol, 266 mg sodium

Preparation time: About 30 minutes
Cooking time: About 15 minutes

Popular family fare south of the border, this wholesome brew is a crowd pleaser here, too. To cut back on fat, the meatballs are made with ground turkey instead of pork or beef; for extra convenience, make them in advance.

- Meatballs (recipe follows)
- 1 can (about 15 oz.) pear-shaped tomatoes
- 6 cups low-sodium chicken broth
- 4 cups low-sodium beef broth
- 2 cups chopped onions
- 6 medium-size carrots (about 1½ lbs. *total*), thinly sliced
- 1 teaspoon dry oregano leaves
- 2 teaspoons chili powder
- ¾ pound stemmed spinach leaves, rinsed well and drained
- ⅓ cup chopped cilantro (coriander)
- 1 or 2 limes, cut into wedges

Prepare Meatballs; set aside.

In an 8- to 10-quart pan, combine tomatoes (break up with a spoon) and their liquid, chicken broth, beef broth, onions, carrots, oregano, and chili powder. Bring to a boil over high heat; then reduce heat to low. Add meatballs and cook for 10 minutes. Stir in spinach and cilantro and cook until wilted (about 3 more minutes). Ladle into bowls and offer with lime. Makes 6 to 8 servings.

Meatballs. Mix 1 pound **fresh ground turkey**, ½ cup cooked **brown or white rice**, ¼ cup *each* **all-purpose flour** and **water**, and 1 teaspoon **ground cumin**. Shape mixture into 1- to 1½-inch balls and place, slightly apart, in a 10- by 15-inch baking pan. Bake in a 450° oven until well browned (about 15 minutes). Pour off fat. If made ahead, let cool; then cover and refrigerate until next day.

Serve up a triple dose of spinach with Tortellini
& Chicken Soup (recipe on facing page), brimming with
spinach pasta, chopped spinach, and chunks of chicken,
and Mini-Calzones (recipe on page 180), tiny turnovers
stuffed with spinach and ham.

TORTELLINI & CHICKEN SOUP

■

Per serving: 201 calories, 19 g protein, 21 g carbohydrates, 4 g total fat (0.8 g saturated fat), 37 mg cholesterol, 247 mg sodium

Preparation time: About 15 minutes
Cooking time: About 15 minutes

Plump tortellini and tender chicken float in a vegetable- and rice-filled broth for a simple yet substantial soup. Look for fresh tortellini in the refrigerator case of your supermarket or in a pasta shop.

- 4½ **quarts low-sodium chicken broth**
- 1 **package (9 oz.) fresh cheese-filled spinach tortellini**
- ¾ **pound stemmed spinach leaves, rinsed well, drained, and chopped**
- 1 **pound boneless and skinless chicken breasts, cut into ½-inch chunks**
- ½ **pound mushrooms, sliced**
- 1 **medium-size red bell pepper (about 6 oz.), stemmed, seeded, and diced**
- 1 **cup cooked white or brown rice**
- 2 **teaspoons dry tarragon leaves**
  Grated Parmesan cheese (optional)

In an 8- to 10-quart pan, bring chicken broth to a boil over high heat. Add tortellini; cook until al dente (about 4 minutes).

Add spinach, chicken, mushrooms, bell pepper, rice, and tarragon; return to a boil over high heat. Reduce heat, cover, and simmer until chicken in center is no longer pink; cut to test (about 2 minutes). Ladle into bowls and offer with Parmesan, if desired. Makes 10 to 12 servings.

SHRIMP & RICE CHOWDER

■

Per serving: 282 calories, 23 g protein, 31 g carbohydrates, 7 g total fat (1 g saturated fat), 148 mg cholesterol, 292 mg sodium

Preparation time: About 15 minutes
Cooking time: About 35 minutes

Jalapeños add sizzle to this sturdy chowder of rice, peas, and shrimp. A squeeze of lime adds a tart counterbalance.

- 2 **jalapeño chiles (about 3 inches long *each*), stemmed**
- 2 **tablespoons salad oil**
- 1 **large onion, finely chopped**
- 2 **cloves garlic, minced or pressed**
- ½ **teaspoon cumin seeds**
- 6 **cups low-sodium chicken broth**
- ⅔ **cup short-grain (pearl) rice**
- 1 **pound small cooked shrimp**
- 3 **medium-size pear-shaped tomatoes (about ½ lb. *total*), finely chopped**
- 1 **package (10 oz.) frozen tiny peas, thawed**
- 1 **lime, cut into wedges**

Cut 1 of the chiles in half lengthwise. Thinly slice remaining chile crosswise and set aside.

Heat oil in a 5- to 6-quart pan over medium-high heat. Add onion, garlic, cumin, and 1 or both of the chile halves (to taste). Cook, stirring often, until onion is soft (about 5 minutes). Add chicken broth and rice. Bring to a boil over high heat; reduce heat, cover, and simmer until rice is tender (20 to 25 minutes).

Set aside ½ cup of the shrimp. Add remaining shrimp, tomatoes, and peas to pan. Simmer, uncovered, until hot (2 to 3 minutes). Remove chile halves and discard. Ladle chowder into bowls and top with reserved shrimp and chile slices. Offer with lime. Makes 6 servings.

Salads

Spinach Salad with Garlic Croutons ■ Napa

Cabbage Slaw ■ Orange-Onion Salad ■ Jicama

& Apples with Pomegranate ■ Red & Yellow

Pepper Salad ■ Corn & Black Bean Salad ■

Potato & Avocado Salad ■ Bulgur & Vegetables

with Lemon-Curry Dressing ■ Tuscan Bean

Salad ■ Orzo with Spinach & Pine Nuts ■

Pepper, Pasta & Orange Salad ■ Chef's Salad

with Fruit ■ Chicken & Pears with Mint

Vinaigrette ■ Turkey & Rice Salad ■ Panzanella

■ Crab & Cucumber Salad

Eat to your heart's content! There's no need to worry about overindulging when it comes to salads. Fresh fruits and vegetables are excellent sources of vitamins and minerals, whole grains and legumes offer valuable complex carbohydrates and fiber, and morsels of poultry and seafood contribute protein. Used in salads, they all add up to great nutrition in every bite. What about dressings? We've lightened them up. You'll find delicate blends of mild vinegars, citrus juices, and fresh herbs, with just a trace of oil. Even the old standards that defined your favorite green salad— French or Italian dressing, or creamy Roquefort— have been re-created in delicious, lean versions. For all your salad preparations, seek out the freshest possible ingredients. Peel and cut fruits and vegetables at the last minute to avoid discoloration and nutrient loss.

Better yet, leave the vitamin-packed peels on when possible. Offered as a first course, a side dish, or an entrée, salads feature abundant variety and wholesome eating for any occasion.

■ *Pictured on facing page*

SPINACH SALAD WITH GARLIC CROUTONS

Preparation time: About 20 minutes
Broiling time: About 4 minutes

When Popeye's favorite—iron-rich spinach—teams up with sweet onion rings, vibrant red bell peppers, mushrooms, and garlicky croutons, it becomes a festival in a bowl. A tangy feta dressing adds a Greek accent.

1½ **pounds spinach, stems removed, rinsed well, and dried**

1 **medium-size red onion (about 6 oz.), cut into thin rings**

½ **pound mushrooms, thinly sliced**

1 **large red bell pepper (about ½ lb.), stemmed, seeded, and thinly sliced**

2 **ounces (about ½ cup) crumbled feta cheese**

½ **cup lemon juice**

4 **teaspoons olive oil**

½ **teaspoon dry oregano leaves**

2 **cloves garlic**

1 **small French bread baguette (about ½ lb.)**

■ *Per serving: 255 calories, 10 g protein, 38 g carbohydrates, 8 g total fat (3 g saturated fat), 11 mg cholesterol, 471 mg sodium*

Tear spinach into bite-size pieces, if desired. Place in a bowl with onion, mushrooms, and bell pepper; set aside.

In a blender, whirl feta, lemon juice, oil, oregano, and 1 clove of the garlic until smooth; set aside.

Cut baguette into ½-inch-thick slices. Place in a single layer on a baking sheet and broil 4 inches below heat, turning once, until golden brown on both sides (about 4 minutes *total*). Let cool briefly. Rub remaining garlic clove over tops of croutons.

Pour dressing over vegetables and toss well. Transfer to individual salad plates and top with croutons. Makes 4 to 6 servings.

■ NAPA CABBAGE SLAW

■ *Per serving: 76 calories, 2 g protein, 18 g carbohydrates, 0.3 g total fat (0.1 g saturated fat), 0 mg cholesterol, 44 mg sodium*

Preparation time: About 15 minutes

Fresh and crunchy, this salad will remind you of traditional coleslaw, but without the mayonnaise. Pale green napa cabbage and a touch of ginger give this slaw an Oriental flavor.

1½ **pounds carrots, finely shredded**

4 **cups finely slivered napa cabbage**

⅓ **cup white wine vinegar**

2 **tablespoons sugar**

1 **clove garlic, minced or pressed**

1 **teaspoon minced fresh ginger**
  Salt

In a salad bowl, gently mix carrots, cabbage, vinegar, sugar, garlic, and ginger. Season to taste with salt. If made ahead, cover and refrigerate for up to 4 hours. Makes 6 servings.

Keep things light with Spinach Salad with Garlic Croutons (recipe on facing page). Fresh, iron-rich spinach, red bell pepper, onion, and mushrooms are tossed with a lean feta dressing; top each serving with toasty homemade croutons.

ORANGE-ONION SALAD

Per serving: 117 calories, 2 g protein, 21 g carbohydrates, 4 g total fat (0.5 g saturated fat), 0 mg cholesterol, 5 mg sodium

Preparation time: About 20 minutes
Cooking time: About 8 minutes

This colorful salad, perfect at holiday time, won't add unwanted calories.

- 1¼ **cups fresh or frozen cranberries**
- ⅓ **cup sugar**
- 4 **medium-size oranges (about 2 lbs.** *total***)**
- 2 **tablespoons** *each* **salad oil and red wine vinegar**
- 12 **cups (about 1½ lbs.) bite-size pieces mixed greens, such as butterhead lettuce, chicory, and escarole, rinsed and crisped**
- ½ **cup thinly sliced red onion rings**
  Salt and pepper

In a 1½- to 2-quart pan, stir together cranberries and sugar. Cover and cook over low heat, shaking pan occasionally, just until a few cranberries begin to burst (about 8 minutes for fresh, 15 minutes for frozen). Let cool.

Grate enough orange peel to make 1 teaspoon. Ream 1 of the oranges to make 3 tablespoons juice.

Mix orange peel, orange juice, oil, and vinegar; gently stir into cranberry mixture. (At this point, you may cover and refrigerate for up to 2 days.)

Remove peel and white membrane from remaining oranges; thinly slice crosswise. In a salad bowl, combine orange slices, greens, and onion. Pour cranberry dressing over salad. Toss well. Season to taste with salt and pepper. Makes 8 servings.

JICAMA & APPLES WITH POMEGRANATE

Per serving: 40 calories, 0.6 g protein, 10 g carbohydrates, 0.2 g total fat (0 g saturated fat), 0 mg cholesterol, 5 mg sodium

Preparation time: About 15 minutes

Typical of the crunchy, fresh salads served alongside spicy dishes in Mexico, this one contains no oil. For a festive presentation, fan out the jicama and apple slices on salad plates and cluster pomegranate seeds in the center.

- ½ **small jicama, peeled and rinsed**
- 1 **large tart green apple (about 6 oz.), such as Granny Smith or Newtown Pippin**
- 6 **tablespoons lime juice**
- 1 **teaspoon sugar**
- 6 **tablespoons pomegranate seeds**
  Salt
  Cilantro (coriander) sprigs (optional)

Cut jicama crosswise into 18 thin, half-circle slices. Core and halve apple; cut each half into 18 thin slices. Place jicama and apple in a bowl and coat with lime juice. Lift slices from juice, add sugar to lime juice, and set aside. Arrange 3 jicama slices and 6 apple slices in a fan pattern on each of 6 salad plates. (At this point, you may cover and refrigerate for up to 5 hours.)

Just before serving, spoon 1 tablespoon of the pomegranate seeds in center of each salad. Sprinkle with lime juice mixture and season to taste with salt. Garnish with cilantro, if desired. Makes 6 servings.

CORN & BLACK BEAN SALAD

Per serving: 183 calories, 8 g protein, 29 g carbohydrates, 5 g total fat (0.7 g saturated fat), 0 mg cholesterol, 388 mg sodium

Preparation time: About 15 minutes
Cooking time: About 5 minutes

Summer calls for outdoor eating. Offer this fiber-packed combination of beans and corn alongside sandwiches or cold chicken. Look for canned black beans in your grocery store or in Latin American markets.

- 4 **cups fresh or frozen corn kernels**
- 2 **cans (about 15 oz.** *each***) black beans, drained and rinsed**
- 3 **medium-size tomatoes (about 1 lb.** *total***), seeded and chopped**
- ¼ **cup minced cilantro (coriander)**
- ½ **cup minced red onion**
   Cumin Dressing (recipe follows)

In a 4- to 5-quart pan, bring 2 quarts water to a boil over high heat. Add corn and cook until tender (about 5 minutes). Drain, rinse with cold water until cool, and drain again. In a salad bowl, stir together corn, beans, tomatoes, cilantro, and onion.

Prepare Cumin Dressing. Pour over vegetables and toss well. If made ahead, cover and refrigerate until next day. Makes 10 servings.

Cumin Dressing. Stir together ¼ cup **lime juice,** ⅓ cup **sherry vinegar** or red wine vinegar, 1 tablespoon **Dijon mustard,** and 2 teaspoons **ground cumin.** Add 3 tablespoons **salad oil;** whisk until blended.

RED & YELLOW PEPPER SALAD

Per serving: 59 calories, 1 g protein, 10 g carbohydrates, 2 g total fat (0.3 g saturated fat), 0 mg cholesterol, 4 mg sodium

Preparation time: About 20 minutes
Cooking time: 2 minutes

This brilliant mosaic of red and yellow bell peppers is a sparkling choice for outdoor meals. This sweet, colorful vegetable is an exceptional source of vitamin C. If yellow peppers are unavailable in your market, use all red.

- 1 **large red onion (about ¾ lb.), thinly sliced and separated into rings**
- 1 **tablespoon balsamic or red wine vinegar**
- 2 **medium-size red bell peppers (about ¾ lb.** *total***), stemmed, seeded, and cut into strips**
- 1 **medium-size yellow bell pepper (about 6 oz.), stemmed, seeded, and finely diced**
- 2 **medium-size cucumbers (about 1¼ lbs.** *total***), thinly sliced**
   Tarragon Vinaigrette (recipe follows)

In a wide frying pan, combine onion and vinegar. Cook over medium heat, stirring, for 2 minutes. Let cool.

In a large bowl, combine onion mixture, red and yellow bell peppers, and cucumbers. Prepare Tarragon Vinaigrette. Pour over vegetables and toss well. If made ahead, cover and refrigerate until next day, stirring several times. Makes 8 servings.

Tarragon Vinaigrette. Mix ⅓ cup **white wine vinegar;** 1 tablespoon **olive oil** or salad oil; 2 teaspoons **sugar;** 1 teaspoon **dry tarragon leaves;** 1 clove **garlic,** minced or pressed; and ¼ teaspoon **pepper.**

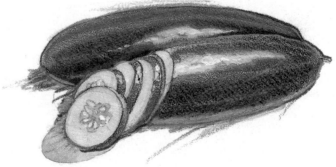

Iceberg
lettuce

Escarole

Chicory

Green leaf
lettuce

Butterhead
lettuce

Red leaf lettuce

Romaine
lettuce

Radicchio

Arugula

Watercress

Belgian endive

Limestone
lettuce

*Take your pick! Garden-fresh greens give
character to salads. Compose a medley for contrasting
taste, texture, and color, or feature one kind in a solo
performance. Individual descriptions and availabilities
are detailed on the facing page.*

Not too long ago, making a green salad meant choosing among a few familiar lettuces: iceberg, romaine, butterhead, and perhaps looseleaf. For more unusual selections, you had to seek out a farmer's market or grow your own.

All that has changed. Now, numerous wonderful lettuces, chicories, and greens are available in most supermarkets. Flavors range from mild to peppery, colors from palest celadon to emerald to vivid magenta. From a nutritional standpoint, all are low in calories and add varying amounts of potassium, vitamin A, vitamin C, calcium, and iron to your diet.

When purchasing salad greens, look for crisp, fresh-looking leaves with deep color. At home, gently rinse and dry the leaves; then tear them into bite-size pieces. To crisp, place them in a bowl, cover with a dry paper towel, and refrigerate for up to 4 hours. Dress the leaves with quality oils and vinegars, applying them with a light hand. (For lowfat dressings, see page 77.)

Here's a guide to 10 of the most common salad greens (pictured on facing page). Other leafy greens worth considering for your salad include spinach, dandelion, and sorrel.

Arugula (rocket, roquette). The bright green, deeply serrated leaves of arugula have a spicy, mustardy tang. Mix with milder-tasting greens.

Belgian endive (French endive). A member of the chicory family, endive is grown in a light-deprived environment and is almost white in color. The flavor is pleasantly bitter and the texture crisp. Availability peaks from September through May.

Butterhead lettuce (Bibb, Boston, buttercrunch, limestone). These lettuces are named for their delicate, almost buttery flavor. The heads are small with loose, pliable leaves.

Chicory (curly endive). Distinguished by its tousled-looking head, chicory has ragged, dark outer leaves that are more bitter and tough than the pale inner ones. Baby chicory (frisée) is more softly textured.

Escarole. Also a chicory, escarole is sturdy and broad leafed with a distinctive, slightly bitter flavor that blends well with looseleaf greens.

Iceberg lettuce (head lettuce). This best-seller, available all year, is composed mostly of water. It has a firm, tightly bound head with pale, crisp leaves. Iceberg is lower in vitamins and minerals than the darker green lettuces.

Looseleaf lettuce (green leaf, red leaf). All looseleaf lettuces are tender and mildly flavored. Colors range from red to bronze to dark green, and leaves can be smooth or ruffled.

Radicchio (red chicory, Italian chicory). This rising star on the salad circuit has been popular in Northern Europe for years. The most common variety in U.S. markets is a tight, round head of magenta leaves striated with white. It has the same slightly bitter bite as its cousin, chicory.

Romaine lettuce. Deep green in color, romaine is distinguished by its long, straight, exceptionally crisp leaves. It stands up well to heavy dressings.

Watercress. Tingly and peppery, watercress adds distinctive flavor to salads. It provides more vitamins A and C than the other greens.

Mixed Greens with Vinaigrette

Because the vinegar used in this dressing is so mild, you'll need very little oil.

> 4 cups bite-size pieces tender mixed greens, such as red leaf, butterhead, and escarole, rinsed and crisped
> 1 cup arugula or lightly packed watercress, rinsed and crisped
> 1 cup chopped Belgian endive or radicchio (or ½ cup *each*), rinsed and crisped
> ½ cup unseasoned rice vinegar
> 1 teaspoon Dijon mustard
> 1 tablespoon minced shallots (optional)
> 1 tablespoon olive oil
> Salt and pepper

In a salad bowl, gently toss lettuce, arugula, and endive. In a small bowl, whisk vinegar, mustard, and, if desired, shallots. Add oil; whisk until blended. Pour over greens and toss well. Season to taste with salt and pepper. Makes 6 servings.

Per serving: 32 calories, 0.8 g protein, 2 g carbohydrates, 2 g total fat (0.3 g saturated fat), 0 mg cholesterol, 31 mg sodium

POTATO & AVOCADO SALAD

Per serving: 185 calories, 4 g protein, 37 g carbohydrates, 3 g total fat (0.4 g saturated fat), 0 mg cholesterol, 20 mg sodium

Preparation time: About 20 minutes
Cooking time: About 15 minutes

Although higher in fat than other fruits, avocados have exquisite flavor and contain lots of potassium (1,200 milligrams on average). They're a nutritious addition to your diet when eaten in moderation, as in this spicy potato salad.

2 pounds small red thin-skinned potatoes (about 16), quartered
½ cup thinly sliced green onions (including tops)
6 tablespoons lime juice
1 or 2 jalapeño or other small hot chiles, stemmed, seeded, and minced
2 teaspoons minced fresh ginger
1 tablespoon chopped cilantro (coriander)
½ teaspoon sugar
1 small firm-ripe avocado (about ¼ lb.)

In a 4- to 5-quart pan, bring 2 quarts water to a boil over high heat. Add potatoes; reduce heat, cover, and simmer until tender when pierced (about 15 minutes). Drain and let cool.

In a large bowl, mix potatoes, onions, lime juice, chiles, ginger, cilantro, and sugar. (At this point, you may cover and refrigerate for up to 3 hours.)

Pit and peel avocado; cut into ½-inch cubes. Add to potato mixture and stir gently. Makes 4 to 6 servings.

BULGUR & VEGETABLES WITH LEMON-CURRY DRESSING

Per serving: 327 calories, 8 g protein, 53 g carbohydrates, 10 g total fat (1 g saturated fat), 0 mg cholesterol, 316 mg sodium

Preparation time: About 20 minutes (plus 1 hour standing time)

A versatile, fiber-rich whole grain, bulgur is familiar to many as the main ingredient in tabbouleh. Here, it's showcased as a tart and spicy main-dish salad.

1 cup bulgur
2 cups boiling water
Lemon-Curry Dressing (recipe follows)
1 can (about 15½ oz.) garbanzo beans, drained and rinsed
2 celery stalks, thinly sliced
3 medium-size tomatoes (about 1 lb. *total*), seeded and diced
½ cup minced cilantro (coriander)
Salt

In a large bowl, combine bulgur and water; cover with foil. Let stand until bulgur is soft and most of the liquid is absorbed (about 1 hour).

Meanwhile, prepare Lemon-Curry Dressing and set aside.

Drain off excess liquid from bulgur. Add beans, celery, tomatoes, and cilantro; stir well. Pour in dressing and stir again; season to taste with salt. If made ahead, cover and refrigerate for up to 8 hours. Serve at room temperature. Makes 4 to 6 servings.

Lemon-Curry Dressing. Stir together ¼ cup **lemon juice**, 1 teaspoon **Dijon mustard**, and 1 teaspoon **curry powder.** Add 3 tablespoons **salad oil;** whisk until blended.

■ *Pictured on page 55*

TUSCAN BEAN SALAD

■ *Per serving: 215 calories, 8 g protein, 31 g carbohydrates, 8 g total fat (1 g saturated fat), 0 mg cholesterol, 434 mg sodium*

Preparation time: About 15 minutes
Cooking time: About 13 minutes

White beans and sage are considered a poetic match in central Italian cuisine. The addition of tender red potatoes and crisp asparagus makes this dish a colorful springtime classic.

- 8 small red thin-skinned potatoes (about 1 lb. *total*), cut into small chunks
- ½ pound asparagus, tough ends snapped off, cut into 1-inch pieces
- 2 cans (about 15 oz. *each*) cannellini (white kidney beans), drained and rinsed
- ½ cup finely chopped red onion
- 2 large tomatoes (about 1 lb. *total*), seeded and diced
- ¼ cup sherry vinegar or red wine vinegar
- 1 tablespoon Dijon mustard
- ¼ cup olive oil (preferably extra virgin)
- 3 tablespoons minced fresh sage leaves; or 2 teaspoons dry sage leaves mixed with 2 tablespoons minced parsley
  Freshly ground pepper

In a 4- to 5-quart pan, bring 2 quarts water to a boil over high heat; add potatoes and cook just until tender when pierced (about 10 minutes). Add asparagus and continue cooking until tender-crisp (about 3 more minutes). Drain, rinse with cold water until cool, and drain again.

In a large bowl, combine potatoes, asparagus, beans, onion, and tomatoes. In a small bowl, stir together vinegar and mustard; add oil and whisk until blended. Stir in sage. Pour dressing over bean mixture and stir gently; season to taste with pepper. If made ahead, cover and refrigerate until next day. Serve at room temperature, stirring before serving. Makes 8 servings.

ORZO WITH SPINACH & PINE NUTS

■ *Per serving: 226 calories, 8 g protein, 32 g carbohydrates, 7 g total fat (3 g saturated fat), 13 mg cholesterol, 177 mg sodium*

Preparation time: About 20 minutes
Cooking time: About 15 minutes

This pasta salad is excellent either as a prelude to a light dinner or as picnic fare. Orzo, a rice-shaped pasta, is sometimes labeled *semi di mellone*.

- ½ pound orzo or very small pasta shells
- 2 tablespoons pine nuts
- 1 tablespoon olive oil
- ½ cup minced red onion
- ¼ pound stemmed spinach leaves, rinsed well and chopped
- 2 pear-shaped tomatoes (about ⅓ lb. *total*), seeded and diced
- 3 ounces (about ¾ cup) crumbled feta cheese
- ¼ cup chopped parsley
  Freshly ground pepper

In a 3- to 4-quart pan, cook orzo in 2 quarts boiling water until al dente (about 5 minutes). Drain, rinse with cold water until cool, and drain again.

In a medium-size frying pan, cook pine nuts over medium heat, stirring, until golden (about 3 minutes). Remove nuts and set aside. Heat oil in pan. Add onion and cook, stirring, until soft (about 5 minutes). Add spinach and continue cooking, stirring, just until wilted (about 2 more minutes).

In a large bowl, combine orzo, pine nuts, and spinach mixture; toss well. Add tomatoes, feta, and parsley; season to taste with pepper. Toss again. If made ahead, cover and refrigerate for up to 4 hours. Serve at room temperature. Makes 6 servings.

■ *Pictured on page 1*

PEPPER, PASTA & ORANGE SALAD

Preparation time: About 20 minutes
Cooking time: 7 to 9 minutes

Golden bell peppers and gleaming oranges star with pasta, onion, and basil in this warm-weather main dish. For extra punch, add chili oil to the dressing.

- 10 ounces dry pasta, such as shells, gnocchi shape, or corkscrews
- 4 large yellow or red bell peppers (about 2 lbs. *total*), stemmed, seeded, and quartered
- 2 large oranges (about 1¼ lbs. *total*)
- ¼ cup olive oil (preferably extra virgin)
- ¼ cup balsamic or red wine vinegar
- 2 teaspoons hot chili oil (optional)
- 1 medium-size red onion (about 6 oz.), thinly sliced
- ¼ cup finely chopped fresh basil leaves Basil sprigs (optional)

■

Per serving: 331 calories, 8 g protein, 53 g carbohydrates, 11 g total fat (1 g saturated fat), 0 mg cholesterol, 5 mg sodium

In an 8- to 10-quart pan, cook pasta in 6 quarts boiling water until al dente (7 to 9 minutes or according to package directions). Drain, rinse with cold water until cool, and drain again. Set aside.

Meanwhile, place bell peppers, skin sides up, on a foil-lined baking sheet and broil 3 inches below heat until charred (about 7 minutes). Let cool slightly; then peel off skins under cool running water and discard. Pat dry and cut into thin strips.

Peel oranges and remove white membrane. Holding oranges over a small bowl, cut between segments to release fruit; squeeze juice from membrane into bowl and reserve.

In a large bowl, mix pasta, olive oil, vinegar, and, if desired, chili oil. Mound pasta mixture on a platter or in a bowl, and top with peppers, onion, and oranges. Sprinkle with orange juice and chopped basil. Garnish with basil sprigs, if desired. Toss lightly. Makes 6 servings.

■ *Pictured on facing page*

CHEF'S SALAD WITH FRUIT

Preparation time: About 25 minutes

Here's a fresh look at chef's salad: this inspired version features vegetables, fruit, lowfat cheese, and succulent turkey. It's a lovely main course for a warm-evening supper.

- Honey-Mustard Dressing (recipe follows)
- 12 cups (about 1½ lbs.) bite-size pieces red leaf lettuce, rinsed and crisped
- 2 large red Bartlett or other firm-ripe pears (about 1 lb. *total*)
- 4 kiwi fruit (about 1 lb. *total*), peeled and thinly sliced crosswise
- 2 large carrots (about ¾ lb. *total*), coarsely grated
- 3 ounces part-skim mozzarella cheese, finely shredded
- ¼ pound thinly sliced cooked skinless turkey breast, cut into julienne strips

■

Per serving: 286 calories, 12 g protein, 40 g carbohydrates, 11 g total fat (3 g saturated fat), 21 mg cholesterol, 110 mg sodium

Prepare Honey-Mustard Dressing and set aside.

Place lettuce in a large shallow bowl or on a platter. Core and slice pears. Arrange pears, kiwis, carrots, mozzarella, and turkey in separate mounds on lettuce. Offer with dressing. Makes 6 servings.

Honey-Mustard Dressing. Mix ½ cup **cider vinegar**, 3 tablespoons *each* **salad oil** and **honey**, and 2 teaspoons **dry mustard.** If made ahead, cover and refrigerate for up to 2 days.

*Rediscover a main-course classic with a light
twist. Chef's Salad with Fruit (recipe on facing page)
stars vitamin-rich kiwi, garnet-edged pears, and crunchy
carrots atop red leaf lettuce; slivered turkey breast
and mozzarella cheese add protein.*

CHICKEN & PEARS WITH MINT VINAIGRETTE

Per serving: 350 calories, 35 g protein, 44 g carbohydrates, 4 g total fat (1 g saturated fat), 91 mg cholesterol, 76 mg sodium

Preparation time: About 20 minutes
Steeping time: 16 to 18 minutes

Steeping chicken guarantees moist, tender results with absolutely no added fat. A splash of mint-infused dressing adds contrast to this main-dish salad.

1 **whole chicken breast (about 1 lb.), split**

½ **cup unseasoned rice vinegar or white wine vinegar**

1½ **tablespoons sugar**

3 **tablespoons chopped fresh mint leaves**

4 **to 6 lettuce leaves, rinsed and crisped**

2 **large firm-ripe pears (about 1 lb.** *total***)**

Mint sprigs (optional)

In a 3- to 4-quart pan, bring 2 quarts water to a boil over high heat. Add chicken, pushing into water to cover completely. Cover pan and remove from heat; let chicken steep until meat in center is no longer pink; cut to test (16 to 18 minutes).

Meanwhile, combine vinegar, sugar, and chopped mint in a small bowl; stir until sugar is dissolved. Line 2 dinner plates with lettuce. Set aside.

Lift out chicken and immerse in ice water until cool; drain. Discard skin and bones; cut meat diagonally into thin slices. Peel pears, if desired; core and thinly slice. Arrange chicken and pears on lettuce; spoon on dressing. Garnish with mint sprigs, if desired. Makes 2 servings.

TURKEY & RICE SALAD

Per serving: 290 calories, 30 g protein, 20 g carbohydrates, 9 g total fat (2 g saturated fat), 64 mg cholesterol, 81 mg sodium

Preparation time: About 15 minutes
Cooking time: About 45 minutes

When holiday turkey leftovers overrun the refrigerator, put them to wholesome use by mixing them with crisp vegetables, rice, and a lively Oriental dressing. Or simmer a turkey breast anytime and treat yourself to this superb light dish.

Simmered Turkey Breast (recipe follows) or 4 cups diced cooked skinless turkey breast

2 **celery stalks, thinly sliced**

½ **cup minced cilantro (coriander)**

2 **green onions (including tops), thinly sliced**

2 **cups cooled cooked brown or white rice**

2 **tablespoons salad oil**

2 **teaspoons sesame oil**

½ **cup** *each* **lime juice and low-sodium chicken broth**

⅓ **cup minced fresh ginger**

Prepare Simmered Turkey Breast. Cut meat away from bone and dice (you should have about 4 cups).

In a salad bowl, combine turkey, celery, cilantro, onions, and rice. In a small bowl, stir together salad oil, sesame oil, lime juice, chicken broth, and ginger; pour over turkey mixture and toss well. If made ahead, cover and refrigerate until next day. Makes 6 servings.

Simmered Turkey Breast. Place 1 **turkey breast half** (about 3 lbs.) in a 6- to 8-quart pan. Add cold **water** to cover and bring to a boil over high heat; skim off any foam. Add 1 **celery stalk,** chopped; 1 small **onion,** quartered; 1 small **bay leaf;** and 10 **black peppercorns.** Reduce heat and simmer, uncovered, until meat near bone is no longer pink; cut to test (about 45 minutes). Lift out turkey and let cool briefly; pull off and discard skin.

Feature LOWFAT DRESSINGS

Diet-conscious people often put salad on the menu. But to keep a salad healthy, you need to be aware of what goes on top. Many a well-intentioned bowlful is nutritionally undermined by the addition of a high-fat dressing.

Below, some favorite dressings are presented in their slimmest guise. Each recipe contains 1 gram or less of fat per tablespoon. For best flavor, start with the right oil. Olive oil has the most distinctive taste and is high in monounsaturated fat. If you prefer a more neutral flavor, choose canola, corn, peanut, or safflower oil.

Use the savory dressings on mixed greens, cold vegetables, or meat-based salads; drizzle Honey-Yogurt Dressing over fresh fruit. It's best to limit the amount you use to 3 tablespoons or less for each serving.

Orange-Basil Vinaigrette. In a small pan, stir together ½ cup freshly squeezed **orange juice** and 1 teaspoon **cornstarch** until cornstarch is dissolved. Bring to a boil over medium heat and cook, stirring, for 30 seconds. Pour into a small bowl or measuring cup and refrigerate until cold.

Add 3 tablespoons **white wine vinegar,** 1 teaspoon *each* **Dijon mustard** and **dry basil leaves,** and 1 teaspoon **olive oil** (preferably extra virgin); whisk until blended. If made ahead, cover and refrigerate until next day. Makes about ½ cup.

Per tablespoon: 15 calories, 0.1 g protein, 2 g carbohydrates, 0.7 g total fat (0.1 g saturated fat), 0 mg cholesterol, 19 mg sodium

Spicy French Dressing. In a small pan, stir together ½ cup *each* **sugar** and **cider vinegar** and 1 tablespoon **all-purpose flour.** Cook over medium heat, stirring, until bubbling (about 5 minutes).

Place in a blender with 1 teaspoon *each* **salt** and **Worcestershire;** 1 medium-size **onion,** finely chopped; and 1 clove **garlic,** minced or pressed. Whirl until smooth. With blender on lowest speed, slowly pour in 2 tablespoons **salad oil.** Transfer to a bowl and stir in ⅓ cup **catsup** and 1 teaspoon **celery seeds.** If made ahead, cover and refrigerate for up to 1 month. Makes about 2 cups.

Per tablespoon: 25 calories, 0.1 g protein, 4 g carbohydrates, 0.9 g total fat (0.1 g saturated fat), 0 mg cholesterol, 100 mg sodium

Italian Dressing. In a small pan, stir together 1 cup cold **water,** ⅓ cup **red wine vinegar,** and 2 teaspoons **cornstarch** until cornstarch is dissolved. Bring to a boil over medium heat and cook, stirring, until slightly thickened (about 1 minute). Pour into a small bowl or measuring cup and refrigerate until cold.

Add 1 teaspoon **Dijon mustard,** ½ teaspoon **garlic powder,** ¼ teaspoon *each* **salt** and **pepper,** 1 teaspoon *each* **dry basil leaves** and **dry oregano leaves,** 2 tablespoons finely minced **red or green bell pepper,** and 2 teaspoons **olive oil;** whisk until blended. If made ahead, cover and refrigerate for up to 1 week. Makes about 1 cup.

Per tablespoon: 8 calories, 0 g protein, 0.7 g carbohydrates, 0.6 g total fat (0.1 g saturated fat), 0 mg cholesterol, 43 mg sodium

Creamy Blue Cheese. In a blender or food processor, combine ¾ cup **lowfat buttermilk;** 2 tablespoons *each* chopped **parsley, plain nonfat yogurt, white wine vinegar,** and **blue-veined cheese;** 1 teaspoon **salad oil;** and 1 tablespoon minced **shallot.** Whirl until smooth. Season to taste with **ground white pepper.** If made ahead, cover and refrigerate for up to 1 week. Makes about 1 cup.

Per tablespoon: 13 calories, 0.7 g protein, 0.9 g carbohydrates, 0.7 g total fat (0.3 g saturated fat), 1 mg cholesterol, 28 mg sodium

Honey-Yogurt Dressing. Stir together 1½ tablespoons grated **orange peel,** 1 teaspoon minced **fresh ginger,** 1 cup **plain lowfat yogurt,** 2 tablespoons **honey,** and 1 tablespoon **lemon juice** until smooth. Stir in 2 teaspoons **poppy seeds,** if desired. If made ahead, cover and refrigerate for up to 1 week. Makes about 1¼ cups.

Per tablespoon: 14 calories, 0.6 g protein, 3 g carbohydrates, 0.2 g total fat (0.1 g saturated fat), 0.7 mg cholesterol, 8 mg sodium

A sophisticated choice for light dining, Crab & Cucumber Salad (recipe on facing page) is peppered with toasted black sesame seeds and spooned over romaine lettuce leaves. Chilled white wine and breadsticks are easy menu partners.

PANZANELLA

Per serving: 239 calories, 16 g protein, 30 g carbohydrates, 7 g total fat (1 g saturated fat), 15 mg cholesterol, 367 mg sodium

Preparation time: About 25 minutes

A thrifty cook's dream, this rustic Tuscan salad uses leftover bread. It delivers complex carbohydrates with little fat and lots of flavor.

½ **pound stale whole wheat Italian or French bread, torn into coarse pieces**

1 **pound ripe tomatoes, seeded and chopped**

½ **cup *each* chopped fresh basil leaves and chopped parsley**

1 **cup chopped red onion**

2 **cloves garlic, minced or pressed**

1 **can (about 6½ oz.) tuna packed in water, drained**

½ **cup red wine vinegar**

2 **tablespoons olive oil (preferably extra virgin)**

Freshly ground pepper

In a large bowl, combine bread with just enough cold water (about 2 cups) to moisten. Let bread soak for about 5 minutes. Place in a colander. With back of a spoon, press bread to extract excess moisture; then break up large chunks. Transfer to a salad bowl.

Add tomatoes, basil, parsley, onion, garlic, and tuna to bread; mix well. In a measuring cup, stir together vinegar and oil; pour over salad and mix well. Season to taste with pepper. Makes 4 to 6 servings.

■ *Pictured on facing page*

CRAB & CUCUMBER SALAD

Per serving: 124 calories, 18 g protein, 9 g carbohydrates, 2 g total fat (0.2 g saturated fat), 85 mg cholesterol, 243 mg sodium

Preparation time: About 15 minutes
Cooking time (optional): 3 to 5 minutes

Delicate crab and crunchy cucumber are tossed with radishes and a whisper of rice vinegar in this exquisite entrée. A sprinkling of black sesame seeds (available in Asian markets) adds distinction.

1 **teaspoon black sesame seeds (optional)**

1 **large English cucumber (about 1 lb.)**

1 **green onion (including top), thinly sliced**

10 **medium-size radishes, thinly sliced**

½ **to 1 pound flaked crabmeat**

⅓ **to ½ cup seasoned rice vinegar; or ⅓ to ½ cup white wine vinegar mixed with 4 teaspoons sugar**

Romaine lettuce leaves, rinsed and crisped

Slivered green onion tops and whole radishes (optional)

In a small frying pan, toast sesame seeds, if used, over low heat, shaking pan often, until fragrant (3 to 5 minutes). Set aside.

Quarter cucumber lengthwise; then thinly slice crosswise. In a large bowl, lightly mix cucumber, sliced onion, sliced radishes, crab, and vinegar.

Line individual plates with lettuce, top with crab mixture, and sprinkle with sesame seeds, if used. Garnish with slivered onion tops and whole radishes, if desired. Makes 4 servings.

Meats

Curry Beef in Lettuce ■ Chile Beef Stir-fry on

Mixed Greens ■ Souvlaki in Pitas ■ Sweet &

Sour Flank Steak ■ Grilled Orange-Coriander

Steak ■ Italian Pork Stew with Polenta ■ Cool

Pork with Zucchini & Wheat Berries ■ Spicy Pork

Tenderloins ■ Lamb Chops with Papaya

Chutney ■ Dilled Lamb Stew with Peas ■

Oregon Spring Stew with Vegetables ■ Chayote

with Spiced Lamb Filling ■ Veal Curry with Fruit

■ Mediterranean Veal Ragout

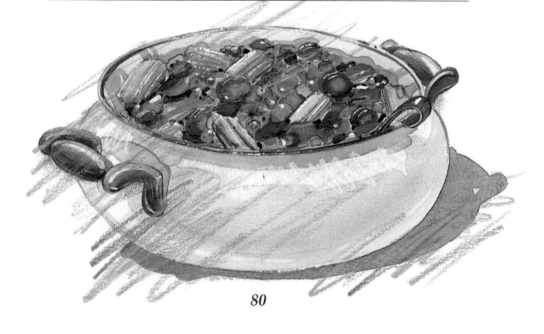

Can you include red meat as part of a healthy, balanced diet? Absolutely. Meat is a superb source of complete protein; it also provides essential B vitamins, zinc, and readily absorbable iron. What about saturated fat and cholesterol? Today, cattle, hogs, and sheep are bred to be leaner than in the past. Because fat content varies from place to place on these animals, the solution is to choose cuts composed of lean muscle, with outside fat that can be trimmed away. As for cholesterol, it's best controlled by portion size; the ideal serving of cooked meat is 3 ounces, which translates to 4 ounces boneless raw meat. (See the chart on page 84 for nutritional information.) As the recipes in this chapter illustrate, you can maximize tenderness and succulence by choosing the right cooking method for the cut of meat you're using. More tender cuts can be grilled, broiled, roasted, or stir-fried; slice the meat thinly across the grain and offer it on the rare side to ensure juiciness. Tougher cuts benefit from braising and stewing.

CURRY BEEF IN LETTUCE

Per serving: 197 calories, 22 g protein, 17 g carbohydrates, 4 g total fat (1 g saturated fat), 49 mg cholesterol, 118 mg sodium

Preparation time: About 15 minutes
Cooking time: About 25 minutes

When casual and quick are the main requirements for dinner, try this easy ground beef dish. A spicy filling, bolstered with a potato, is scooped into lettuce leaves.

- 1 medium-size thin-skinned potato (about ½ lb.), quartered
- ¾ pound lean top round, freshly ground
- 1 medium-size onion, chopped
- 2 tablespoons *each* curry powder, tomato paste, and vinegar
- ½ cup water
- ¼ pound mushrooms, chopped
- 1 medium-size head butterhead lettuce (about ¼ lb.), separated into leaves, rinsed, and crisped

In a 2- to 3-quart pan, bring 1 quart water to a boil over high heat; add potato and cook until tender when pierced (about 10 minutes). Drain and let cool; then dice. Set aside.

Crumble beef into a medium-size frying pan; add onion. Cook over medium-high heat, stirring, until meat is browned and onion is limp (about 7 minutes). Pour off any fat. Stir in curry, tomato paste, vinegar, the ½ cup water, and mushrooms. Reduce heat, cover, and simmer until mushrooms are soft (about 5 minutes). Uncover, increase heat to high, and cook, stirring often, until almost all the liquid has evaporated. Add potatoes; cook, stirring, until hot.

Spoon meat mixture into lettuce leaves and roll up. Makes 4 servings.

Pictured on facing page

CHILE BEEF STIR-FRY ON MIXED GREENS

Per serving: 262 calories, 25 g protein, 12 g carbohydrates, 13 g total fat (4 g saturated fat), 68 mg cholesterol, 226 mg sodium

Preparation time: About 15 minutes
Marinating time: At least 30 minutes
Cooking time: 3 to 5 minutes

An intriguing interplay of hot and cold sets this stir-fry apart. The mixed greens add crunch and contrast.

- 1 pound lean boneless top sirloin steak (about 1 inch thick), fat trimmed
- 1 jalapeño or other small hot chile, stemmed, seeded, and minced
- 2 cloves garlic, minced or pressed
- ½ to ¾ teaspoon ground red pepper (cayenne)
- 1 tablespoon reduced-sodium soy sauce
- ½ teaspoon sugar
- ⅓ cup seasoned rice vinegar; or ⅓ cup white wine vinegar mixed with 2 tablespoons sugar
- 3 teaspoons salad oil
- 8 cups (about 1 lb.) bite-size pieces mixed greens, such as watercress, chicory, arugula, radicchio, butterhead lettuce, and looseleaf lettuce, rinsed and crisped

  Freshly ground black pepper

Slice steak across grain into ⅛-inch-thick strips about 3 inches long. In a medium-size bowl, mix chile, garlic, red pepper, soy sauce, and sugar. Add steak, turning to coat. Cover and refrigerate for at least 30 minutes or until next day.

Just before serving, stir together vinegar and 2 teaspoons of the salad oil in a large bowl. Add greens, turning to coat; arrange on individual plates and set aside.

Heat remaining oil in a wide nonstick frying pan over high heat. Add steak mixture and cook, stirring, until steak is browned (3 to 5 minutes). Spoon over greens and season to taste with black pepper. Makes 4 servings.

Quickly cook marinated lean red meat and present
it in a tempting new guise with Chile Beef Stir-fry on
Mixed Greens (recipe on facing page), a tantalizing
contrast of tastes and textures.

83

■ Nutritional Values of Meat

For many people, meat is their primary source of protein. Yet we tend to consume far more of it than necessary. In fact, adults need only about 6 ounces of meat per day to help meet their protein requirements.

Along with protein, meat supplies iron, B vitamins, and zinc. But it can also be high in cholesterol and saturated fat. That's why it's important to choose meat cuts wisely. Look for cuts with minimal marbling, the web of fat interlaced in the muscle, and with fat that can be trimmed away (often referred to as knife-separable fat), leaving good, lean muscle for cooking. To assure minimum fat in ground meats, select a lean cut, such as beef top round or lamb sirloin, and have your butcher grind it for you.

The chart below is designed to help you choose those cuts of meat that are naturally lean. The figures are based on a portion size of 3 ounces cooked (4 ounces raw boneless) meat.

Portion: 3 ounces cooked	Calories	Protein (g)	Total fat (g)	Saturated fat (g)	Cholesterol (mg)
BEEF					
Top round, lean only, broiled	165	24	7	2	70
Bottom round, lean only, braised	191	27	8	3	82
Sirloin, lean only, broiled	179	26	8	3	76
Flank steak, lean only, broiled	207	22	13	5	60
Prime rib, lean and fat, roasted	328	19	28	12	72
Ground, extra lean, broiled	218	22	14	5	71
Ground, lean, broiled	231	21	16	6	74
Ground, regular, broiled	246	20	18	7	77
Chuck roast, lean only, braised	199	28	9	3	86
Liver, pan-fried	185	23	7	2	410
PORK					
Bacon, pan-fried	490	26	42	15	72
Canadian bacon, pan-fried	157	21	7	2	49
Center loin, lean and fat, roasted	259	22	19	7	77
Shoulder, lean only, braised	250	27	15	5	99
Tenderloin, roasted	141	24	4	1	79
Leg, lean only, roasted	187	24	9	3	80
Ham, extra lean, roasted	123	18	5	2	45
LAMB					
Loin chops, lean only, broiled	184	26	8	3	81
Sirloin, lean only, roasted	174	24	8	3	78
Shoulder, lean only, broiled	179	22	10	3	77
VEAL					
Leg, lean only, braised	173	31	4	2	115
Shoulder, lean only, braised	168	28	6	2	134
Ground, broiled	146	21	6	3	88
Loin chops, lean only, roasted	149	22	6	2	90

SOUVLAKI IN PITAS

Per serving: 560 calories, 42 g protein, 82 g carbohydrates, 8 g total fat (2 g saturated fat), 70 mg cholesterol, 831 mg sodium

Preparation time: About 20 minutes
Marinating time: At least 30 minutes
Broiling time: 5 to 7 minutes

For an out-of-the-ordinary dinner, try spicy grilled beef enfolded in whole wheat pita bread and moistened with yogurt sauce.

- 1 **pound lean top round steak (about 1 inch thick), fat trimmed**
- ¼ **cup** *each* **lemon juice and dry white wine**
- 2 **cloves garlic, minced or pressed**
- 1 **teaspoon ground cumin**
  Souvlaki Sauce (recipe follows)
- 8 **whole wheat pita breads (6-inch diameter)**
  Nonstick cooking spray or salad oil
- 2 **large tomatoes (about 1 lb.** *total***), cut into thin wedges**
- 2 **cups shredded romaine lettuce**
- 1 **small red onion (about ¼ lb.), cut into thin rings**

Slice steak across grain into long, ½-inch-thick strips. In a medium-size bowl, mix lemon juice, wine, garlic, and cumin. Add steak, turning to coat. Cover and refrigerate for at least 30 minutes or until next day. Meanwhile, prepare Souvlaki Sauce.

Wrap pita breads, 4 at a time, in foil; place in a 250° oven until warm (about 10 minutes).

Meanwhile, lightly coat a broiler pan rack with cooking spray. Drain steak and place on rack. Broil 3 to 4 inches below heat, turning once, until lightly browned but still juicy; cut to test (5 to 7 minutes *total*).

Place 2 or 3 pieces of meat in center of each pita bread. Top with sauce, tomatoes, lettuce, and onion and fold up. Makes 4 servings (2 souvlaki *each*).

Souvlaki Sauce. Stir together 1 cup **plain lowfat yogurt,** 1 teaspoon **dry oregano leaves,** and 2 tablespoons **water.** Cover and refrigerate for at least 30 minutes or until next day.

SWEET & SOUR FLANK STEAK

Per serving: 254 calories, 22 g protein, 14 g carbohydrates, 12 g total fat (5 g saturated fat), 58 mg cholesterol, 473 mg sodium

Preparation time: About 15 minutes
Marinating time: At least 4 hours
Grilling time: 8 to 10 minutes

To maximize the flavor of lean flank steak, soak it in a piquant marinade and grill it just until rare. You may want to have the butcher pass the meat through a tenderizer first.

- ⅓ **cup cider vinegar**
- ¼ **cup** *each* **honey and reduced-sodium soy sauce**
- 1 **clove garlic, minced or pressed**
- ⅛ **teaspoon liquid hot pepper seasoning**
- 1½ **pounds flank steak, fat trimmed**
  Parsley sprigs (optional)

In a small pan, cook vinegar, honey, soy sauce, garlic, and hot pepper seasoning over medium heat, stirring often, until honey is dissolved and mixture is well blended (about 5 minutes). Let cool briefly.

Place steak in a shallow nonmetal bowl just large enough to hold it; pour in marinade. Cover and refrigerate for at least 4 hours or until next day, turning once or twice.

Lift out steak and drain, reserving marinade. Place on a lightly greased grill 4 to 6 inches above a solid bed of medium-hot coals. Cook, turning once and basting often with marinade, until done to your liking; cut to test (8 to 10 minutes *total* for rare).

Meanwhile, bring any remaining marinade to a boil in a small pan over high heat. Slice steak thinly across grain. Garnish with parsley, if desired, and offer with marinade. Makes 6 servings.

*Abbondanza! Enjoy the gusto of an Italian meal
and get a healthy balance of protein and carbohydrates
at the same time with Italian Pork Stew with Polenta
(recipe on facing page). Offer lightly sautéed summer
squash and red bell peppers alongside.*

GRILLED ORANGE-CORIANDER STEAK

Per serving: 190 calories, 28 g protein, 6 g carbohydrates, 6 g total fat (2 g saturated fat), 71 mg cholesterol, 53 mg sodium

Preparation time: About 15 minutes
Marinating time: At least 4 hours
Grilling time: About 8 minutes

Beef aficionados will applaud this juicy top round steak, soaked in a tangy citrus marinade and then grilled to perfection. Slice thinly and serve with the extra marinade.

- 1 teaspoon grated orange peel
- ¾ cup orange juice
- 1 medium-size onion, minced
- 3 cloves garlic, minced or pressed
- ¼ cup white wine vinegar
- 1½ tablespoons ground coriander
- 1 teaspoon *each* cracked pepper and dry basil leaves
- 1½ pounds lean top round steak (about 1 inch thick), fat trimmed
  Finely shredded orange peel (optional)

Stir together grated orange peel, orange juice, onion, garlic, vinegar, coriander, pepper, and basil. Measure out ½ cup of the mixture; cover and refrigerate.

Place steak in a shallow nonmetal bowl just large enough to hold it; pour in remaining marinade. Cover and refrigerate for at least 4 hours or until next day, turning meat once or twice.

Lift out steak and drain, reserving marinade. Place on a lightly greased grill 4 to 6 inches above a solid bed of medium-hot coals. Cook, turning once and basting often with marinade, until done to your liking; cut to test (about 8 minutes *total* for rare).

Meanwhile, bring the ½ cup refrigerated marinade to a boil in a small pan over medium-high heat. Slice steak thinly across grain. Garnish with shredded orange peel, if desired, and offer with heated marinade. Makes 6 servings.

■ *Pictured on facing page*

ITALIAN PORK STEW WITH POLENTA

Per serving: 399 calories, 31 g protein, 49 g carbohydrates, 8 g total fat (2 g saturated fat), 77 mg cholesterol, 321 mg sodium

Preparation time: About 15 minutes
Cooking time: About 2 hours

Perfect fare for cool autumn nights, this earthy stew will warm you up without weighing you down. Look for polenta (coarsely ground cornmeal) in Italian delicatessens and well-stocked supermarkets.

- 1½ pounds lean boneless pork (cut from leg or shoulder), fat trimmed, cut into 1½-inch chunks
- 3½ cups water
- ¾ pound small mushrooms, halved
- 1 large onion, chopped
- 2 cloves garlic, minced or pressed
- 1 can (28 oz.) pear-shaped tomatoes
- 1 cup dry red wine
- ½ teaspoon *each* dry rosemary and dry marjoram, dry oregano, and dry thyme leaves
- 4 cups low-sodium chicken broth
- 2 cups polenta
- ½ cup chopped Italian parsley
  Rosemary sprigs (optional)

Place pork and ½ cup of the water in a 5- to 6-quart pan. Cover and cook over medium-high heat for 10 minutes. Uncover and continue cooking, stirring, until juices have evaporated and meat is browned (about 5 more minutes). Add mushrooms, onion, and garlic; reduce heat to medium and cook, stirring often, until onion is soft (about 5 minutes).

Add tomatoes (break up with a spoon) and their liquid, wine, dry rosemary, marjoram, oregano, and thyme, stirring to loosen browned bits. Bring to a boil; reduce heat and simmer, partially covered, until pork is tender (about 1½ hours).

About 30 minutes before stew is done, bring chicken broth and remaining water to a boil in a heavy 3- to 4-quart pan over high heat. Stir in polenta in a thin stream. Cook, stirring, until polenta begins to thicken; reduce heat to low and continue cooking, stirring often, until no longer grainy (20 to 25 minutes).

Spoon onto a platter and top with stew; sprinkle with parsley. Garnish with rosemary sprigs, if desired. Makes 6 servings.

Lean cuts of red meat *can* fit into a light and healthy diet. The challenge is learning how to enhance the flavor of the meat without adding extra fat. Here we present a variety of lean marinades and sauces you can use when you're grilling, stir-frying, or sautéing meat. By varying the cooking styles and seasonings, you can create an entire repertoire of easy, meat-based meals.

Suggested cuts. Use tender, boneless, fat-trimmed cuts of meat, such as beef tenderloin, sirloin, or top round; veal leg or loin cutlets; pork tenderloin; or lamb sirloin or loin cuts. The chart on page 84 provides a listing of the calories, protein, fat, and cholesterol content of each cut of meat; nutritional information for each marinade and sauce is given with the recipe.

Grilled Marinated Meat

Fajita Marinade, Lemon-Soy Marinade, or Orange-Anise Marinade (recipes follow)

1 pound lean boneless meat (suggestions above), cut into cubes or steaks
   Nonstick cooking spray or salad oil

Prepare marinade of your choice. Add meat, turning to coat. Cover and refrigerate, stirring occasionally, for at least 1 hour or until next day. Lift out meat and drain, reserving marinade. Thread cubes, if used, on skewers.

To barbecue, place meat on a lightly greased grill about 6 inches above a solid bed of hot coals. Cook, basting several times with reserved marinade and turning as needed, until done to your liking; cut to test.

To broil, lightly coat a broiler pan rack with cooking spray. Place meat on rack and broil 3 to 4 inches below heat, basting several times with reserved marinade and turning as needed, until done to your liking; cut to test. Makes 4 servings.

Fajita Marinade. In a nonmetallic bowl, mix 2 tablespoons **lime juice,** ¼ cup **water,** ½ teaspoon **ground cumin,** 1 teaspoon **ground coriander,** and 1 clove **garlic,** minced or pressed.

Per serving (marinade only): 4 calories, 0.1 g protein, 0.9 g carbohydrates, 0.1 g total fat (0 g saturated fat), 0 mg cholesterol, 2 mg sodium

Lemon-Soy Marinade. In a nonmetallic bowl, mix 3 tablespoons **reduced-sodium soy sauce;** ¼ cup **lemon juice;** 2 cloves **garlic,** minced or pressed; and 1 tablespoon finely chopped **fresh ginger** or ¼ teaspoon ground ginger.

Per serving (marinade only): 14 calories, 0.9 g protein, 3 g carbohydrates, 0.1 g total fat (0 g saturated fat), 0 mg cholesterol, 454 mg sodium

Orange-Anise Marinade. In a nonmetallic bowl, mix 2 tablespoons **frozen orange juice concentrate,** thawed; ⅓ cup **dry red wine;** and ½ teaspoon **anise or fennel seeds,** crushed.

Per serving (marinade only): 17 calories, 0.3 g protein, 4 g carbohydrates, 0.1 g total fat (0 g saturated fat), 0 mg cholesterol, 1 mg sodium

Stir-fried Meat with Sauce

Barbecue Stir-fry Sauce, Ginger-Sherry Stir-fry Sauce, or Rosemary-Pear Stir-fry Sauce (recipes follow)

2 teaspoons salad oil

½ pound lean boneless meat (suggestions at left), cut across grain into ⅛-inch-thick strips about 2 inches long

Prepare stir-fry sauce of your choice and set aside.

Heat oil in a wok or medium-size frying pan over high heat. Add meat and cook, stirring, until done to your liking. Lift out meat and keep warm. Stir sauce and add to pan. Boil until thickened. Return meat to pan, stirring to coat. Makes 2 servings.

Barbecue Stir-fry Sauce. Mix ⅓ cup **low-sodium beef broth;** 1 tablespoon *each* **brown sugar, red wine vinegar,** and **Worcestershire;** 1 clove **garlic,** minced or pressed; 1 teaspoon **cornstarch;** and ½ teaspoon **dry mustard.**

Per serving (sauce only): 46 calories, 0.6 g protein, 11 g carbohydrates, 0.3 g total fat (0 g saturated fat), 0 mg cholesterol, 86 mg sodium

Ginger-Sherry Stir-fry Sauce. Mix ¼ cup *each* **dry sherry** and **low-sodium chicken broth;** 1 tablespoon **reduced-sodium soy sauce;** 1 teaspoon minced **fresh ginger;** 1 clove **garlic,** minced or pressed; 1 teaspoon **cornstarch;** and ⅛ to ¼ teaspoon **crushed dried hot red chiles.**

Per serving (sauce only): 31 calories, 0.9 g protein, 6 g carbohydrates, 0.2 g total fat (0.1 g saturated fat), 0 mg cholesterol, 310 mg sodium

Rosemary-Pear Stir-fry Sauce. Mix ½ cup canned **pear nectar,** 2 to 3 teaspoons **white wine vinegar,** 1 teaspoon chopped **fresh rosemary** or ½ teaspoon dry rosemary, ¼ teaspoon **coarsely ground pepper,** and ¾ teaspoon **cornstarch.**

Per serving (sauce only): 43 calories, 0.1 g protein, 11 g carbohydrates, 0 g total fat (0 g saturated fat), 0 mg cholesterol, 3 mg sodium

Mustard-Tarragon Sauce. Mix ⅓ cup **low-sodium beef broth,** 1 teaspoon *each* **red wine vinegar** and **Dijon mustard,** ½ teaspoon **cornstarch,** and ½ teaspoon chopped **fresh tarragon leaves** or ¼ teaspoon dry tarragon leaves.

Per serving (sauce only): 9 calories, 0.1 g protein, 2 g carbohydrates, 0.3 g total fat (0 g saturated fat), 0 mg cholesterol, 76 mg sodium

Wine–Blue Cheese Sauce. Mix ⅓ cup **low-sodium beef broth,** 2 tablespoons **dry red wine,** 1 teaspoon **cornstarch,** and ¼ teaspoon **Worcestershire.** After pouring heated sauce over meat, sprinkle with 1 tablespoon crumbled **blue-veined cheese.**

Per serving (sauce only): 24 calories, 1 g protein, 2 g carbohydrates, 1 g total fat (0.8 g saturated fat), 3 mg cholesterol, 67 mg sodium

Thyme Sauce. Mix ⅓ cup **low-sodium chicken broth,** 1 teaspoon chopped **fresh thyme leaves** or ½ teaspoon dry thyme leaves, and ½ teaspoon **cornstarch.**

Per serving (sauce only): 8 calories, 0.4 g protein, 1 g carbohydrates, 0.3 g total fat (0.1 g saturated fat), 0 mg cholesterol, 9 mg sodium

Sautéed Meat with Pan Sauce

Mustard-Tarragon Sauce, Wine–Blue
Cheese Sauce, or Thyme Sauce
(recipes follow)

2 teaspoons salad oil
½ pound lean boneless meat (suggestions on facing page), thinly sliced and pounded about ¼ inch thick

Prepare sauce of your choice and set aside.

Heat oil in a wide frying pan over medium-high heat. Add meat and cook, turning once, until done to your liking. Lift out, transfer to heated plates, and keep warm.

Stir sauce and add to pan, stirring to loosen browned bits. Bring to a boil and pour over meat. Makes 2 servings.

COOL PORK WITH ZUCCHINI & WHEAT BERRIES

Per serving: 408 calories, 35 g protein, 42 g carbohydrates, 12 g total fat (3 g saturated fat), 72 mg cholesterol, 531 mg sodium

Preparation time: About 30 minutes
Cooking time: About 1½ hours

Pork loin teams up with chewy wheat berries (available in health food stores) and zucchini in this balanced meal, served at room temperature.

 1 tablespoon salad oil
 1 boneless, fat-trimmed, rolled, and tied pork loin roast (about 1½ lbs.)
 1½ cups low-sodium chicken broth
 1 piece fresh ginger (about 1 oz.), thinly sliced
 ½ cup sake or dry white wine
 ¼ cup reduced-sodium soy sauce
 1 clove garlic, minced or pressed
 ½ cup chopped green onions (including tops)
   Steamed Zucchini (directions follow)
   Simmered Wheat Berries (recipe follows)
 ½ cup lemon juice
 6 lettuce leaves, rinsed and crisped
 1 lemon, cut into wedges

Heat oil in a 5- to 6-quart pan over medium-high heat. Add pork and cook, turning, until browned (10 to 15 minutes). Pour off any fat. Add chicken broth, ginger, sake, soy sauce, garlic, and onions. Reduce heat, cover, and simmer until a meat thermometer inserted in center registers 155°F (about 40 minutes). Meanwhile, prepare Steamed Zucchini and Simmered Wheat Berries.

Lift out pork and let cool. Discard fat and ginger from pan juices. (At this point, you may cover and refrigerate pork and juices separately until next day.)

Add lemon juice to pan juices and set aside. Line a platter with lettuce. Thinly slice pork and arrange on platter; add zucchini and wheat berries. Season with juice mixture. Serve at room temperature with lemon wedges. Makes 6 servings.

Steamed Zucchini. Slice 6 small **zucchini** (about 1½ lbs. *total*) into ½-inch rounds. Place on a rack in a pan above 1 inch boiling water; cover and steam over high heat until barely tender when pierced (about 5 minutes). Immerse in ice water until cool; drain. If made ahead, cover and refrigerate until next day.

Simmered Wheat Berries. In a 5- to 6-quart pan, bring 1½ cups **wheat berries** and 3 cups **low-sodium chicken broth** to a boil over high heat; reduce heat, cover, and simmer until tender (about 1½ hours). Drain and let cool. If made ahead, cover and refrigerate until next day.

■ *Pictured on facing page*

SPICY PORK TENDERLOINS

Per serving: 201 calories, 26 g protein, 12 g carbohydrates, 5 g total fat (2 g saturated fat), 84 mg cholesterol, 283 mg sodium

Preparation time: About 10 minutes
Marinating time: At least 4 hours
Grilling time: About 20 minutes (plus 10 minutes standing time)

The tender eye of the loin is one of the leanest cuts of pork. It's ideal for grilling, especially when coated with a hot-sweet blend of mustard, honey, and spices.

 ¼ cup *each* honey and prepared mustard
 ¼ teaspoon *each* salt and chili powder
 2 pork tenderloins (about ¾ lb. *each*), fat and silvery membrane trimmed

In a large bowl, stir together honey, mustard, salt, and chili powder. Add pork, turning to coat. Cover and refrigerate for at least 4 hours or until next day, turning meat several times.

Lift out pork and drain, reserving marinade. Place pork on a lightly greased grill 4 to 6 inches above a solid bed of medium-hot coals. Cook, basting once with reserved marinade, until no longer pink in center (cut to test) or until a meat thermometer inserted in center registers 155°F (about 20 minutes). Cover with foil and let stand for 10 minutes; cut across grain into thin, slanting slices. Makes 6 servings.

Quickly grilled Spicy Pork Tenderloins (recipe on facing page) offer delicious eating with surprisingly little fat. To round out the menu, add sliced Oriental eggplants and bell peppers to the barbecue, and arrange the meat on a bed of herbed rice.

LAMB CHOPS WITH PAPAYA CHUTNEY

Per serving: 338 calories, 21 g protein, 47 g carbohydrates, 9 g total fat (3 g saturated fat), 51 mg cholesterol, 98 mg sodium

Preparation time: About 15 minutes
Cooking time: About 8 minutes

Broiled lamb chops topped with fresh papaya chutney and seasoned yogurt are sure to please. Purchase loin chops with the rib attached; trim off all the visible fat before cooking and broil until pink and juicy inside.

    Spiced Yogurt Sauce (recipe follows)

1   **medium-size English cucumber (about ¾ lb.)**
    Nonstick cooking spray or salad oil

8   **single-rib lamb chops (about 1½ lbs. *total*), fat trimmed**

¼   **cup *each* sugar and cider vinegar**

1   **small onion, minced**

½   **cup golden raisins**

1   **teaspoon *each* ground cinnamon and ground ginger**

1   **large papaya (about 1¼ lbs.), peeled, seeded, and diced**

Prepare Spiced Yogurt Sauce and set aside. With a vegetable peeler, slice cucumber lengthwise into paper-thin strips; set aside.

Lightly coat a broiler pan rack with cooking spray. Place chops on rack and broil 3 to 4 inches below heat, turning once, until well browned but still pink in center; cut to test (about 8 minutes *total*).

Meanwhile, cook sugar, vinegar, onion, raisins, cinnamon, and ginger in a wide frying pan over medium-high heat, stirring occasionally, until onion is soft (about 5 minutes). Add papaya and cook, stirring gently, until hot (about 3 more minutes). Place 2 chops on each of 4 plates and top with papaya mixture; arrange cucumber alongside. Offer with yogurt sauce. Makes 4 servings.

Spiced Yogurt Sauce. Stir together 1 cup **plain nonfat yogurt**, 2 tablespoons **water**, 1 tablespoon **mustard seeds**, 1 teaspoon **sugar**, ¼ teaspoon **ground cumin**, and ⅛ teaspoon **chili powder.**

DILLED LAMB STEW WITH PEAS

Per serving: 306 calories, 29 g protein, 32 g carbohydrates, 7 g total fat (2 g saturated fat), 75 mg cholesterol, 149 mg sodium

Preparation time: About 20 minutes
Cooking time: About 1¼ hours

Who can resist a stew with rich, meaty flavor and a built-in sauce? Ask for stew meat cut from the leg; it's leaner and requires less cooking time than a shoulder cut.

1½   **pounds lean boneless lamb stew meat (cut from leg), fat trimmed, cut into 1-inch chunks**

2   **cups dry red wine**

½   **cup chopped fresh dill or 1 tablespoon dry dill weed**

4   **small onions, cut into eighths**

2   **pounds carrots, cut into ½-inch lengths**

2   **cups fresh or frozen peas**

½   **cup plain lowfat yogurt**

1   **tablespoon cornstarch**

In a 5- to 6-quart pan, bring lamb and ½ cup of the wine to a boil over high heat. Reduce heat, cover, and simmer for 30 minutes. Uncover and cook over medium-high heat until liquid has evaporated; continue cooking lamb, turning once, until browned (about 5 more minutes). Lift out and set aside. Pour off any fat.

Add remaining wine and dill to pan, stirring to loosen browned bits. Return meat to pan and add onions and carrots. Reduce heat, cover, and simmer, stirring occasionally, until lamb is very tender when pierced (about 35 minutes).

Stir in peas and cook until tender (about 5 more minutes). Remove from heat. In a small measuring cup, mix yogurt and cornstarch; add to pan and stir just until blended. Makes 6 servings.

OREGON SPRING STEW WITH VEGETABLES

Per serving: 298 calories, 28 g protein, 24 g carbohydrates, 10 g total fat (3 g saturated fat), 71 mg cholesterol, 120 mg sodium

Preparation time: About 20 minutes
Cooking time: About 2 hours

From the Oregon countryside comes this bountiful combination of beef and lamb, simmered with plenty of fresh vegetables. A handful of barley adds extra goodness. If the stew is made ahead, the flavor improves.

- 1 tablespoon salad oil
- 1 pound *each* lean boneless lamb shoulder and beef bottom round, fat trimmed, cut into 1-inch chunks
- 1 pound medium-size carrots, sliced
- 1 large onion, chopped
- 1 large turnip (about 10 oz.), peeled and diced
- ½ cup pearl barley, rinsed and drained
- 5 cups low-sodium beef broth
- 2 cups water
- ½ teaspoon pepper
- ½ pound green beans, ends trimmed, cut into 1-inch pieces
- 1 pound fresh peas, shelled, or 1½ cups frozen tiny peas

Heat oil in a 5- to 6-quart ovenproof pan over high heat. Add lamb and beef and cook, stirring, until browned (about 5 minutes); lift out and set aside. Reduce heat to medium-high. Add carrots, onion, and turnip and cook, stirring often, until onion is limp (about 10 minutes). Pour off fat.

Return meats to pan with barley, beef broth, water, and pepper. Bring to a boil over high heat. Cover and bake in a 325° oven until meat is very tender when pierced (about 1½ hours). At this point, you may cool, cover, and refrigerate for up to 2 days; lift off any fat and discard. Reheat to simmering before continuing.

Stir in beans and peas; continue baking until beans are tender (about 10 minutes). Makes 8 servings.

CHAYOTE WITH SPICED LAMB FILLING

Per serving: 199 calories, 19 g protein, 23 g carbohydrates, 5 g total fat (1 g saturated fat), 50 mg cholesterol, 281 mg sodium

Preparation time: About 50 minutes
Baking time: About 25 minutes

Similar in taste to zucchini, chayote is a tropical summer squash sometimes called mirliton. For an unusual entrée, serve it stuffed with a lightly spiced lamb filling. Ask your butcher to grind lamb sirloin; or grind it yourself in a food processor. It's a lot leaner than regular ground lamb.

- 3 chayotes (about ¾ lb. *each*)
- 1 pound lean lamb sirloin, freshly ground
- 1 medium-size onion, minced
- 4 cloves garlic, minced or pressed
- ½ teaspoon *each* ground allspice and coarsely ground pepper
- ⅛ teaspoon ground cloves
- ⅓ cup raisins
- 1 can (6 oz.) tomato paste
- 2 tablespoons dry red wine

In a 4- to 5-quart pan, bring 2 quarts water to a boil over high heat. Add chayotes; reduce heat, cover, and simmer until tender when pierced (about 40 minutes). Drain and let cool; halve lengthwise and discard pit. Scoop out and reserve pulp, leaving ½-inch-thick shells. Invert shells on paper towels to drain. Chop pulp.

Meanwhile, crumble lamb into a wide frying pan; add onion, garlic, allspice, pepper, and cloves. Cook over medium-high heat, stirring occasionally, until lamb is well browned (about 15 minutes). Stir in chayote pulp, raisins, tomato paste, and wine.

Spoon lamb mixture into shells. Place in a 9- by 13-inch baking pan. Cover and bake in a 350° oven for 20 minutes; uncover and continue baking until hot (about 5 more minutes). Makes 6 servings.

Subtle spices and a creamy sauce give Veal Curry with
Fruit (recipe on facing page) an irresistible flavor. Spoon
over brown rice, garnish with fresh cilantro, and offer
pita bread alongside for a stunning main course.

94

■ *Pictured on facing page*

VEAL CURRY WITH FRUIT

■ *Per serving: 495 calories, 30 g protein, 70 g carbohydrates, 12 g total fat (3 g saturated fat), 93 mg cholesterol, 217 mg sodium*

Preparation time: About 20 minutes
Cooking time: About 40 minutes

Fresh fruit acts as a perfect foil to tender veal simmered in a creamy sauce.

- 1 **pound boneless veal loin, fat trimmed**
- 2 **tablespoons margarine**
- 1 **medium-size onion, finely chopped**
- 1 **large carrot (about 5 oz.), finely chopped**
- 3 **tablespoons all-purpose flour**
- 1½ **teaspoons curry powder**
- ½ **teaspoon ground coriander**
- ¼ **teaspoon *each* ground cardamom and ground white pepper**
- 1 **cup low-sodium chicken broth**
- ½ **cup lowfat (2%) milk**
- 6 **tablespoons dry sherry**
- 2 **small bananas (about 10 oz. *total*)**
- 2 **teaspoons lemon juice**
- 2 **cups hot cooked brown or white rice**

- 1 **cup sliced peaches, papaya, or apricots; or 1 cup drained canned sliced peaches or apricots**
- ½ **cup golden raisins**

Slice veal across grain into ½-inch-thick strips about 3 inches long. In a wide frying pan, melt margarine over medium-high heat. Add veal and cook, stirring often, until lightly browned (about 7 minutes); lift out and set aside.

Add onion and carrot to pan and cook, stirring, until lightly browned (about 5 minutes). Stir in flour, curry powder, coriander, cardamom, and pepper; cook for 1 minute. Stir in chicken broth, milk, and 4 tablespoons of the sherry; bring to a boil. Return veal to pan; reduce heat, cover, and simmer until veal is tender (about 25 minutes). Stir in remaining sherry.

Slice bananas; coat with lemon juice. Spoon rice onto individual plates. Top with curry. Offer with bananas, peaches, and raisins. Makes 4 servings.

MEDITERRANEAN VEAL RAGOUT

■ *Per serving: 203 calories, 28 g protein, 14 g carbohydrates, 4 g total fat (1 g saturated fat), 89 mg cholesterol, 236 mg sodium*

Preparation time: About 20 minutes
Cooking time: About 50 minutes

Using a "sweating" technique, you can brown the meat and onions for this stew with very little fat.

- 1 **pound lean boneless veal stew meat (cut from leg or shoulder), fat trimmed, cut into 1-inch chunks**
- 2 **medium-size onions, thinly sliced**
- ½ **cup water**
- 1 **teaspoon olive oil (preferably extra virgin)**
- 1 **cup low-sodium chicken broth**
- 1 **pound tomatoes, finely chopped**
- 3 **cloves garlic, minced or pressed**
- 2 **teaspoons dry thyme leaves**
- ½ **teaspoon dry rosemary**
- 1 **package (9 oz.) frozen artichoke hearts, thawed**
- 2 **tablespoons drained and rinsed capers**

- ½ **teaspoon anchovy paste or 1 teaspoon chopped canned anchovy fillets (optional)**
- 1 **tablespoon red wine vinegar**

In a 5- to 6-quart pan, bring veal, onions, water, and oil to a boil over high heat; reduce heat, cover, and simmer, stirring occasionally, for 30 minutes.

Uncover, increase heat to medium-high, and cook, stirring often, until veal is lightly browned and onions begin to caramelize (about 5 minutes).

Add chicken broth, stirring to loosen browned bits. Reserve ¼ cup of the tomatoes; add remaining tomatoes, garlic, thyme, rosemary, artichokes, capers, and, if desired, anchovy paste. Reduce heat, cover, and simmer until veal is tender and artichokes are hot (about 15 minutes). Stir in vinegar and reserved tomatoes. Makes 4 servings.

Poultry

Oven-fried Chicken ■ Chicken Yakitori ■
Chicken-on-a-Stick with Couscous ■ Honeyed
Chicken ■ Chicken in a Squash Shell ■ Baked
Chicken with Pears ■ Apricot-Mustard Chicken
■ Sake-steamed Chicken ■ Cool Spiced Chicken
■ Chicken Enchilada Bake ■ Raspberry-glazed
Turkey Tenderloins ■ Grilled Turkey with
Peaches ■ Summer Turkey Stir-fry ■ Turkey &
Corn Chili ■ Turkey Burgers with Tomato Salad
■ White Wine Turkey Loaf ■ Turkey & Eggplant
Parmigiana ■ Chili-Citrus Rabbit

From simple stewed chicken to the regal Thanksgiving bird, poultry has long been a favorite on dinner tables everywhere. Lately, consumption of poultry has been increasing, due mostly to an awareness of its role in a healthy diet. Relative to other meat sources, poultry provides ample protein with less saturated fat, particularly when skinless pieces of white meat are used (see page 100 for detailed nutritional information). In addition to its nutritive value, poultry is amazingly versatile. It takes well to all the lean cooking methods, such as baking, grilling, poaching, and stir-frying, and its mild flavor is accepting of both bold seasonings and subtle sauces. Depending on the occasion, poultry can be presented in an elegant guise or in simple attire. The recipes here concentrate on those cuts that contain minimal fat—skinless chicken breasts and turkey breasts and tenderloins. Also included is rabbit, which, while not a bird, has naturally lean meat similar to white meat chicken. When using ground turkey, look for it freshly ground, rather than frozen thawed. Buy turkey labeled lean ground, if available.

■ *Pictured on page 159*

OVEN-FRIED CHICKEN

■
Per serving: 204 calories, 35 g protein, 8 g carbohydrates, 2 g total fat (0.5 g saturated fat), 86 mg cholesterol, 404 mg sodium

Preparation time: About 15 minutes
Marinating time: 20 minutes
Baking time: About 20 minutes

Give up fried chicken? If that's not what you have in mind, you can still enjoy tender, juicy chicken in a crunchy crust with this slim variation.

- 2 **tablespoons dry sherry**
- 2 **cloves garlic, minced or pressed**
- 2 **whole chicken breasts (about 1 lb.** *each***), skinned, boned, and split**
- ½ **cup soft whole wheat bread crumbs**
- 2 **tablespoons cornmeal**
- 1 **teaspoon paprika**
- ½ **teaspoon** *each* **salt, pepper, and dry sage, dry thyme, and dry basil leaves**
  Nonstick cooking spray or salad oil

In a shallow bowl, combine sherry and garlic. Add chicken, turning to coat, and let stand for 20 minutes.

In another shallow bowl, mix bread crumbs, cornmeal, paprika, salt, pepper, sage, thyme, and basil. Lightly coat a large rimmed baking sheet with cooking spray.

Lift chicken from marinade and let drain briefly, discarding marinade. Turn in crumb mixture to coat and place, skinned sides up, on baking sheet. Bake in a 450° oven until meat in thickest part is no longer pink; cut to test (about 20 minutes). Serve hot or at room temperature. Makes 4 servings.

■ *Pictured on facing page*

CHICKEN YAKITORI

■
Per serving: 295 calories, 39 g protein, 16 g carbohydrates, 9 g total fat (1 g saturated fat), 86 mg cholesterol, 332 mg sodium

Preparation time: About 30 minutes
Marinating time: 1 to 8 hours
Grilling time: About 35 minutes

For an elegant summer entrée, present skewers of grilled chicken chunks with meaty shiitake mushrooms and slim Oriental eggplants. An Asian-inspired marinade, made with sesame oil, flavors each ingredient.

- 2 **tablespoons sesame seeds**
- 3 **whole chicken breasts (about 1 lb.** *each***), skinned, boned, and split**
  Sherry-Soy Marinade (recipe follows)
- 6 **medium-size Oriental eggplants (about 1½ lbs.** *total***)**
- 18 **large fresh shiitake mushrooms or regular button mushrooms**

In a small frying pan, toast sesame seeds over medium heat, shaking pan often, until golden (about 3 minutes). Set aside.

Cut each breast half into 6 equal-size chunks; place in a medium-size bowl. Prepare Sherry-Soy Marinade. Pour ¼ cup of the marinade over chicken, turning gently to coat; reserve remaining marinade. Cover and refrigerate chicken and reserved marinade separately for at least 1 hour or up to 8 hours.

Lift chicken from marinade and let drain briefly, discarding marinade in bowl. Thread chicken on skewers. Set aside.

Evenly slash each eggplant lengthwise in 4 or 5 places, making cuts about ⅓ inch deep. Cut mushroom stems flush with caps. Place eggplants on a lightly greased grill 4 to 6 inches above a solid bed of hot coals. Cook, turning often, until very soft when pressed (about 35 minutes).

About 20 minutes before eggplants are done, dip mushrooms in reserved marinade, drain briefly, and place on grill. Cook, turning once, until lightly browned (about 10 minutes *total*). Meanwhile, place chicken on grill and cook, turning occasionally, until meat in center is no longer pink; cut to test (10 to 12 minutes).

Arrange chicken and vegetables on separate platters. Moisten with some of the remaining marinade and sprinkle with sesame seeds. Offer with remaining marinade. Makes 6 servings.

Sherry-Soy Marinade. Stir together ⅓ cup **dry sherry,** 3 tablespoons *each* **sesame oil** and **reduced-sodium soy sauce,** and 1½ teaspoons finely minced **fresh ginger.**

Make dinner an all-grill affair with Chicken Yakitori (recipe on facing page). Skewers of marinated chicken grill alongside tender eggplants and shiitake mushrooms; sesame seeds and a soy-sherry dip provide an Oriental accent. If desired, garnish with lemon leaves and sliced kumquats.

■ Nutritional Values of Poultry

One of the reasons poultry is so popular on healthy menus today is because it's easy to control the amount of fat you're eating; most of it lies just beneath the skin, where it can be removed when the skin is pulled off. What remains is high-quality protein in a relatively lean package.

As indicated in the chart below, breast (light) meat is lower in fat than leg (dark) meat. (Note, however, that some birds, such as duck, contain only dark meat.) The amount of cholesterol in poultry is comparable to that in lean beef.

The chart is based on a portion size of 3 ounces cooked poultry. Although some pieces, such as half a boneless chicken breast, may run larger, they can still be considered an acceptable portion. Although it's clearly not a bird, rabbit is included here; its mild flavor and naturally lean meat make it similar to chicken, and it's prepared in much the same way.

Portion: 3 ounces cooked	Calories	Protein (g)	Total fat (g)	Saturated fat (g)	Cholesterol (mg)
CHICKEN					
Breast, meat and skin, roasted	168	25	7	2	71
Breast, meat only, roasted	140	26	3	1	72
Thigh, meat and skin, roasted	210	21	13	4	79
Thigh, meat only, roasted	178	22	9	3	81
Drumstick, meat and skin, roasted	184	23	9	3	77
Drumstick, meat only, roasted	146	24	5	1	79
Liver, simmered	134	21	5	2	537
TURKEY					
Breast, meat and skin, roasted	161	24	6	2	63
Breast, meat only, roasted	131	25	2	1	59
Leg, meat and skin, roasted	177	24	8	3	72
Leg, meat only, roasted	157	24	6	2	75
Giblets (gizzard, heart, liver), simmered	142	23	4	1	356
Ground, regular, cooked	195	21	12	3	59
GOOSE					
Meat and skin, roasted	259	21	19	6	77
Meat only, roasted	202	25	11	4	82
DUCK					
Meat and skin, roasted	287	16	24	8	71
Meat only, roasted	171	20	10	4	76
RABBIT					
Meat only, roasted	131	19	5	2	54

■ *Pictured on page 7*

CHICKEN-ON-A-STICK WITH COUSCOUS

■
Per serving: 595 calories, 50 g protein, 65 g carbohydrates, 14 g total fat (3 g saturated fat), 91 mg cholesterol, 200 mg sodium

Preparation time: About 30 minutes
Marinating time: At least 30 minutes
Grilling time: About 10 minutes

Compose a balanced meal with little effort by offering chicken kebabs, fluffy couscous, and a calcium-rich yogurt sauce.

    Cumin-Garlic Yogurt Sauce (recipe follows)
2   **whole chicken breasts (about 1 lb. each), skinned, boned, and split**
⅓   **cup *each* lemon juice and olive oil**
¼   **cup dry white wine**
6   **cloves garlic, minced or pressed**
2   **bay leaves, crumbled**
2½ **cups low-sodium chicken broth**
10 **ounces (about 1¾ cups) couscous**
½   **cup sliced green onions (including tops)**

Soak 8 bamboo skewers in hot water to cover for at least 30 minutes. Meanwhile, prepare Cumin-Garlic Yogurt Sauce.

Cut chicken into about ¾-inch chunks. In a medium-size bowl, mix lemon juice, oil, wine, garlic, and bay leaves. Add chicken, turning to coat. Cover and refrigerate for at least 30 minutes or up to 4 hours.

In a 2- to 3-quart pan, bring chicken broth to a boil over high heat. Stir in couscous. Cover, remove from heat, and let stand while chicken is cooking.

Lift chicken from marinade, reserving marinade, and thread on skewers. Place on a lightly greased grill 4 to 6 inches above a solid bed of medium-hot coals. Cook, basting with reserved marinade and turning as needed, until meat in center is no longer pink; cut to test (about 10 minutes).

With a fork, stir onions into couscous and fluff. Spoon couscous onto a platter and top with chicken skewers. Offer with yogurt sauce. Makes 4 servings (2 skewers *each*).

Cumin-Garlic Yogurt Sauce. Stir together 1½ cups **plain lowfat yogurt,** 2 tablespoons minced **cilantro** (coriander), 1 teaspoon **cumin seeds,** and 1 clove **garlic,** minced or pressed. Cover and refrigerate for at least 15 minutes or until next day.

■
HONEYED CHICKEN

■
Per serving: 229 calories, 35 g protein, 12 g carbohydrates, 4 g total fat (0.7 g saturated fat), 86 mg cholesterol, 398 mg sodium

Preparation time: About 10 minutes
Baking time: 15 to 20 minutes

A light, tart-sweet sauce glazes baked chicken breasts. Sesame seeds add delicate crunch.

2   **tablespoons sesame seeds**
3   **tablespoons honey**
¼   **cup *each* dry sherry and Dijon mustard**
1   **tablespoon lemon juice**
3   **whole chicken breasts (about 1 lb. each), skinned, boned, and split**

In a small frying pan, toast sesame seeds over medium heat, shaking pan often, until golden

(about 3 minutes). Transfer to a small bowl and add honey, sherry, mustard, and lemon juice; stir until blended.

Arrange chicken breasts, slightly apart, in a 9- by 13-inch baking pan. Drizzle with honey mixture. Bake in a 400° oven, basting several times with sauce, until meat in thickest part is no longer pink; cut to test (15 to 20 minutes). Transfer chicken to individual plates. Offer with any remaining sauce. Makes 6 servings.

Not only is baked acorn squash full of vitamin A, but it also makes an edible container for Chicken in a Squash Shell (recipe on facing page). A dollop of yogurt, sprinkled with green onions, adds creaminess. Sliced bread and iced tea are no-fuss accompaniments.

102

■ *Pictured on facing page*

CHICKEN IN A SQUASH SHELL

■
Per serving: 282 calories, 29 g protein, 30 g carbohydrates, 6 g total fat (0.9 g saturated fat), 66 mg cholesterol, 396 mg sodium

Preparation time: About 20 minutes
Cooking time: About 40 minutes

Stir-fried chicken and vegetables are spooned into baked acorn squash for a vivid, vitamin-rich entrée. Sichuan peppercorns add tingle; look for them in an Oriental market or specialty food store.

Nonstick cooking spray
2 small acorn squash (about 1 lb. *each*)
   Soy-Ginger Sauce (recipe follows)
1 tablespoon salad oil
1 pound boneless and skinless chicken breasts, cut into ½-inch cubes
½ cup *each* finely diced red bell pepper and jicama
1 small onion, finely chopped
2 small firm-ripe tomatoes (about 6 oz. *total*), peeled and finely diced
1 teaspoon Sichuan peppercorns, coarsely ground, or ½ teaspoon pepper
¼ cup chopped green onions (including tops)
   Plain lowfat yogurt (optional)

Lightly coat a 9- by 13-inch baking pan with cooking spray. With a sharp, heavy knife, cut squash in half lengthwise and scoop out seeds. Arrange squash, cut sides down, in pan. Bake in a 400° oven until tender when pierced (about 40 minutes).

Meanwhile, prepare Soy-Ginger Sauce and set aside.

About 15 minutes before squash is done, heat oil in a wide frying pan or wok over medium-high heat. Add chicken and cook, stirring, until meat in center is no longer pink; cut to test (2 to 3 minutes). Lift out with a slotted spoon and set aside. Add bell pepper, jicama, onion, tomatoes, and peppercorns to pan; cook, stirring, for 5 minutes. Add sauce; boil until thickened. Return chicken and any juices to pan, remove from heat, and keep warm.

Place squash in individual bowls and fill with chicken mixture. Sprinkle with green onions. Offer with yogurt, if desired. Makes 4 servings.

Soy-Ginger Sauce. Stir together 2 tablespoons *each* **reduced-sodium soy sauce** and **dry sherry**, ¾ cup **low-sodium chicken broth**, 1 tablespoon *each* **cornstarch** and firmly packed **brown sugar,** and 1 teaspoon finely minced **fresh ginger.**

BAKED CHICKEN WITH PEARS

■
Per serving: 259 calories, 34 g protein, 25 g carbohydrates, 2 g total fat (0.5 g saturated fat), 86 mg cholesterol, 97 mg sodium

Preparation time: About 10 minutes
Baking time: 15 to 20 minutes

Round out a simple baked chicken dish with liqueur-poached pears and you add valuable vitamins and fiber, as well as subtle flavor, to the dinner menu.

Nonstick cooking spray or salad oil
3 whole chicken breasts (about 1 lb. *each*), skinned, boned, and split
3 tablespoons lemon juice
4 teaspoons cornstarch
1 cup pear-flavored brandy or apple juice
2 large red Bartlett or other firm-ripe pears (about 1 lb. *total*)

Lightly coat a 9- by 13-inch baking pan with cooking spray. Rub chicken breasts with lemon juice and arrange, slightly apart, in pan. Bake in a 425° oven until meat in thickest part is no longer pink; cut to test (15 to 20 minutes).

Meanwhile, stir cornstarch and brandy in a small pan until blended. Core pears; cut lengthwise into ½-inch-thick slices. Add to pan and mix gently. Bring to a boil over medium-high heat; reduce heat, cover, and simmer until pears are tender when pierced (about 5 minutes).

When chicken is done, pour in pear mixture, shaking dish to mix gently. Transfer chicken and pears to individual plates. Drizzle with sauce. Makes 6 servings.

APRICOT-MUSTARD CHICKEN

Per serving: 380 calories, 41 g protein, 46 g carbohydrates, 3 g total fat (0.7 g saturated fat), 86 mg cholesterol, 352 mg sodium

Preparation time: About 10 minutes
Cooking time: 20 to 23 minutes

Delicate chicken breasts cloaked in a rich sauce may sound off-limits, but not if the sauce is based on apricot nectar. Mustard adds tang; fresh basil provides contrast.

- 1 **can (12 oz.) apricot nectar**
- 3 **tablespoons Dijon mustard**
- 3 **whole chicken breasts (about 1 lb.** *each*), **skinned, boned, and split**
- 2½ **cups low-sodium chicken broth**
- 10 **ounces (about 1¾ cups) couscous**
- 2 **tablespoons minced fresh basil leaves**
  Basil sprigs and lime wedges (optional)

In a wide frying pan, combine apricot nectar and mustard. Bring to a boil over high heat. Ar-range chicken breasts, skinned sides down, in pan. Reduce heat, cover, and simmer for 10 minutes. Turn chicken and continue cooking until meat in thickest part is no longer pink; cut to test (5 to 8 more minutes).

Meanwhile, bring chicken broth to a boil in a 2- to 3-quart pan over high heat; stir in couscous. Cover, remove from heat, and let stand until broth is completely absorbed (about 5 minutes).

With a fork, fluff couscous; transfer to a platter. Lift out chicken with a slotted spoon and arrange over couscous; keep warm.

Boil apricot mixture over high heat, stirring often, until reduced to 1 cup (about 5 minutes). Pour over chicken and sprinkle with minced basil. Garnish with basil sprigs and lime, if desired. Makes 6 servings.

SAKE-STEAMED CHICKEN

Per serving: 312 calories, 39 g protein, 31 g carbohydrates, 3 g total fat (0.5 g saturated fat), 86 mg cholesterol, 726 mg sodium

Preparation time: About 20 minutes
Marinating time: At least 30 minutes
Cooking time: About 12 minutes

In an intriguing contrast of tastes, a whisper of Japanese wine seasons steam-cooked chicken, while a dipping sauce thunders with the pungency of horseradish.

- ½ **cup sake or unseasoned rice vinegar**
- ½ **teaspoon salt**
- 3 **whole chicken breasts (about 1 lb.** *each*), **skinned, boned, and split**
- 1 **small head iceberg lettuce (about 1¼ lbs.), separated into leaves, rinsed, and crisped**
  About ⅓ cup reduced-sodium soy sauce
- 1 **tablespoon prepared horseradish**
- 3 **cups hot cooked brown or white rice**
- ½ **cup slivered green onions (including tops)**
  Lemon wedges

In a medium-size bowl, mix sake and salt until salt is dissolved. Add chicken, turning to coat. Cover and refrigerate for at least 30 minutes or up to 2 hours.

Lift out chicken, discarding marinade, and arrange, thickest ends toward outside, in a single layer on a 10- to 11-inch round nonmetal plate or dish. Cover with wax paper or foil and set on a rack in a pan above 1 inch boiling water. Cover and steam over high heat until meat in thickest part is no longer pink; cut to test (about 12 minutes).

Meanwhile, place 1 or 2 large lettuce leaves on each of 6 plates. Finely shred remaining lettuce and mound on leaves. Divide soy sauce among 6 tiny dipping bowls; add ½ teaspoon of the horseradish to each and place bowls on plates.

Cut chicken crosswise into ½-inch-wide strips. Spoon rice and chicken on lettuce. Sprinkle with onions and add lemon. To eat, squeeze lemon into soy mixture and dip chicken into sauce. Or tear lettuce leaves into sections and fill with chicken, rice, and shredded lettuce; season with sauce and eat out-of-hand. Makes 6 servings.

COOL SPICED CHICKEN

Per serving: 191 calories, 28 g protein, 8 g carbohydrates, 4 g total fat (1 g saturated fat), 89 mg cholesterol, 102 mg sodium

Preparation time: About 30 minutes
Baking time: About 1 hour

If you love the succulence of whole roasted chicken but want to avoid the fat in the skin, here's a solution: shred the meat and use the defatted pan juices as a sauce. Sweet red onion, citrus, and aromatic spices round out the flavors.

- 1 whole chicken (about 3½ lbs.)
  Freshly ground pepper
- 2 cloves garlic, minced or pressed
- 3 tablespoons red wine vinegar
- 1 medium-size red onion (about 6 oz.), cut into thin rings
- 1 tablespoon *each* coriander seeds and cumin seeds
- 1 cup orange juice
- 1 tablespoon finely shredded orange peel
- 1 tablespoon chopped cilantro (coriander)
- 6 large butterhead lettuce leaves, rinsed and crisped

Remove giblets from chicken; reserve for other uses. Pull off and discard any lumps of fat; rinse chicken and pat dry. Place, breast side up, on a rack in a roasting pan and sprinkle inside and out with pepper and garlic. Bake in a 400° oven until meat near thighbone is no longer pink; cut to test (about 1 hour). Tip bird to drain juices into pan. Let stand until cool enough to handle.

Meanwhile, bring vinegar and 2 cups water to a boil in a 1- to 1½-quart pan over high heat. Add onion and cook just until bright pink (about 10 seconds). Drain well and place in a large bowl.

Discard skin and bones from chicken; tear meat into bite-size pieces. Add to onion. Skim and discard fat from pan drippings; pour juices into a small frying pan. Add coriander seeds, cumin seeds, orange juice, and orange peel. Bring to a boil over medium-high heat and cook, stirring occasionally, for 3 minutes. Add to chicken mixture along with cilantro; stir well. Season to taste with pepper.

Line individual plates with lettuce. Spoon chicken mixture on top. Makes 6 servings.

CHICKEN ENCHILADA BAKE

Per serving: 254 calories, 19 g protein, 28 g carbohydrates, 8 g total fat (2 g saturated fat), 39 mg cholesterol, 293 mg sodium

Preparation time: About 20 minutes
Baking time: About 30 minutes

Here's proof that even rich casseroles can become lean treats without losing any of the hearty taste.

- 12 corn tortillas (7-inch diameter)
- 5 medium-size tomatoes (about 1½ lbs. *total*), peeled and thinly sliced
- 2 cups skinless and boneless shredded cooked chicken breast
- 1 cup thinly sliced green onions (including tops)
- 1 tablespoon margarine
- 2 tablespoons all-purpose flour
- 2 cups low-sodium chicken broth
- 1 cup plain lowfat yogurt
- 1 can (4 oz.) diced green chiles
- 2 ounces (about ½ cup) grated Cheddar cheese

Dip tortillas, one at a time, in water; let drain briefly. Stack and cut into 8 wedges. Spread a third of the tortillas in a 9- by 13-inch baking pan. Top with half the tomatoes; cover with half the chicken and onions. Repeat layers, ending with tortillas. Set aside.

In a 2- to 3-quart pan, melt margarine over medium heat. Add flour and cook, stirring, for 20 seconds. Whisk in chicken broth and bring to a boil. Remove from heat and add yogurt and chiles, whisking until smooth. Pour over tortilla mixture.

Cover and bake in a 375° oven for 20 minutes. Remove cover, sprinkle with Cheddar, and continue baking, uncovered, until cheese is melted (about 10 more minutes). Makes 8 servings.

■ *Pictured on facing page*

RASPBERRY-GLAZED TURKEY TENDERLOINS

Preparation time: About 15 minutes
Broiling time: 8 to 10 minutes

Pairing poultry with fruit isn't a new idea, but it's worth rediscovering in this updated version. The fruit glaze locks in moisture during broiling and then doubles as a distinctive sauce.

½ cup seedless raspberry jam

6 tablespoons raspberry vinegar

¼ cup Dijon mustard

1 teaspoon grated orange peel

½ teaspoon dry thyme leaves

4 turkey breast tenderloins (about 2¼ lbs. *total*)

■

Per serving: 241 calories, 34 g protein, 18 g carbohydrates, 3 g total fat (0.7 g saturated fat), 90 mg cholesterol, 358 mg sodium

In a 1- to 2-quart pan, stir together jam, vinegar, mustard, orange peel, and thyme. Bring to a boil over high heat and cook, stirring, until reduced by about a fourth (2 to 3 minutes). Reserve about ½ cup of the glaze; brush turkey with some of the remaining glaze.

Place turkey on a rack in a broiler pan. Broil about 4 inches below heat, turning and brushing once with remaining glaze, until meat in center is no longer pink; cut to test (8 to 10 minutes *total*). Slice crosswise. Offer with reserved glaze. Makes 6 to 8 servings.

■ *Pictured on page 214*

GRILLED TURKEY WITH PEACHES

Preparation time: About 10 minutes
Grilling time: 50 to 55 minutes

A shiny glaze of puréed chutney seals in moisture in this grilled boneless turkey breast. You also use the barbecue to cook the peaches and green onions that accompany the meat.

⅔ cup peach or Major Grey's chutney

1 teaspoon minced fresh ginger

1 turkey breast half (about 3 lbs.), boned and skinned

3 large firm-ripe peaches (about 1¼ lbs. *total*) or 6 canned peach halves, drained

2 tablespoons lemon juice (if using fresh peaches)

6 green onions
Mint sprigs (optional)

In a blender or food processor, combine ⅓ cup of the chutney with ginger. Whirl until puréed. Coarsely chop remaining chutney and set aside. Brush turkey all over with some of the chutney mixture.

■

Per serving: 310 calories, 42 g protein, 28 g carbohydrates, 3 g total fat (0.9 g saturated fat), 108 mg cholesterol, 180 mg sodium

Place a lightly greased grill 4 to 6 inches over a medium-hot fire that has a drip pan placed in center; position turkey on grill directly above pan. Cover barbecue and adjust dampers to maintain an even heat. Cook turkey, brushing occasionally with chutney mixture, until a meat thermometer inserted in center registers 155°F (50 to 55 minutes).

Meanwhile, immerse fresh peaches in boiling water for 30 seconds; lift out and let cool for 1 minute. Peel, halve, and pit; coat with lemon juice. Peel off outer layer of onions; trim tops, leaving about 4 inches of green.

About 10 minutes before turkey is done, lay peach halves, cut sides down, and onions on grill directly over coals. Cook, turning once and brushing several times with chutney mixture, until peaches are hot and onion tops are wilted (about 10 minutes).

Slice meat across grain. Arrange on a platter and surround with peaches and onions. Garnish with mint, if desired. Offer with reserved chutney. Makes 6 servings.

*Juicy slices of Raspberry-glazed Turkey
Tenderloins (recipe on facing page), accompanied by
herb-sprinkled pasta and a green salad embellished with
fruit and nuts, provide ample proof that family meals
can be simple as well as nutritious.*

107

SUMMER TURKEY STIR-FRY

Per serving: 384 calories, 33 g protein, 49 g carbohydrates, 6 g total fat (1 g saturated fat), 70 mg cholesterol, 416 mg sodium

Preparation time: About 15 minutes
Cooking time: About 15 minutes

The secret to this vibrant stir-fry lies in its fresh ingredients and subtle sauce. Have all the ingredients chopped and at the ready before you begin cooking.

          Cooking Sauce (recipe follows)
    1 cup bulgur
    1 tablespoon salad oil
    3 cloves garlic, minced or pressed
    2 turkey breast tenderloins (about 1 lb. *total*), cut into ¾-inch chunks
    3 cups thinly sliced carrots
    2 small zucchini (about ½ lb. *total*), sliced
    2 tablespoons minced fresh ginger
    ½ cup thinly sliced green onions (including tops)

Prepare Cooking Sauce and set aside.

In a 2- to 3-quart pan, bring 1½ cups water to a boil over high heat; stir in bulgur. Reduce heat, cover, and simmer until bulgur is soft and water is absorbed (about 15 minutes).

Meanwhile, heat oil in a wide frying pan or wok over high heat. Add garlic and turkey and cook, stirring, until meat in center is no longer pink; cut to test (about 5 minutes). Add carrots, zucchini, ginger, and ¼ cup water. Cover and continue cooking, stirring occasionally, until vegetables are tender-crisp (about 5 more minutes). Uncover and boil until liquid has almost evaporated. Stir in sauce and boil until thickened.

Spoon bulgur onto individual plates and top with turkey mixture. Sprinkle with onions. Makes 4 servings.

Cooking Sauce. Stir together ½ cup **low-sodium chicken broth,** 2 tablespoons **reduced-sodium soy sauce,** and 1 tablespoon **cornstarch.**

TURKEY & CORN CHILI

Per serving: 375 calories, 37 g protein, 39 g carbohydrates, 9 g total fat (2 g saturated fat), 64 mg cholesterol, 794 mg sodium

Preparation time: About 1 hour
Cooking time: About 40 minutes

An all-time favorite for cool-weather meals, this thick, chunky chili uses lean turkey breast.

          Simmered Turkey Breast (page 76) or 4 cups diced cooked skinless turkey breast
    2 tablespoons salad oil
    2 large onions, chopped
    2 large cloves garlic, minced or pressed
    2 teaspoons chili powder
    ¾ teaspoon *each* dry oregano leaves and ground cumin
    ½ teaspoon crushed red pepper flakes
    1 can (28 oz.) peeled tomatoes
    1 can (6 oz.) tomato paste
    2 cups water
    2 cups fresh or frozen corn kernels
    1 can (about 15 oz.) black beans, drained and rinsed
    ½ cup thinly sliced green onions (including tops)
    1 medium-size green bell pepper (about 6 oz.), stemmed, seeded, and finely diced
          Chopped cilantro (coriander)
          Plain lowfat yogurt

Prepare Simmered Turkey Breast. Cut meat away from bone and dice (you should have about 4 cups). Set aside.

Heat oil in a 5- to 6-quart pan over medium heat. Add onions and garlic and cook, stirring often, until onions are limp (about 15 minutes). Add chili powder, oregano, cumin, red pepper flakes, tomatoes (break up with a spoon) and their liquid, tomato paste, and water. Cook, stirring often, until hot (about 10 minutes). Stir in corn and continue cooking until corn is tender (about 10 more minutes). Stir in beans and turkey and cook until hot (about 5 more minutes). Ladle into bowls.

Sprinkle with green onions and bell pepper. Offer with cilantro and yogurt. Makes 6 servings.

TURKEY BURGERS WITH TOMATO SALAD

Per serving: 512 calories, 36 g protein, 59 g carbohydrates, 15 g total fat (4 g saturated fat), 60 mg cholesterol, 545 mg sodium

Preparation time: About 15 minutes
Cooking time: About 17 minutes

What's better for a casual dinner than burgers with all the fixings? You'll applaud the flavor and ease of preparation of these meaty turkey burgers.

        Yogurt Sauce (recipe follows)
    1   medium-size red onion (about 6 oz.)
    1   teaspoon salad oil
    ½   pound fresh ground turkey
    ½   teaspoon ground cumin
        Freshly ground pepper
    ¼   cup water
    2   tablespoons sherry vinegar or white
        wine vinegar
    2   whole wheat pita breads (6-inch
        diameter)
    1   small cucumber (about 6 oz.), peeled
        and thinly sliced
    ½   pound tomatoes, sliced

Prepare Yogurt Sauce; cover and refrigerate. Cut onion in half horizontally. Chop half. Thinly slice remaining half into rings and set aside.

In a nonstick frying pan, combine chopped onion and oil. Cook over medium-high heat, stirring often, until onion is soft (about 5 minutes). Transfer to a small bowl and mix with turkey and cumin; season to taste with pepper. Shape mixture into 2 patties.

Place in pan and cook, turning once, until browned on both sides (about 10 minutes *total*). Pour off fat. Add water and vinegar; reduce heat, cover, and simmer until liquid has almost evaporated and meat in center is no longer pink; cut to test (about 7 more minutes).

Meanwhile, wrap pita breads in foil and place in a 250° oven until hot (about 15 minutes).

In a bowl, mix cucumber, tomatoes, and reserved onion rings with half the sauce. Offer burgers with pita breads, vegetable mixture, and remaining sauce. Makes 2 servings.

Yogurt Sauce. Stir together 1 cup **plain nonfat yogurt,** ¼ cup **sherry vinegar** or white wine vinegar, and 2 tablespoons **dry dill weed.**

WHITE WINE TURKEY LOAF

Per serving: 207 calories, 19 g protein, 10 g carbohydrates, 10 g total fat (3 g saturated fat), 46 mg cholesterol, 134 mg sodium

Preparation time: About 15 minutes
Baking time: 40 to 45 minutes (plus 5 minutes standing time)

The humble meatloaf is actually a relative of the elegant meat pâtés of France. This version returns to that grand tradition with its infusion of dry white wine and thyme, but it uses turkey instead of meat.

    ⅓   cup low-sodium chicken broth
    ⅓   cup thinly sliced green onions
        (including tops)
    1   small green bell pepper (about 5 oz.),
        stemmed, seeded, and diced
    ½   cup dry white wine
    1   cup soft whole wheat bread crumbs
    1   teaspoon dry thyme leaves
    1   pound fresh ground turkey
    1   egg white
        Freshly ground pepper
    1   can (8 oz.) no-salt-added tomato sauce

In a small frying pan, bring chicken broth to a boil over high heat. Add onions and bell pepper and cook, stirring, until liquid has evaporated and vegetables are soft (about 5 minutes). Add wine, bring to a boil, and remove from heat. Stir in bread crumbs and thyme.

In a bowl, mix turkey, bread crumb mixture, and egg white; season to taste with pepper. Pat mixture into a 5- by 9-inch loaf pan. Spread half the tomato sauce over meat.

Bake in a 350° oven for 30 minutes. Remove pan from oven and tip to pour off fat. Spread remaining tomato sauce over loaf and continue baking until meat in center is no longer pink; cut to test (10 to 15 more minutes). Let stand for 5 minutes before slicing. Makes 4 to 6 servings.

TURKEY & EGGPLANT PARMIGIANA

Preparation time: About 30 minutes
Baking time: About 25 minutes

Per serving: 242 calories, 19 g protein, 17 g carbohydrates, 11 g total fat (4 g saturated fat), 43 mg cholesterol, 239 mg sodium

In this light version of a traditional dish, the eggplant is steamed instead of fried.

> 1 large eggplant (about 1½ lbs.)
> 1 pound pear-shaped tomatoes, coarsely chopped
> ¾ pound fresh ground turkey
> 1 medium-size onion, chopped
> 1 clove garlic, minced or pressed
> 1 teaspoon olive oil
> 1 can (8 oz.) no-salt-added tomato sauce
> 1 teaspoon dry oregano leaves
> ¼ teaspoon ground red pepper (cayenne), optional
> Freshly ground black pepper
> Nonstick cooking spray or salad oil
> 4 ounces (about 1 cup) shredded part-skim mozzarella cheese
> ½ cup soft whole wheat bread crumbs
> 1 ounce (about ¼ cup) grated Parmesan cheese

Slice eggplant crosswise ½ inch thick. Place slices, slightly overlapping, on a rack in a pan above 1 inch boiling water. Cover and steam over high heat until tender (about 5 minutes). Meanwhile, place tomatoes in a food processor and coarsely purée. Set vegetables aside separately.

In a wide frying pan, cook turkey, onion, and garlic in oil over medium-high heat, stirring to break up turkey with a fork, until meat is no longer pink (about 7 minutes). Pour off fat. Add tomatoes, tomato sauce, oregano, and, if desired, red pepper. Cook, stirring often, until sauce is thickened (about 10 minutes). Season to taste with black pepper.

Lightly coat a 7- by 11-inch baking pan with cooking spray. Arrange half the eggplant in pan. Spoon on turkey mixture and sprinkle with mozzarella. Top with remaining eggplant. (At this point, you may cool, cover, and refrigerate until next day.)

Sprinkle casserole with bread crumbs and Parmesan. Bake, uncovered, in a 350° oven until crumbs are lightly browned and sauce is bubbling (about 25 minutes; 35 minutes if refrigerated). Makes 6 servings.

■ *Pictured on facing page*

CHILI-CITRUS RABBIT

Preparation time: About 15 minutes
Cooking time: 40 to 50 minutes

Per serving: 417 calories, 35 g protein, 41 g carbohydrates, 12 g total fat (3 g saturated fat), 90 mg cholesterol, 185 mg sodium

Rabbit's delicate flavor and lean meat make it a wonderful choice for light meals.

> 2 large oranges (about 1¼ lbs. *total*)
> 2 tablespoons salad oil
> 1 fryer rabbit (2½ to 3 lbs.), cut into serving-size pieces
> 1 cup orange juice
> ½ cup lime juice
> 1 can (4 oz.) diced green chiles
> 1 teaspoon cumin seeds
> 2 teaspoons cornstarch mixed with 1 tablespoon water
> 1 lime, thinly sliced (optional)
> Watercress sprigs (optional)
> 3 cups hot cooked brown or white rice

Grate 1 tablespoon zest (colored part of peel) from oranges; set aside.

Heat oil in a wide frying pan over medium-high heat. Add rabbit and cook, turning, until browned (about 5 minutes). Lift out and set aside. Pour off fat. Add orange peel, orange juice, lime juice, chiles, and cumin seeds to pan. Stir to loosen browned bits. Add rabbit; reduce heat, cover, and simmer until meat near thighbone is no longer pink; cut to test (30 to 40 minutes). Meanwhile, peel oranges, thinly slice, and arrange on a platter.

Lift out rabbit and place on platter. Boil pan juices over high heat, stirring often, until reduced to 1 cup (about 5 minutes). Stir in cornstarch mixture and boil until thickened; pour over rabbit. Garnish with lime and watercress, if desired. Offer with rice. Makes 6 servings.

Introduce a new lean meat to your family with Chili-Citrus Rabbit (recipe on facing page). They'll love its mild, chickenlike taste; you'll appreciate its ease of preparation. Dress up the platter with watercress and sliced citrus, and offer rice alongside.

Seafood

Halibut with Tomatoes & Dill ■ Fish Pot-au-Feu

■ Baked Sole & Ratatouille ■ Simmered Cod &

Vegetables ■ Curried Fish & Rice ■ Cool Salmon

with Radish Tartar ■ Ahi Steaks with Bacon

■ Swordfish with Mushroom Sauce ■ Chinese-

style Steamed Fish ■ Stuffed Trout ■ Dilled

Roughy in Parchment ■ Shellfish Couscous ■

Clam Paella for Two ■ Oyster Jambalaya

■ San Francisco–style Cioppino ■ Mussels

Provençal ■ Stir-fried Scallops & Asparagus ■

Greek-style Shrimp on Zucchini ■ Shrimp

Fajitas ■ Soft-shell Crab with Ginger

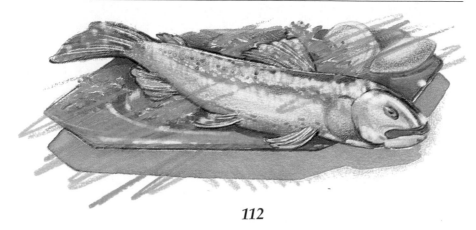

Walk into a seafood market today and you'll be dazzled by a stunning display of fresh and high-quality frozen fish and shellfish. Much of the catch is now available year-round, wonderful news considering seafood's great taste and ease of preparation. But seafood's reputation is based on more than just good taste. A superior source of protein in a low-calorie package, seafood is rich in essential vitamins and minerals, including iron, B vitamins, and selenium; saltwater seafood is a natural source of iodine. If you eat canned salmon, sardines, and herring with their soft bones, you'll also get calcium. Furthermore, fish and shellfish contain mainly unsaturated fats, including polyunsaturated omega-3 fatty acids, believed to have certain health benefits (see page 116). As for cholesterol, the levels in finfish are about the same as in white meat poultry; though such shellfish as crab, shrimp, and squid are higher in cholesterol, they're still a delicious, lean protein source and can be included in a balanced diet. (For more nutritional information on fish and shellfish, turn to page 116.)

■ *Pictured on front cover*

HALIBUT WITH TOMATOES & DILL

Per serving: 236 calories, 37 g protein, 7 g carbohydrates, 6 g total fat (0.9 g saturated fat), 54 mg cholesterol, 103 mg sodium

Preparation time: About 10 minutes
Baking time: About 35 minutes

Few herbs accent fish as perfectly as dill. Here, it enhances a fresh tomato sauce that's spooned over mild-tasting halibut; fish and sauce bake separately in the oven. If halibut is out of season, choose rockfish or cod.

- 1 **pound cherry tomatoes, stemmed and halved**
- ½ **cup thinly sliced green onions (including tops)**
- 2 **cloves garlic, minced or pressed**
- 2 **tablespoons chopped fresh dill or ½ teaspoon dry dill weed**
- 2 **teaspoons olive oil**
- 2 **tablespoons water**
- 1½ **pounds halibut fillets or steaks, or rockfish or cod fillets, rinsed and patted dry**
- 2 **tablespoons lemon juice**
  Dill sprigs (optional)

Arrange tomatoes, cut sides up, in a 9- by 13-inch baking pan. In a small bowl, mix onions, garlic, chopped dill, oil, and water. Distribute over tomatoes. Bake on top rack in a 425° oven for 25 minutes.

Meanwhile, place fish in a baking pan large enough to hold pieces in a single layer; drizzle with lemon juice and cover.

After tomato mixture has baked for 25 minutes, add fish, placing pan on bottom rack. Continue baking until tomatoes are lightly browned and fish looks just opaque but still moist in center; cut to test (8 to 10 minutes).

Lift out fish and transfer to a platter. Add fish juices to tomato mixture and stir well; spoon over fish. Garnish with dill sprigs, if desired. Makes 4 servings.

■ *Pictured on facing page*

FISH POT-AU-FEU

Per serving: 324 calories, 37 g protein, 35 g carbohydrates, 4 g total fat (0.8 g saturated fat), 73 mg cholesterol, 216 mg sodium

Preparation time: About 15 minutes
Cooking time: About 30 minutes

Tender fish fillets and fresh vegetables simmer in a subtly seasoned broth for this country-style stew. Part soup and part knife-and-fork supper, it's deliciously light.

- 5 **cups low-sodium chicken broth**
- 1 **cup dry white wine**
- 1 **tablespoon chopped fresh tarragon leaves or ½ teaspoon dry tarragon leaves**
- 4 **small red thin-skinned potatoes (about ½ lb. *total*)**
- 8 **small, slender carrots (about ¾ lb. *total*)**
- 4 **medium-size leeks (about 2 lbs. *total*), roots and most of dark green tops trimmed**
- 1½ **pounds skinless cod, rockfish, snapper, or orange roughy fillets, rinsed and patted dry**

In a 5- to 6-quart pan, combine chicken broth, wine, and tarragon. Bring to a boil over high heat. Add potatoes and carrots and return to a boil; reduce heat, cover, and simmer for 10 minutes.

Meanwhile, split leeks lengthwise and rinse well. Add to pan, cover, and simmer until leeks are tender when pierced (about 10 minutes). Lift out leeks and keep warm.

Cut fish into 4 portions. Add to broth mixture; cover and simmer until vegetables are tender and fish looks just opaque but still moist in thickest part; cut to test (8 to 10 minutes). Carefully transfer fish, vegetables, and broth to a tureen; add leeks. Serve in wide soup bowls. Makes 4 servings.

Refreshingly light Fish Pot-au-Feu (recipe on facing page), a French specialty, combines lean seafood, fresh vegetables, and starchy potatoes in a satisfying one-pan meal.

115

■ Nutritional Values of Seafood

More abundantly available than ever before, seafood is a naturally lean protein source that supplies many important vitamins and minerals. Fish and shellfish have also received attention for their oils, which contain omega-3 fatty acids. These unique polyunsaturated fats are found in highest concentration in fatty fish, such as mackerel, herring, sardines, and salmon. When consumed through eating seafood, they may reduce the risk of high blood pressure and blood clots.

In the past, there was concern about the amount of cholesterol in shellfish. However, recent studies have shown that the type of cholesterol found in shellfish has minimal effect on blood cholesterol. Moreover, as shown below, many shellfish have very moderate levels of cholesterol, generally less ounce per ounce than lean meat or poultry.

In the chart, data is given for raw seafood where figures for seafood cooked by dry heat were not available.

Portion: 3 ounces cooked, except where noted	Calories	Protein (g)	Total fat (g)	Saturated fat (g)	Cholesterol (mg)
FINFISH					
Catfish, raw (4 oz.)	132	21	5	1	66
Cod, Atlantic, cooked, dry heat	89	19	1	*	47
Halibut, cooked, dry heat	119	23	3	*	35
Mackerel, Atlantic, cooked, dry heat	223	20	15	4	64
Orange roughy, raw (4 oz.)	143	17	8	*	23
Salmon, sockeye, cooked, dry heat	183	23	9	2	74
Salmon, canned, drained solids with bone**	120	18	5	1	33
Sardines, canned in oil, drained solids with bone**	177	21	10	1	121
Sea bass, cooked, dry heat	105	20	2	1	45
Snapper, cooked, dry heat	109	22	1	*	40
Sole, cooked, dry heat	100	21	1	*	58
Swordfish, cooked, dry heat	132	22	4	1	43
Trout, rainbow, cooked, dry heat	128	22	4	1	62
Tuna, yellowfin (ahi), raw (4 oz.)	122	27	1	*	51
Tuna, white, canned in oil, drained	158	23	7	N/A	26
Tuna, white, canned in water, drained	116	23	2	1	36
SHELLFISH					
Clams, cooked, moist heat	126	22	2	*	57
Crab, cooked, moist heat	87	17	2	*	85
Lobster, cooked, moist heat	83	17	1	*	61
Mussels, cooked, moist heat	146	20	4	1	48
Oysters, cooked, moist heat	117	12	4	1	93
Scallops, raw (4 oz.)	100	19	1	*	37
Shrimp, cooked, moist heat	84	18	1	*	166
Squid, raw (4 oz.)	104	18	2	*	264

*Contains less than 1 gram   **Because these products include soft, edible bones, they're good sources of calcium.

BAKED SOLE & RATATOUILLE

Per serving: 238 calories, 31 g protein, 12 g carbohydrates, 8 g total fat (2 g saturated fat), 75 mg cholesterol, 176 mg sodium

Preparation time: About 15 minutes
Baking time: About 50 minutes

Fresh fish and vegetables cook together in the oven for an easy-to-prepare entrée. Because the flavors of this dish are mild and delicate, even fish skeptics will approve.

> Nonstick cooking spray or salad oil
> ½ pound medium-size zucchini, sliced
> 1 medium-size eggplant (about ¾ lb.), cut into ½-inch cubes
> 1 *each* large green and red bell peppers (about 1 lb. *total*), stemmed, seeded, and cut into thin strips
> 1 tablespoon *each* dry basil leaves and olive oil
> 1 teaspoon dry oregano leaves
> 4 sole fillets (about 5 oz. *each*), rinsed and patted dry
> 1 ounce Havarti or jack cheese, shredded

Lightly coat a 9- by 13-inch baking pan with cooking spray. Add zucchini, eggplant, bell peppers, basil, oil, and oregano; stir gently. Cover and bake in a 425° oven for 40 minutes.

Stir vegetables, pushing to sides of pan. Lay fish in center, overlapping slightly if necessary. Cover and continue baking until fish looks just opaque but still moist in thickest part; cut to test (about 8 minutes). Uncover and sprinkle with Havarti; continue baking, uncovered, until cheese is melted (1 to 2 more minutes). Makes 4 servings.

SIMMERED COD & VEGETABLES

Per serving: 276 calories, 26 g protein, 38 g carbohydrates, 2 g total fat (0.1 g saturated fat), 49 mg cholesterol, 672 mg sodium

Preparation time: About 10 minutes
Cooking time: About 20 minutes

For a quick meal on busy nights, use fish directly from the freezer to make this low-calorie, high-protein main dish. Other frozen white-fleshed fish fillets, such as ocean perch, haddock, sole, or orange roughy, can be substituted for the cod.

> 12 small red thin-skinned potatoes (about 1½ lbs. *total*), halved
> ½ pound broccoli flowerets
> 1 bottle (8 oz.) clam juice
> 1 cup dry white wine
> 1 pound individually frozen cod or other white-fleshed fish fillets (suggestions above)
> 1 tablespoon *each* cornstarch, water, and prepared horseradish
> ¼ cup coarse-grained Dijon mustard

Place potatoes in a 3- to 4-quart pan and add enough water to cover by 1 inch. Bring to a boil over high heat; cover and cook for 15 minutes. Add broccoli; cover and continue cooking until vegetables are tender when pierced (about 5 more minutes). Drain.

Meanwhile, combine clam juice, wine, and fish in a wide frying pan. Bring to a boil over high heat; reduce heat, cover, and simmer until fish looks just opaque but still moist in thickest part; cut to test (about 8 minutes). Lift out fish and transfer to a platter; keep warm.

Boil fish liquid over high heat until reduced to 1 cup (about 5 minutes). In a small measuring cup, mix cornstarch, water, horseradish, and mustard and stir into pan. Cook, stirring, until mixture boils and thickens (about 1 minute); pour into a bowl.

Arrange potatoes and broccoli alongside fish. Offer with sauce. Makes 4 servings.

CURRIED FISH & RICE

Per serving: 459 calories, 41 g protein, 44 g carbohydrates, 13 g total fat (3 g saturated fat), 75 mg cholesterol, 185 mg sodium

Preparation time: About 20 minutes
Cooking time: About 20 minutes

Enjoy the intriguing contrast of hot fish and cool rice in this nutritionally balanced dish. A curry-yogurt sauce flavors both fish and rice.

  1 **small head romaine lettuce (about ¾ lb.), separated into leaves, rinsed, and crisped**

  2 **tablespoons salad oil**

  1 **cup sliced green onions (including tops)**

  1 **large red bell pepper (about ½ lb.), stemmed, seeded, and finely chopped**

  2 **teaspoons curry powder**

1½ **cups plain lowfat yogurt**

 ⅓ **cup water**

2½ **cups cooled cooked brown or white rice**

  4 **Chilean sea bass fillets (about 6 oz. *each*), ¾ to 1 inch thick, rinsed and patted dry**

Finely shred about a third of the lettuce. Arrange remaining whole leaves on a platter; mound shredded lettuce over half the leaves. Set aside.

Heat 1 tablespoon of the oil in a wide nonstick frying pan over medium-high heat. Add onions and bell pepper and cook, stirring often, until limp (about 10 minutes). Add curry powder; cook, stirring, for 1 more minute. Transfer vegetables to a large bowl and stir in yogurt and water; set aside 1¼ cups of the mixture. Add rice to remaining vegetable mixture and stir well; mound on shredded lettuce. Set aside.

Heat remaining oil in pan over medium-high heat. Add fish and cook, turning once, until just opaque but still moist in thickest part; cut to test (8 to 10 minutes *total*). Arrange fish on lettuce leaves; spoon reserved yogurt mixture over fish. Makes 4 servings.

■ *Pictured on facing page*

COOL SALMON WITH RADISH TARTAR

Per serving: 515 calories, 49 g protein, 48 g carbohydrates, 14 g total fat (3 g saturated fat), 113 mg cholesterol, 274 mg sodium

Preparation time: About 15 minutes
Cooking time: About 40 minutes

If "one-pot meal" sounds dull to you, this refreshing combination will change your mind. Each ingredient is cooked in sequence in the same pan.

  1 **pound green beans**

  4 **salmon steaks (6 to 8 oz. *each*), rinsed and patted dry**

12 **small red thin-skinned potatoes (about 1½ lbs. *total*)**

  4 **butterhead lettuce leaves, rinsed and crisped**

  1 **pound cherry tomatoes, stemmed**
    Radish Tartar (recipe follows)
    Lemon wedges (optional)

In a 5- to 6-quart pan, bring 3 quarts water to a boil over high heat. Add beans; cook until barely tender (about 5 minutes). Lift out, immerse in ice water until cool, and drain. Set aside.

Return water in pan to boiling. Add fish; cover pan tightly and remove from heat. Let fish stand until just opaque but still moist in thickest part; cut to test (about 12 minutes). Lift out, immerse in ice water until cool, and drain; pat dry. Set aside.

Return water in pan to boiling. Add potatoes; reduce heat, cover, and simmer until tender when pierced (20 to 25 minutes). Drain, immerse in ice water until cool, and drain again. Set aside.

Arrange lettuce on a platter. Lay salmon on lettuce. Arrange beans, potatoes, and tomatoes around fish. If made ahead, cover and refrigerate until next day.

Prepare Radish Tartar and offer with fish. Garnish with lemon, if desired. Makes 4 servings.

Radish Tartar. Stir together 1 cup **plain lowfat yogurt**, ¾ cup chopped **red radishes**, ⅓ cup minced **green onions** (including tops), 2 tablespoons drained and rinsed **capers,** and 1 tablespoon **prepared horseradish.**

*As colorful as it is nutritious, Cool Salmon with Radish
Tartar (recipe on facing page) furnishes impressive
sustenance on a warm summer evening. A crusty loaf of
bread is all you'll need alongside.*

119

AHI STEAKS WITH BACON

Per serving: 248 calories, 41 g protein, 1 g carbohydrates, 8 g total fat (2 g saturated fat), 82 mg cholesterol, 453 mg sodium

Preparation time: About 5 minutes
Cooking time: About 17 minutes

Meaty yellowfin tuna, called ahi in Hawaii, is a seafood luxury not to be missed. For best flavor, cook the steaks until browned on the outside but still pink inside. Top with a soy-wine glaze and a sprinkling of crisp bacon.

- 2 slices bacon
- 4 ahi (yellowfin tuna) steaks (about 6 oz. *each*), about 1 inch thick, rinsed and patted dry
- 2 teaspoons margarine
- 2 tablespoons reduced-sodium soy sauce
- ½ cup dry white wine

In a wide frying pan, cook bacon over medium heat until crisp (about 7 minutes). Lift out and drain on paper towels. Discard all but 1 tablespoon of the drippings from pan.

Add fish to pan, increase heat to high, and cook, turning once, until browned on both sides (about 4 minutes *total*). Dot fish with margarine; add soy sauce and wine. Reduce heat to medium, cover, and cook until fish is pale pink in center; cut to test (about 4 minutes). Lift out and arrange on a platter; keep warm.

Increase heat to high and boil sauce until reduced to about 3 tablespoons (about 2 minutes). Meanwhile, crumble bacon. Top fish with sauce and sprinkle with bacon. Makes 4 servings.

SWORDFISH WITH MUSHROOM SAUCE

Per serving: 210 calories, 31 g protein, 4 g carbohydrates, 7 g total fat (2 g saturated fat), 59 mg cholesterol, 332 mg sodium

Preparation time: About 15 minutes
Marinating time: 30 minutes
Broiling time: 8 to 10 minutes

Firm swordfish is extra juicy when soaked in a lemony marinade and topped with a wine-laced mushroom sauce. If you like, use shark steaks instead of swordfish.

- 2 pounds swordfish or shark steaks, rinsed and patted dry
- 6 tablespoons lemon juice
- ½ cup dry white wine or water
- 1 clove garlic, minced or pressed
- ½ teaspoon *each* dry oregano leaves, salt, and pepper
- ¼ teaspoon fennel seeds, crushed
  Nonstick cooking spray
- ½ pound mushrooms, sliced
- 1 teaspoon salad oil
- ½ cup thinly sliced green onions (including tops)
- 3 cups watercress sprigs

Cut fish into serving-size pieces, if necessary. In a 9- by 13-inch baking pan, stir together lemon juice, wine, garlic, oregano, salt, pepper, and fennel seeds. Add fish and let stand, turning occasionally, for 30 minutes. Lift out fish and drain briefly, reserving marinade.

Lightly coat a broiler pan rack with cooking spray. Place fish on rack and broil 3 to 4 inches below heat, turning once or twice, until fish looks just opaque but still moist in center; cut to test (8 to 10 minutes *total*).

Meanwhile, combine mushrooms and oil in a nonstick frying pan over medium-high heat. Cook, stirring, until mushrooms are soft (about 5 minutes). Stir in reserved marinade and boil gently for 2 minutes; stir in onions and remove from heat.

Arrange watercress on individual plates. Add fish and top with mushroom sauce. Makes 6 servings.

CHINESE-STYLE STEAMED FISH

Per serving: 170 calories, 32 g protein, 2 g carbohydrates, 3 g total fat (0.6 g saturated fat), 60 mg cholesterol, 254 mg sodium

Preparation time: About 15 minutes
Steaming time: 8 to 10 minutes per inch of thickness

For a dramatic main dish, present a whole fish steamed with Asian-inspired seasonings. The moist heat intensifies the flavors of fresh ginger and chile.

- 1 scaled and cleaned whole rockfish, snapper, or black sea bass (about 2 lbs.), head removed, if desired, rinsed, and patted dry
  Salt
- 3 tablespoons slivered fresh ginger
- 3 green onions (including tops), thinly sliced lengthwise
- 1 dried hot red chile (about 3 inches long)
- 1 tablespoon unseasoned rice vinegar or wine vinegar
- 1 tablespoon reduced-sodium soy sauce
  Cilantro (coriander) sprigs (optional)

Make 3 diagonal slashes across fish on each side. Place on a rimmed plate that will fit on a steamer rack in a pan. (If fish is too long, cut in half crosswise and place halves side by side.) Season to taste with salt. Place half the ginger and onions inside cavity; put chile and remaining ginger and onions on top. Pour vinegar and soy sauce over fish.

Loosely cover with foil and place plate on a rack in a pan above 1 inch boiling water. Cover and steam until fish looks just opaque but still moist in thickest part; cut to test (8 to 10 minutes per inch of thickness).

Arrange fish on a large platter (reassemble halves, if necessary). Garnish with cilantro, if desired. To serve, cut through fish to backbone and slide a spatula between flesh and ribs to lift off each serving. Remove backbone to serve bottom half. Makes 4 servings.

STUFFED TROUT

Per serving: 363 calories, 38 g protein, 18 g carbohydrates, 14 g total fat (2 g saturated fat), 100 mg cholesterol, 279 mg sodium

Preparation time: About 35 minutes
Baking time: About 20 minutes

Small boned whole fish, such as trout and baby salmon, are good candidates for stuffing. The stuffing stays moist because it bakes inside the fish.

- Toasted Bread Cubes (directions follow)
- 2 tablespoons finely chopped parsley
- ½ cup thinly sliced green onions (including tops)
- 1 medium-size red or green bell pepper (about 6 oz.), stemmed, seeded, and finely chopped
- ⅓ cup dry white wine or low-sodium chicken broth
- 1 tablespoon melted margarine
  Salt and freshly ground pepper
- 6 boned and butterflied whole trout (about 8 oz. *each*), rinsed and patted dry
  Nonstick cooking spray or salad oil
  About ¼ cup lemon juice
  Parsley sprigs and lemon wedges (optional)

Prepare Toasted Bread Cubes. In a bowl, stir together bread cubes, chopped parsley, onions, bell pepper, wine, and margarine. Season to taste with salt and pepper. Lightly pack stuffing into cavities of fish; sew openings with heavy thread or close with wooden picks. (Wrap any extra stuffing in foil and bake in pan alongside fish.)

Lightly coat a 9- by 13-inch baking pan with cooking spray. Add fish and brush with lemon juice. Cover and bake in a 400° oven for 10 minutes. Uncover and continue baking until fish looks just opaque but still moist in thickest part; cut to test (about 10 more minutes).

Transfer fish to a platter and remove thread. Garnish with parsley sprigs and lemon, if desired. Makes 6 servings.

Toasted Bread Cubes. Cut about 6 ounces **French or Italian bread** into ½-inch cubes (you should have about 4 cups). Spread in a single layer on a baking sheet and bake in a 400° oven until crisp (about 10 minutes).

*Light and elegant—it's easy to cook that way
when you prepare Dilled Roughy in Parchment (recipe on
facing page) and offer it with steamed squash and diced
bell peppers. A fresh fruit garnish adds flourish.*

■ *Pictured on facing page*

DILLED ROUGHY IN PARCHMENT

Preparation time: About 25 minutes
Baking time: 7 to 10 minutes

Baking fish in parchment is one of the lightest ways to cook fish. It maximizes flavor, locks in moisture, and makes for a burst of delicious aroma when the packets are opened. Practice the folding method once or twice before preparing the fish packets.

- 1 tablespoon salad oil
- 3 tablespoons *each* white wine vinegar and chopped green onions (including tops)
- 1 teaspoon chopped fresh dill or ½ teaspoon dry dill weed
- 1 teaspoon shredded tangerine or orange peel
- 1 large can (about 1 lb.) mandarin oranges, drained
  Nonstick cooking spray
- 4 orange roughy fillets (about 5 oz. *each*), rinsed and patted dry

■ *Per serving: 283 calories, 21 g protein, 19 g carbohydrates, 14 g total fat (0.6 g saturated fat), 28 mg cholesterol, 97 mg sodium*

Mix oil, vinegar, onions, dill, tangerine peel, and oranges. Set aside.

Cut 4 pieces of parchment paper, each about 4 times wider and 6 inches longer than each fish fillet. Coat each sheet with cooking spray, starting 1 inch from long side and covering an area the size of a fish fillet. Place a fillet on sprayed area of each sheet; spoon orange mixture over each fillet.

Fold long edge of parchment closest to fish over fish; then roll over several times to wrap fish in parchment. With seam side down, double fold each end, pressing lightly to crease and tucking ends under packet.

Place packets, folded ends underneath, slightly apart on a baking sheet; spray packets lightly with cooking spray. Bake in a 500° oven until fish looks just opaque but still moist in thickest part; cut a tiny slit through parchment into fish to test (7 to 10 minutes). Slash packets open and pull back parchment to reveal fish. Makes 4 servings.

SHELLFISH COUSCOUS

Preparation time: About 20 minutes
Cooking time: About 25 minutes

Couscous—pellet-shaped pasta made from semolina wheat—swells to edible tenderness when steeped in hot liquid. Here, this nutritious carbohydrate is paired with shellfish for an easy main dish.

- 3 slices bacon, chopped
- ¾ pound large shrimp (about 18 *total*), shelled and deveined
- ¾ pound bay scallops, rinsed and patted dry
- 1 cup dry vermouth
- 2½ cups low-sodium chicken broth
- ½ cup orange juice
- 2 cups couscous
- ¼ cup dried tomatoes packed in oil, drained, rinsed, and slivered
- ⅔ cup minced chives
- 2 large oranges (about 1¼ lbs. *total*), thinly sliced

■ *Per serving: 484 calories, 30 g protein, 66 g carbohydrates, 10 g total fat (2 g saturated fat), 94 mg cholesterol, 477 mg sodium*

In a 4- to 5-quart pan, cook bacon over medium heat, stirring often, until crisp (about 7 minutes). Discard all but 2 tablespoons of the drippings from pan. Increase heat to medium-high and add shrimp and scallops. Cook, stirring often, until opaque in center; cut to test (about 5 minutes). Lift out shellfish and bacon; keep warm.

Add vermouth to pan; increase heat to high and boil until reduced by about half (about 5 minutes). Add chicken broth and orange juice. Bring to a boil; stir in couscous, tomatoes, and ⅓ cup of the chives. Cover, remove from heat, and let stand until liquid is absorbed (about 5 minutes).

Mound couscous on a platter and top with shellfish and bacon; sprinkle with remaining chives. Tuck oranges around couscous. Makes 6 servings.

It's no wonder that the microwave is so popular for cooking seafood. It produces moist, luscious results with no added fat. Moreover, it brings out seafood's natural flavor. For a superb lean entrée, try one of the following microwave recipes. Or simply microwave seafood plain and then top with a light sauce or a squeeze of lemon.

When microwaving seafood, refer to the chart on the facing page for cooking and standing times. Check the food for doneness after the standing time. If it's not completely cooked, continue microwaving in 30-second increments. Remember that it's better to undercook delicate seafood and add more cooking time later than to overcook it.

Fennel-seasoned Salmon with Vegetables

4   small red thin-skinned potatoes (about ½ lb. *total*)

2   salmon steaks or fillets (6 to 8 oz. *each*), about ¾ inch thick, rinsed and patted dry

¼   teaspoon fennel seeds

½   pound asparagus, tough ends snapped off
    Orange wedges

Peel a thin strip from center of each potato; evenly arrange potatoes around edge of a rimmed microwave-safe platter. Cover loosely with plastic wrap and microwave on **HIGH (100%)** for 5 minutes.

Arrange fish pieces opposite each other on platter, with thickest portions toward outside of dish. Fold tips of steaks inward or fold under any thin edges of fillets. Sprinkle with fennel seeds. Cover and microwave on **HIGH (100%)** for 2 minutes.

Place asparagus in a single layer in center of platter. Cover and microwave on **HIGH (100%)** for 3 to 5 minutes. Let stand, covered, for 2 minutes. Asparagus should be tender-crisp and fish should look just opaque but still moist in thickest part; cut to test. Squeeze orange wedges over fish and vegetables. Makes 2 servings.

Per serving: 388 calories, 43 g protein, 23 g carbohydrates, 13 g total fat (2 g saturated fat), 109 mg cholesterol, 97 mg sodium

Sole Fillets with Capers

½   pound sole fillets, rinsed and patted dry

1   teaspoon lemon juice

1   tablespoon finely chopped chives

½   teaspoon *each* finely shredded lemon peel and drained and rinsed capers

⅛   teaspoon crushed red pepper flakes
    Lemon wedges

Place fish in a single layer, overlapping thin edges, on a 9- to 10-inch microwave-safe plate. Drizzle with lemon juice and sprinkle with chives, lemon peel, capers, and red pepper flakes. Cover loosely with plastic wrap and microwave on **HIGH (100%)** for 1½ to 2 minutes. Let stand, covered, for 1 to 2 minutes. Fish should look just opaque but still moist in thickest part; cut to test. Offer with lemon wedges. Makes 2 servings.

Per serving: 105 calories, 21 g protein, 0.3 g carbohydrates, 1 g total fat (0.3 g saturated fat), 54 mg cholesterol, 111 mg sodium

Pictured on page 126

Sea Bass with Ginger

¾   pound sea bass fillets (1 to 1½ inches thick)

2   tablespoons orange juice

4   teaspoons reduced-sodium soy sauce

2   teaspoons finely shredded fresh ginger

1   teaspoon finely shredded orange peel
    Orange wedges

Cut each fillet in half horizontally almost all the way through; lay flat. On both sides of each fillet, make crosswise cuts all the way through at 1-inch intervals, cutting toward center and leaving about a 1-inch-wide strip uncut at center. Rinse and pat dry.

Arrange fish in a 9- by 13-inch microwave-safe baking dish. Drizzle with orange juice and soy sauce, and sprinkle with ginger and orange peel. Cover loosely with plastic wrap and microwave on **HIGH (100%)** for 2 minutes. Let stand, covered, for 3 minutes. Fish should look just opaque but still moist in thickest part; cut to test. Arrange fish on individual plates and offer with orange wedges.

Per serving: 181 calories, 32 g protein, 3 g carbohydrates, 3 g total fat (0.9 g saturated fat), 70 mg cholesterol, 517 mg sodium

■ Cooking Chart

To prevent overcooking, use shortest cooking time; let stand before testing for doneness. If necessary, continue microwaving in 30-second increments. Cooking times below are for a 600- to 700-watt microwave oven. If yours is different, consult manufacturer's instructions.

To grease plate, lightly coat with nonstick cooking spray or salad oil. Use wax paper or heavy-duty plastic wrap to cover seafood for cooking.

Seafood	Preparation	Cooking Time (CT) Standing Time (ST)
Fish steaks or fillets, ½ to ¾ inch thick (1 lb. *total*)	If frozen, thaw completely. Rinse and pat dry. In a greased 7- by 11-inch microwave-safe baking dish, arrange fish in an even layer, with thickest portions toward outside of dish. Sprinkle with lemon juice or dry white wine and, if desired, season to taste with paprika, dry dill weed, or dry thyme leaves. Cover.	**CT:** 3 to 4 minutes Microwave on **HIGH (100%),** giving pieces a half-turn after 2 minutes. **ST:** 3 minutes, covered Fish should look just opaque but still moist in thickest part; cut to test.
Whole trout, baby salmon, or other small fish (cleaned and dressed), 1 or 2 (8 to 10 oz. *each*)	If frozen, thaw completely. Rinse and pat dry. If desired, stuff with lemon or onion slices. In a greased 7- by 11-inch microwave-safe baking dish, arrange fish lengthwise, with backbone toward outside of dish. Sprinkle with lemon juice. Cover.	**CT:** 1 fish: 2½ to 3½ minutes 2 fish: 5 to 7 minutes Microwave on **HIGH (100%),** turning fish over and bringing cooked portion to inside of dish halfway through cooking. **ST:** 3 minutes, covered Fish should look just opaque but still moist in thickest part; cut to test.
Hard-shell clams in shell, 1 dozen	Scrub well. On a flat 10-inch microwave-safe plate, arrange clams in a circle, with hinge sides toward outside of plate. Cover loosely.	**CT:** 3 to 4 minutes Microwave on **HIGH (100%)** until shells open. Lift out opened clams; continue microwaving remaining clams, checking at 30-second intervals, until shells open. **ST:** 1 minute, covered
Crab in shell (cooked, cleaned, and cracked), 1 large (about 2 lbs.)	Rinse; do not dry. Place crab in a 7- by 11-inch microwave-safe baking dish, with meaty portions toward outside of dish. Cover.	**CT:** 2 to 3 minutes Microwave on **HIGH (100%).** Meat in shells should be hot. **ST:** 1 to 2 minutes, covered
Mussels in shell, 1 dozen	Same as for hard-shell clams in shell	Same as for hard-shell clams in shell
Oysters in shell Eastern: 10 to 12 Pacific: 8 medium-size	Same as for hard-shell clams in shell	**CT:** 4 to 5 minutes Microwave on **HIGH (100%)** until shells open. Edges of oysters should be curled. **ST:** 2 minutes, covered
Oysters, shucked Eastern: 8 to 10 Pacific, small: 1 jar (10 oz.)	On a flat 10-inch microwave-safe plate, arrange oysters in a circle. Sprinkle with juices. Cover.	**CT:** About 3 minutes Microwave on **HIGH (100%),** turning over after 1½ minutes. Oysters should be hot and edges curled. **ST:** 1 to 2 minutes, covered
Scallops, 1 pound	Rinse and pat dry; if large, cut in half. Place in a 1½-quart microwave-safe baking dish. Sprinkle with lemon juice or dry white wine. Cover.	**CT:** About 3 minutes Microwave on **HIGH (100%),** stirring after 1½ minutes. **ST:** 4 minutes, covered Scallops should be opaque in center; cut to test.
Shrimp, 1 pound medium-size (about 35 *total*)	Rinse and pat dry. Shell and devein, if desired. On a flat 12-inch microwave-safe plate, arrange shrimp in a single layer, with thickest parts toward outside of plate. Sprinkle with dry white wine. Cover.	**CT:** About 4 minutes Microwave on **HIGH (100%),** bringing cooked portion to inside of plate after 2 minutes. **ST:** 2 minutes, covered Shrimp should be opaque in center; cut to test.

Short on time? Prepare dinner in minutes with Sea Bass with Ginger (recipe on page 124). Cooking fish in the microwave ensures tender, juicy results. Delicate snow peas are the perfect vegetable companion.

CLAM PAELLA FOR TWO

Per serving: 450 calories, 29 g protein, 61 g carbohydrates, 9 g total fat (1 g saturated fat), 61 mg cholesterol, 312 mg sodium

Preparation time: About 15 minutes
Cooking time: About 30 minutes

Unlike more traditional paella recipes, this version is not a complex affair. It cooks quickly and needs only a green salad alongside, making it a simple dinner on any night.

- 1 tablespoon olive oil
- 1 clove garlic, minced or pressed
- ¼ teaspoon ground turmeric
- ⅔ cup long-grain white rice
- 2 tablespoons finely chopped parsley
- ½ pound cherry tomatoes, stemmed and halved
- ⅔ cup dry white wine
- ¾ cup bottled clam juice or low-sodium chicken broth
- 24 small hard-shell clams in shells, scrubbed

Heat oil in a wide frying pan over medium heat. Add garlic, turmeric, and rice. Cook, stirring often, until rice begins to look opaque (3 to 5 minutes). Stir in parsley, tomatoes, wine, and clam juice. Reduce heat, cover, and simmer for 15 minutes.

Arrange clams over rice. Cover and continue cooking until shells open and rice is tender (8 to 10 more minutes). Discard any unopened clams. Makes 2 servings.

OYSTER JAMBALAYA

Per serving: 388 calories, 20 g protein, 59 g carbohydrates, 8 g total fat (2 g saturated fat), 66 mg cholesterol, 573 mg sodium

Preparation time: About 25 minutes
Cooking time: About 45 minutes

This dynamite Cajun rice specialty is laced with hot pepper, fresh vegetables, and herbs. The oysters provide valuable minerals—zinc, copper, and iron.

- 2 jars (10 oz. *each*) small shucked oysters, drained and rinsed
- 1 tablespoon salad oil
- 6 ounces Canadian bacon, diced
- 1 large onion, chopped
- 3 cloves garlic, minced or pressed
- 2 large green bell peppers (about 1 lb. *total*), stemmed, seeded, and chopped
- 1 cup chopped celery
- 4 large tomatoes (about 2 lbs. *total*), chopped
- 1 can (8 oz.) no-salt-added tomato sauce
- 2 bay leaves, crumbled
- 1 teaspoon dry thyme leaves
- 1½ teaspoons ground white pepper
- ½ teaspoon ground red pepper (cayenne)
- ½ cup chopped parsley
- 1½ cups long-grain white rice
- 2½ cups low-sodium chicken broth

Cut oysters into small pieces and set aside.

Heat oil in a 6- to 8-quart pan over medium heat. Add bacon and cook, stirring often, until lightly browned (about 5 minutes). Add onion, garlic, bell peppers, and celery. Cook, stirring occasionally, until vegetables are limp (about 10 minutes). Add tomatoes, tomato sauce, bay leaves, thyme, white pepper, red pepper, and parsley. Cook, stirring, until sauce boils.

Add rice and chicken broth. Bring to a boil; reduce heat, cover, and simmer for 20 minutes. Stir in oysters, cover, and continue cooking until rice is tender and oysters are opaque in center; cut to test (about 10 more minutes). Makes 6 servings.

SAN FRANCISCO–STYLE CIOPPINO

Per serving: 296 calories, 38 g protein, 18 g carbohydrates, 8 g total fat (1 g saturated fat), 167 mg cholesterol, 664 mg sodium

Preparation time: About 25 minutes
Cooking time: About 45 minutes

This vibrant fish stew, a favorite ever since sailors introduced it to the West Coast, features Dungeness crabs, clams, and shrimp in an herbed tomato sauce.

- 2 tablespoons olive oil
- 1 large onion, chopped
- 2 cloves garlic, minced or pressed
- 1 large green bell pepper (about ½ lb.), stemmed, seeded, and chopped
- ⅓ cup chopped parsley
- 1 can (15 oz.) no-salt-added tomato sauce
- 1 can (28 oz.) peeled tomatoes
- 1 cup dry red or white wine
- 1 bay leaf
- 1 teaspoon dry basil leaves
- ½ teaspoon dry oregano leaves
- 12 small hard-shell clams in shells, scrubbed
- 1 pound large shrimp (about 25 *total*), shelled and deveined
- 2 cooked Dungeness crabs (about 4 lbs. *total*), cleaned and cracked

Heat oil in a 6- to 8-quart pan over medium heat. Add onion, garlic, bell pepper, and parsley. Cook, stirring often, until onion is soft (about 5 minutes). Stir in tomato sauce, tomatoes (break up with a spoon) and their liquid, wine, bay leaf, basil, and oregano. Bring to a boil; reduce heat, cover, and simmer for 20 minutes.

Add clams, shrimp, and crabs. Cover and simmer until clams open and shrimp are opaque in center; cut to test (about 20 minutes). Discard any unopened clams. Ladle sauce and shellfish into wide, shallow bowls. Makes 6 servings.

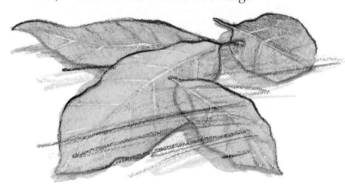

MUSSELS PROVENÇAL

Per serving: 159 calories, 13 g protein, 15 g carbohydrates, 5 g total fat (0.8 g saturated fat), 26 mg cholesterol, 569 mg sodium

Preparation time: About 15 minutes
Cooking time: About 30 minutes

A heady aroma of garlic, tomatoes, and wine wafts up from each bowl of these steamed mussels. Offer with crusty French bread to soak up the sauce.

- 3½ pounds fresh mussels, scrubbed
- 1 tablespoon olive oil
- 3 cloves garlic, minced or pressed
- 1 large onion, chopped
- 1 cup chopped celery
- 2 cans (15 oz. *each*) peeled tomatoes
- 1 cup dry white wine or low-sodium chicken broth
- ½ cup minced parsley
- ½ teaspoon pepper

Discard any mussels that don't close when lightly tapped. With a swift tug, pull beard (clump of fibers along side of shell) off each mussel. Set mussels aside.

Heat oil in a 6- to 8-quart pan over medium-high heat. Add garlic, onion, and celery. Cook, stirring occasionally, until limp (about 7 minutes). Add tomatoes (break up with a spoon) and their liquid. Bring to a boil; reduce heat to medium, cover, and cook for 15 minutes. Add wine, parsley, and pepper. Cover and continue cooking until mixture boils.

Add mussels. Cover and cook until shells open (about 8 minutes). Discard any unopened shells. With a slotted spoon, transfer mussels to wide, shallow bowls; ladle sauce over each portion. Makes 4 to 6 servings.

STIR-FRIED SCALLOPS & ASPARAGUS

Preparation time: About 15 minutes
Cooking time: About 10 minutes

For an elegant, quick-to-fix main course, stir-fry scallops and asparagus and serve atop thin pasta strands. Quick cooking keeps the shellfish tender and retains the nutrients in the asparagus.

- ½ **pound bay or sea scallops, rinsed and patted dry**
- ½ **cup unseasoned rice vinegar; or ½ cup white wine vinegar mixed with 1 teaspoon sugar**
- 2 **tablespoons sugar**
- 1 **teaspoon** *each* **sesame oil and reduced-sodium soy sauce**
- 2 **tablespoons salad oil**
- 1 **pound asparagus, tough ends snapped off, cut diagonally into ½-inch pieces**
- 3 **tablespoons water**
- 8 **ounces dry vermicelli or spaghettini**
- 1 **clove garlic, minced or pressed**
- 1 **tablespoon minced fresh ginger**

Per serving: 378 calories, 19 g protein, 55 g carbohydrates, 9 g total fat (1 g saturated fat), 19 mg cholesterol, 149 mg sodium

Cut sea scallops, if used, into ½-inch pieces. Set aside. In a small bowl, stir together vinegar, sugar, sesame oil, and soy sauce. Set aside.

Heat 1 tablespoon of the salad oil in a wok or wide frying pan over high heat. Add asparagus, stirring to coat. Add the 3 tablespoons water. Cover and cook until asparagus is tender-crisp (about 5 minutes). Lift out and keep warm. Set pan aside.

In a 5- to 6-quart pan, cook pasta in 3 quarts boiling water until al dente (about 5 minutes or according to package directions).

Meanwhile, heat remaining oil in wok over high heat. Add garlic, ginger, and scallops. Cook, stirring, until scallops are opaque in center; cut to test (2 to 3 minutes). Return asparagus to pan and add vinegar mixture, stirring just until sugar is dissolved. Remove from heat.

Drain pasta; place in a large, warm bowl. Add scallop mixture and stir well. Makes 4 servings.

GREEK-STYLE SHRIMP ON ZUCCHINI

Preparation time: About 25 minutes
Cooking time: About 15 minutes

Slender strands of steamed zucchini stand in for pasta as a bed for simmered shrimp and tomatoes.

- 2 **teaspoons olive oil**
- 2 **small carrots (about 5 oz.** *total***), sliced**
- 1 **celery stalk, chopped**
- 1 **medium-size onion, chopped**
- 1 **clove garlic, minced or pressed**
- ¼ **cup dry white wine**
- 1 **can (15 oz.) peeled tomatoes**
- ¼ **cup chopped fresh basil leaves; or ¼ cup chopped parsley and 2 teaspoons dry basil leaves**
- 1 **teaspoon dry oregano leaves**
  Freshly ground pepper
  Zucchini Noodles (directions follow)
- 1 **pound medium-size shrimp (about 35** *total***), shelled and deveined**
- ⅓ **cup crumbled feta cheese**

Per serving: 209 calories, 23 g protein, 16 g carbohydrates, 6 g total fat (2 g saturated fat), 148 mg cholesterol, 442 mg sodium

Heat oil in a wide nonstick frying pan over medium-high heat. Add carrots, celery, and onion. Cook, stirring often, until soft (about 5 minutes). Add garlic and cook, stirring, for 2 more minutes. Add wine, tomatoes (break up with a spoon) and their liquid, basil, and oregano. Season to taste with pepper. Bring to a boil; reduce heat and simmer, uncovered, until thickened (about 10 minutes).

Meanwhile, prepare Zucchini Noodles. Arrange on a platter and keep warm.

Add shrimp to sauce and cook, stirring, until opaque in center; cut to test (about 5 minutes). Stir in feta. Spoon over zucchini. Makes 4 servings.

Zucchini Noodles. Slice 1 pound **zucchini** lengthwise ⅛ inch thick. Stack slices and cut lengthwise into ⅛-inch-thick strips. In a 2-quart pan, bring 1 quart **water** to a boil over high heat. Add zucchini and cook just until tender (2 to 3 minutes). Drain.

Drizzle cilantro-laced shrimp and vegetables
with yogurt and roll in a warm tortilla for zesty Shrimp
Fajitas (recipe on facing page); add green salsa to taste.
Decorate the plate with a still life of lime, cilantro,
and pickled chile pepper.

130

■ *Pictured on facing page*

SHRIMP FAJITAS

Preparation time: About 20 minutes
Marinating time: 20 minutes
Cooking time: About 15 minutes

■ *Per serving: 220 calories, 17 g protein, 28 g carbohydrates, 4 g total fat (0.6 g saturated fat), 94 mg cholesterol, 285 mg sodium*

When tender shrimp are marinated in a lively cilantro sauce, sautéed with peppers and onions, and rolled in tortillas, an absolutely delicious version of the popular fajita is born. It's an easy meal that offers balanced nutrition in a single package.

- 1 **pound medium-size shrimp (about 35** *total*), **shelled and deveined**
- 1 **cup lightly packed chopped cilantro (coriander)**
- 1 **clove garlic, minced or pressed**
- ⅓ **cup lime juice**
- 4 **to 6 flour tortillas (9-inch diameter)**
- 1 **tablespoon salad oil**
- 2 **large green bell peppers (about 1 lb.** *total*), **stemmed, seeded, and thinly sliced**
- 1 **large onion, thinly sliced**
- ½ **cup plain nonfat yogurt**
  Bottled green tomatillo salsa

Stir together shrimp, cilantro, garlic, and lime juice. Let stand at room temperature for 20 minutes.

Meanwhile, wrap tortillas in foil and place in a 350° oven until hot (about 15 minutes).

Heat oil in a wide nonstick frying pan over medium-high heat. Add bell peppers and onion. Cook, stirring occasionally, until limp (about 10 minutes). Remove vegetables and keep warm. Add shrimp mixture to pan, increase heat to high, and cook, stirring often, until shrimp are opaque in center; cut to test (about 3 minutes). Return vegetables to pan, stirring to mix with shrimp.

Spoon shrimp mixture into tortillas, top with yogurt, and roll up. Offer with salsa. Makes 4 to 6 servings.

SOFT-SHELL CRAB WITH GINGER

Preparation time: About 15 minutes
Cooking time: About 8 minutes

■ *Per serving: 122 calories, 22 g protein, 3 g carbohydrates, 2 g total fat (0.2 g saturated fat), 108 mg cholesterol, 306 mg sodium*

Small and wholly edible, soft-shell crab is a seafood specialty available fresh in the summer or frozen the year around. Have your fishmonger clean live crabs. Since they're small, plan on serving two per person.

- 6 **cleaned soft-shell blue crabs (thawed if frozen)**
- ⅓ **cup unseasoned rice vinegar**
- 2 **tablespoons thinly sliced green onions (including tops)**
- 1½ **tablespoons minced fresh ginger**
- 1 **teaspoon sugar**

Place crabs, back sides up, on a rack in a pan above 1 inch boiling water. Cover and steam over high heat until crabs are opaque in center of body; cut to test (about 8 minutes).

Meanwhile, stir together vinegar, onions, ginger, and sugar in a small bowl.

Transfer crabs to individual plates. Offer with ginger sauce. Makes 3 servings.

Pasta

Farfalle with Fresh Tomatoes & Basil ■ Penne
with Broccoli & Ricotta ■ Pasta with Parsley-Lemon
Pesto ■ Vermicelli with Vegetable Sauce ■ Winter
Garden Pasta ■ Summertime Pasta al Fresco ■
Pasta with Beans ■ Orecchiette with Spinach &
Garlic ■ Vegetable Lasagne ■ Spinach &
Tofu Manicotti ■ Noodles with Cabbage &
Gruyère ■ Perciatelli with Turkey Marinara
■ Tortellini & Peas in Creamy Lemon Sauce ■
Seafood Linguine ■ Chilled Oriental Pasta with
Shrimp ■ Cool Pasta Shells with Scallops

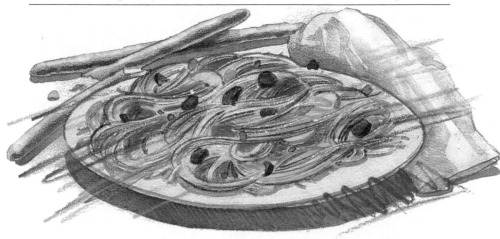

Like a painter's canvas, pasta is a neutral background for countless innovative creations; sauces and toppings are the brush strokes that bring it to life. The end result is a feast for the senses. Happily, pasta is also nutritious, which is one of the reasons it has become so popular today. It provides protein and complex carbohydrates with almost no fat, especially if you use eggless noodles made from semolina (hard durum wheat) or whole wheat. Versatile enough to be a filling lunch, an elegant first course, or a dinner entrée, pasta is also easy to cook. For best results, boil it in ample water—about 6 quarts for a pound of dry pasta. (You may want to buy a special 8- to 10-quart pan equipped with a perforated insert that makes draining pasta a snap.) Cook the pasta until it's just tender-firm to bite with no raw taste, a texture known as al dente (literally, "to the teeth"). Start tasting the pasta about 2 minutes before the package says it will be done. Finally, when adding Parmesan to the finished dish, use a light hand; a tablespoon of Parmesan adds about 2 grams of fat and 114 milligrams of sodium to the pasta.

■ *Pictured on facing page*

FARFALLE WITH FRESH TOMATOES & BASIL

Preparation time: About 10 minutes
Cooking time: 7 to 9 minutes

Typical of the simple goodness of Italian food, this dish can be tossed together in minutes, but it's full of lasting flavor and nutrition. Use *farfalle* ("butter-flies"), also known as bow-tie pasta, or another whimsical shape.

>   12 ounces farfalle or other dry pasta shape
>   1 tablespoon olive oil
>   2 cloves garlic, minced or pressed
>   1 pound ripe pear-shaped tomatoes, coarsely chopped
>   1 cup tightly packed fresh basil leaves, torn into pieces
>   Coarsely ground pepper
>   Grated Parmesan cheese

■ *Per serving: 382 calories, 13 g protein, 72 g carbohydrates, 5 g total fat (0.7 g saturated fat), 0 mg cholesterol, 16 mg sodium*

In an 8- to 10-quart pan, cook pasta in 6 quarts boiling water until al dente (7 to 9 minutes or according to package directions).

Meanwhile, heat oil in a wide frying pan over medium heat. Add garlic and cook, stirring, for 1 minute. Add tomatoes and cook, stirring, just until tomatoes begin to soften (about 3 minutes). Remove from heat.

Drain pasta and place in a large, warm bowl or platter. Add tomato mixture and basil; toss well. Season to taste with pepper and offer with Parmesan. Makes 4 servings.

PENNE WITH BROCCOLI & RICOTTA

Preparation time: About 10 minutes
Cooking time: 7 to 9 minutes

Nutritionists praise broccoli, a member of the cruciferous family of vegetables, for its fiber, vitamins, calcium, and iron. You'll appreciate its goodness in this creamy entrée, made with *penne* ("quills").

>   12 ounces penne, macaroni, or other dry pasta shape
>   2 tablespoons olive oil
>   5 green onions (including tops), thinly sliced
>   1 pound broccoli flowerets, cut into bite-size pieces
>   ¼ cup water
>   Coarsely ground pepper
>   1½ cups part-skim ricotta cheese
>   Grated Parmesan cheese

■ *Per serving: 539 calories, 25 g protein, 75 g carbohydrates, 16 g total fat (6 g saturated fat), 29 mg cholesterol, 147 mg sodium*

In an 8- to 10-quart pan, cook pasta in 6 quarts boiling water until al dente (7 to 9 minutes or according to package directions).

Meanwhile, heat oil in a wide frying pan over medium-high heat. Add onions and cook, stirring often, for 1 minute. Add broccoli and cook, stirring often, until bright green (about 3 more minutes). Add the ¼ cup water to vegetable mixture and bring to a boil; reduce heat, cover, and simmer until broccoli is tender-crisp (about 5 minutes). Remove from heat and season to taste with pepper.

Drain pasta, reserving about ¼ cup of the cooking water; place pasta in a large, warm bowl. Add broccoli mixture and ricotta; stir well. If mixture is too dry, stir in enough of the reserved pasta water to moisten. Offer with Parmesan. Makes 4 servings.

When summer is here and the pace is easy, choose Farfalle with Fresh Tomatoes & Basil (recipe on facing page). This quick-to-fix meal needs only fresh fruit and cool lemonade to complete the feast.

135

In an ideal world, we would pluck fruits and vegetables from our garden each day and enjoy eggs straight from the chicken coop. In reality, most of us depend on supermarkets for our fresh food items. We trust a vast network of people to deliver them in as short a time and with as little damage as possible. Once we take our groceries home, however, keeping them fresh becomes our responsibility.

How important is it to keep food fresh? Very important. With meat, poultry, and seafood, proper storage is essential not only for best flavor but also for safety. As produce ages, its quality deteriorates: crispness and texture fade, flavor weakens, and water-soluble nutrients, especially vitamin C, evaporate with the natural moisture in the fruit or vegetable. Light, heat, bruising, and cutting can also encourage deterioration.

CHOOSING A GROCERY

Seek out a market that stocks the freshest food available and displays it with care. Meat, poultry, seafood, and dairy products should be stored in refrigerated cases; highly perishable produce, like lettuce and celery, should be chilled; and cold- or moisture-sensitive vegetables and fruits—tomatoes, dry onions, and bananas, for example—should be displayed at room temperature. Most importantly, be sure the market's inventory turns over rapidly.

PLAN CAREFULLY

To ensure that fresh food doesn't languish in your refrigerator past its prime, plan meals carefully. Use the most perishable items first. For instance, seafood is best when prepared the day it's purchased; asparagus won't last long, either. Roasts and Swiss chard, on the other hand, keep well and can be used later in the week.

STORING FRESH FOOD AT HOME

Choose your storage method by the type of food you're storing and how long you want to keep it. To facilitate proper storage, keep an assortment of wraps and containers on hand, including freezer paper and plastic wrap, plastic and paper bags, airtight containers and jars, and baskets or perforated bowls for storing fruit at room temperature. When cutting up raw meat, poultry, or fish, use nonwood surfaces and scrub them after each use.

Refrigerators are best for storing most fresh foods. The temperature (it should be between 35°F and 40°F) is just right to slow down natural deterioration with the least impact on quality. Some compartments, such as meat drawers and vegetable crispers, may be colder. To check your refrigerator's temperature, use a reliable thermometer; also, locate the coldest spots—they're handy for certain items.

Keep your refrigerator clean. Drippings, especially those from meat or poultry, and stuck-on food can be prime sources of microbe infestation.

Freezers are popular for preserving food, but freezing can alter texture and flavor. For long-term storage, a freezer should register 0°F or colder, and food must be properly packaged. Wrap the food airtight in plastic wrap; then double-wrap in freezer paper, freezer bags, or heavy-duty foil. Use freezer tape to label and date the package.

Cool, dry, dark cellars (about 32°F to 50°F) are ideal for storing apples and such hardy vegetables as winter squash and potatoes, but they're a rarity in these days of insulated, heated basements.

Storing Meats

For short-term storage, keep raw meat in the coldest part of the refrigerator away from other foods to prevent cross-contamination. The surface of the meat should be exposed to a little dry air, so porous packaging, such as butcher paper slightly open at the ends, or loosely wrapped plastic is good. Prewrapped meat from the supermarket can be left as is for up to 2 days; after that time, it's best to rewrap it loosely in fresh plastic.

Plan to use ground meat and stew meat within 1 or 2 days; because they've been handled more than other meats, they're very perishable. Chops, steaks, roasts, and cutlets can be kept from 3 to 5 days, but check them daily for any off-odors.

To freeze meat, wrap serving-size portions as directed for freezers (see facing page). For best quality, use frozen pork sausage and bacon within 1 month, and ground meat and stew meat within 3 months. Pork chops and veal cutlets should be used within 3 to 4 months, and pork roasts within 4 to 8 months. Lamb and veal chops and roasts keep from 6 to 9 months. Beef roasts and steaks have the longest freezer life—from 6 to 12 months.

Storing Poultry

Fresh poultry loses flavor quickly and is very prone to spoilage. For best results, remove the store packaging, rinse and dry the poultry, and rewrap loosely in fresh paper, plastic, or foil (store giblets separately from whole birds). Place in the coldest part of your refrigerator away from other foods to prevent cross-contamination. Use within 2 days.

For longer storage, you can freeze poultry. Wrap it as directed for freezers (see facing page). It's best to use frozen poultry within 6 months, frozen giblets within 3 months.

Storing Seafood

Fish and shellfish require special care to maintain freshness. Once you leave the market, keep your purchases cool and refrigerate them promptly.

At home, unwrap and rinse with cool water. Eviscerate whole fish before storing. Place the seafood in an open container and cover with damp paper towels. Store it in the coldest part of your refrigerator and use on the day of purchase, if possible, or within 2 days at the most. Shucked oysters refrigerated in their original container should stay fresh for a week after shucking. Never store live shellfish in water or in an airtight container—this will kill them, making them unsuitable to eat.

Purchased frozen seafood can be stored in the freezer in its original packaging; date the package and use within 2 months. Fresh fish can be frozen, but changes during freezer storage eventually cause fish to lose moisture and even become unpalatable. To freeze, wrap serving-size portions as directed for freezers (see facing page).

Lean fish, such as cod, sole, snapper, and catfish, can remain frozen for up to 6 months. Fattier fish, such as tuna, salmon, and mackerel, keep well for only 3 months; for extra protection against rancidity, dip them before freezing in a solution of 2 tablespoons ascorbic acid and 1 quart water.

To freeze shucked raw or lightly cooked clams, oysters, mussels, and scallops, place in an airtight plastic container and fill with water to within ½ inch of the top; close tightly and freeze. Pack shrimp into a rigid, airtight container, leaving no headroom, and freeze. Lobster, crab, and crayfish should be cooked before freezing; pick out the meat and freeze it in an airtight container. For best results, use frozen shellfish within 3 months.

Storing Eggs

If you want your eggs to last, store them in the refrigerator—a day at room temperature equals a week chilled. Eggs need to be covered to prevent odor absorption and moisture loss, so it's best to keep them in their original carton. If very fresh when purchased (check the date on the carton), eggs will keep for up to a month. If an egg cracks, use it right away or it will spoil.

Storing Vegetables

The storage requirements for vegetables vary. Sturdy winter squash and some root vegetables, such as dry onions and russet potatoes, do best in cool, dark, dry places. Other vegetables require high humidity to minimize moisture evaporation; wrap them in plastic and refrigerate. For details, see the information beginning on page 219.

Cuts, tears, and bruises encourage vitamin depletion, so don't wash vegetables or cut them up until you're ready to use them. Sort through prepackaged vegetables at home, weeding out any damaged or spoiled ones.

Storing Fruit

Like vegetables, fruits have individual storage requirements (see the section beginning on page 219).

In general, fruits that have not yet ripened need to do so at room temperature (enclose them in a paper bag to accelerate the process). Already ripe fruits and those that don't ripen further after picking, such as berries, should be wrapped in plastic and refrigerated. Sort through prepackaged fruits at home, discarding any that are damaged; like the proverbial apple, a bad one can spoil the whole bunch. Most fruits can be washed and dried before storage; berries and cherries, however, should not be washed until just before using.

■ Pictured on facing page

PASTA WITH PARSLEY-LEMON PESTO

Preparation time: About 10 minutes
Cooking time: 7 to 9 minutes

The sprightly flavors of parsley and lemon stand in for basil in this twist on a classic pesto.

- 1 pound penne, rigatoni, or other dry pasta shape
- 1 large lemon (about 5 oz.)
- 2 cups lightly packed chopped fresh parsley (preferably Italian)
- 2 cloves garlic
- 3 ounces (about ¾ cup) grated Parmesan cheese
- 3 tablespoons extra-virgin olive oil
  Coarsely ground pepper

■
Per serving: 487 calories, 18 g protein, 71 g carbohydrates, 14 g total fat (4 g saturated fat), 12 mg cholesterol, 289 mg sodium

In an 8- to 10-quart pan, cook pasta in 6 quarts boiling water until al dente (7 to 9 minutes or according to package directions).

Meanwhile, use a vegetable peeler to pare zest (colored part of peel) from lemon in large strips (reserve lemon for other uses). In a food processor, whirl lemon zest, parsley, garlic, and Parmesan until finely minced, scraping down sides of bowl as needed. (Or mince lemon zest, parsley, and garlic by hand; stir in cheese.)

Drain pasta and place in a large, warm bowl. Add parsley mixture and oil; toss well. Season to taste with pepper. Makes 4 to 6 servings.

■

VERMICELLI WITH VEGETABLE SAUCE

Preparation time: About 20 minutes
Cooking time: About 50 minutes

Delicate, thin pasta strands team up with a slowly simmered vegetable sauce so rich in flavor that you'll never miss the meat. To peel fresh tomatoes, drop them into boiling water for 10 seconds; then slip off the skins.

- 2 tablespoons olive oil or salad oil
- 1 medium-size onion, finely chopped
- 1 teaspoon *each* fennel seeds and dry basil, dry tarragon, and dry oregano leaves
- 1 clove garlic, minced or pressed
- 1 small zucchini (about 3 oz.), thinly sliced
- ¼ pound mushrooms, thinly sliced
- 1 small green bell pepper (about 4 oz.), stemmed, seeded, and finely chopped
- ½ cup dry red wine
- 1 pound tomatoes, peeled, seeded, and chopped
- 1 can (6 oz.) tomato paste
- 1 teaspoon sugar
- 12 ounces dry vermicelli (not coiled) or spaghettini
  Grated Parmesan cheese

■
Per serving: 466 calories, 15 g protein, 83 g carbohydrates, 9 g total fat (1 g saturated fat), 0 mg cholesterol, 355 mg sodium

Heat oil in a 4- to 5-quart pan over medium-high heat. Add onion, fennel seeds, basil, tarragon, and oregano. Cook, stirring often, until onion is soft (about 5 minutes). Stir in garlic, zucchini, mushrooms, and bell pepper. Cook, stirring often, until mushrooms begin to brown (about 10 minutes). Add wine, tomatoes, tomato paste, and sugar. Increase heat to high and bring to a boil; reduce heat, cover, and simmer until thickened (about 35 minutes), stirring occasionally.

About 10 minutes before sauce is done, cook pasta in 6 quarts boiling water in an 8- to 10-quart pan until al dente (7 to 9 minutes or according to package directions).

Drain pasta and arrange on warm plates; top with sauce. Offer with Parmesan. Makes 4 servings.

A fresh new sauce makes its debut in Pasta with Parsley-Lemon Pesto (recipe on facing page). If desired, top each serving with lemon zest and a pretty parsley leaf. A colorful salad of yellow and red tomatoes and sliced onion is ideal alongside.

WINTER GARDEN PASTA

Per serving: 455 calories, 16 g protein, 82 g carbohydrates, 8 g total fat (1 g saturated fat), 0 mg cholesterol, 171 mg sodium

Preparation time: About 15 minutes
Cooking time: About 25 minutes

Robust winter vegetables add sustenance to this quick pasta entrée. Swiss chard is an excellent source of vitamin A and fiber.

- ¾ **pound Swiss chard, rinsed and drained**
- 2 **tablespoons olive oil**
- 1 **pound mushrooms, sliced**
- 1 **medium-size onion, chopped**
- 3 **cloves garlic, minced or pressed**
- ½ **cup low-sodium chicken broth**
- 1½ **pounds pear-shaped tomatoes, chopped**
  Freshly ground pepper
- 1 **pound penne, rigatoni, or other dry pasta shape**
  Grated Parmesan cheese

Trim off and discard discolored ends of Swiss chard stems. Cut white stalks from leaves. Finely chop leaves and stalks separately. Set leaves aside.

Heat oil in a wide frying pan over medium-high heat. Stir in chard stalks, mushrooms, onion, and garlic; cover and cook until vegetables are soft (about 10 minutes). Uncover and cook, stirring, until liquid has evaporated (about 3 minutes).

Add chicken broth and chard leaves; cover and cook until leaves are wilted (about 2 minutes). Stir in tomatoes and season to taste with pepper. Cover, remove from heat, and set aside.

In an 8- to 10-quart pan, cook pasta in 6 quarts boiling water until al dente (7 to 9 minutes or according to package directions).

Drain pasta and place in a large, warm bowl. Add chard mixture; mix well. Offer with Parmesan. Makes 4 to 6 servings.

SUMMERTIME PASTA ALFRESCO

Per serving: 283 calories, 11 g protein, 56 g carbohydrates, 2 g total fat (0.7 g saturated fat), 2 mg cholesterol, 97 mg sodium

Preparation time: About 25 minutes
Chilling time: At least 2 hours
Cooking time: 7 to 9 minutes

When the weather turns warm, present cool pasta with marinated fresh vegetables. Although it's made without oil, this dish has rich flavor.

- 3 **small tomatoes (about 12 oz. *total*), peeled and chopped**
- 1 **cup *each* thinly sliced green onions (including tops), finely chopped celery, finely chopped green bell pepper, and diced zucchini**
- 2 **cloves garlic, minced or pressed**
- 3 **tablespoons white wine vinegar**
- 1 **tablespoon sugar**
- ⅓ **cup chopped fresh basil leaves**
- 1 **teaspoon chopped fresh rosemary**
- ¾ **teaspoon chopped fresh oregano leaves**
  Coarsely ground pepper
- 8 **ounces rotelle (corkscrews), ruote (wheels), or other dry pasta shape**
- 2 **tablespoons grated Parmesan cheese**

Combine tomatoes, onions, celery, bell pepper, zucchini, garlic, vinegar, sugar, basil, rosemary, and oregano. Season to taste with pepper; mix well. Cover and refrigerate for at least 2 hours or up to 8 hours.

Shortly before serving, cook pasta in 3 quarts boiling water in a 5- to 6-quart pan until al dente (7 to 9 minutes or according to package directions). Drain, rinse with cold water until cool, and drain again.

Transfer pasta to a serving bowl. Add tomato mixture and mix lightly. Sprinkle with Parmesan and mix again. Makes 4 servings.

PASTA WITH BEANS

Per serving: 523 calories, 21 g protein, 98 g carbohydrates, 6 g total fat (0.8 g saturated fat), 0 mg cholesterol, 1,069 mg sodium

Preparation time: About 20 minutes
Cooking time: About 25 minutes

Inspired by the Italian dish *pasta e fagioli*, this upbeat combination of multicolored corkscrew pasta, two kinds of beans, and crunchy vegetables is packed with nutrition and fiber. It's cooked to the consistency of very thick soup, but you can eat it with a fork.

- 1 tablespoon olive oil
- 1 large carrot (about 6 oz.), finely chopped
- 2 celery stalks, finely chopped
- 1 medium-size onion, chopped
- 2 cloves garlic, minced or pressed
- 2 teaspoons dry marjoram leaves or dry oregano leaves
- 1 can (28 oz.) peeled tomatoes
- 1 can (about 15½ oz.) garbanzo beans, drained and rinsed
- 1 can (about 15 oz.) cannellini (white kidney beans), drained and rinsed
- 1 cup water
- 8 ounces multicolored rotelle (corkscrews) or other dry pasta shape
- ¼ cup minced parsley
  Grated Parmesan cheese

Heat oil in a 4- to 5-quart pan over medium-high heat. Add carrot, celery, onion, and garlic. Cook, stirring often, until vegetables are soft (about 10 minutes). Add marjoram, tomatoes (break up with a spoon) and their liquid, garbanzos, cannellini, and water. Bring to a boil; reduce heat and simmer until slightly thickened (about 10 minutes).

About 5 minutes before sauce is done, cook pasta in 3 quarts boiling water in a 5- to 6-quart pan until slightly underdone (about 5 minutes or two-thirds of the cooking time indicated on package). Drain. Return to pan and stir in vegetable mixture. Bring to a boil; reduce heat and simmer, stirring often, until most of the liquid is absorbed and pasta is al dente (about 5 more minutes).

Transfer to a large, warm bowl. Sprinkle with parsley and offer with Parmesan. Makes 4 servings.

ORECCHIETTE WITH SPINACH & GARLIC

Per serving: 434 calories, 14 g protein, 68 g carbohydrates, 12 g total fat (2 g saturated fat), 0 mg cholesterol, 78 mg sodium

Preparation time: About 15 minutes
Cooking time: 10 to 12 minutes

Garlic lovers rejoice! Here's a sauce full of the exuberance of your favorite seasoning. Charming *orecchiette* ("little ears") are a novel pasta shape to add to your repertoire.

- 12 ounces orecchiette, ruote (wheels), or other dry pasta shape
- 3 tablespoons olive oil
- 6 cloves garlic, minced or pressed
- ½ teaspoon crushed red pepper flakes
- ⅓ cup low-sodium chicken broth
- ¾ pound stemmed spinach leaves, rinsed well and coarsely chopped
  Grated Parmesan cheese

In an 8- to 10-quart pan, cook pasta in 6 quarts boiling water until al dente (10 to 12 minutes or according to package directions).

Meanwhile, heat oil in a wide frying pan over medium heat. Add garlic and red pepper flakes. Cook, stirring occasionally, until garlic is slightly golden (about 2 minutes). Stir in chicken broth. Remove from heat and set aside.

Just before pasta is done, add spinach to pasta. Cook, stirring to distribute spinach, just until water returns to a full boil. Drain and place in a large, warm bowl.

Add sauce to pasta; mix well. Offer with Parmesan. Makes 4 servings.

■ Pictured on facing page

VEGETABLE LASAGNE

Per serving: 458 calories, 31 g protein, 53 g carbohydrates, 16 g total fat (6 g saturated fat), 28 mg cholesterol, 505 mg sodium

Preparation time: About 45 minutes
Baking time: About 25 minutes (plus 5 minutes standing time)

If you have a meatless main dish in mind, this tofu-enriched lasagne will fit the bill. Lots of fresh vegetables and cheese make for a very satisfying meal.

- 1 pound firm tofu
- 8 ounces dry lasagne noodles
- 1 pound carrots, thinly sliced
- 1 pound zucchini, thinly sliced
- 1 tablespoon salad oil
- 1 large onion, chopped
- 1 pound mushrooms, thinly sliced
- 1 teaspoon *each* dry basil, dry thyme, and dry oregano leaves
- 2 cans (15 oz. *each*) no-salt-added tomato sauce
- 1 can (6 oz.) tomato paste
- 2 packages (10 oz. *each*) frozen chopped spinach, thawed and squeezed dry
- 1 cup part-skim ricotta cheese
- 2 cups (8 oz.) shredded part-skim mozzarella cheese
- ¼ cup grated Parmesan cheese

Break tofu into coarse chunks; drain. With paper towels, press to remove excess liquid. Set aside.

In a 5- to 6-quart pan, cook pasta in 3 quarts boiling water until al dente (about 10 minutes or according to package directions). Lift out pasta, rinse, and drain well; set aside. Add carrots to pan and cook for 6 minutes. Add zucchini; continue cooking until vegetables are tender-crisp (about 4 more minutes). Drain and set aside.

Heat oil in pan over medium-high heat. Add tofu, onion, mushrooms, basil, thyme, and oregano. Cook, stirring often, until liquid has evaporated (about 7 minutes). Stir in tomato sauce and tomato paste. Remove from heat and set aside.

In a bowl, mix spinach and ricotta; set aside.

Spread a third of the sauce in a 9- by 13-inch baking pan. Top with half the noodles and sprinkle with half each of the carrot mixture, spinach mixture, and mozzarella. Repeat layers. Spread remaining sauce on top and sprinkle with Parmesan.

Set pan on a baking sheet. Bake in a 400° oven until hot in center (about 25 minutes). Let stand for 5 minutes before serving. Makes 8 servings.

SPINACH & TOFU MANICOTTI

Per serving: 293 calories, 14 g protein, 43 g carbohydrates, 9 g total fat (2 g saturated fat), 5 mg cholesterol, 672 mg sodium

Preparation time: About 40 minutes
Baking time: About 50 minutes

A protein alternative to meat, tofu (soybean curd) is rich in calcium. Look for tofu cakes in the refrigerated dairy case of your supermarket.

- 2 tablespoons olive oil
- 1 medium-size onion, chopped
- 3 celery stalks, chopped
- 2 cloves garlic, minced or pressed
- 2 teaspoons dry oregano leaves
- 2 cans (15 oz. *each*) tomato purée
- 1 cup *each* dry red wine and water
- 1 pound soft tofu, drained and rinsed
- 1 package (10 oz.) frozen chopped spinach, thawed and squeezed dry
- 12 dry mánicotti tubes
- ½ cup shredded part-skim mozzarella cheese

Heat oil in a 4- to 5-quart pan over medium-high heat. Add onion, celery, garlic, and oregano. Cook, stirring often, until onion is limp (about 7 minutes). Add tomato purée, wine, and water. Bring to a boil; reduce heat, cover, and simmer for 25 minutes, stirring often.

Meanwhile, mix tofu and spinach in a bowl. Stuff manicotti with mixture.

Spread 1¾ cups of the tomato sauce in a 9- by 13-inch baking pan. Set manicotti in sauce; top with remaining sauce. Cover and bake in a 375° oven until pasta is tender (about 50 minutes). Sprinkle with mozzarella. Makes 6 servings (2 manicotti *each*).

*Hearty and nutritious, Vegetable Lasagne
(recipe on facing page) is bursting with carrots, zucchini,
mushrooms, spinach, tofu, and cheese. Quick-cooked
green beans and crookneck squash, plus a loaf of crusty
bread, complete this meatless menu.*

143

NOODLES WITH CABBAGE & GRUYÈRE

Per serving: 446 calories, 25 g protein, 72 g carbohydrates, 9 g total fat (4 g saturated fat), 32 mg cholesterol, 696 mg sodium

Preparation time: About 10 minutes
Cooking time: About 20 minutes

Toss whole wheat noodles with slow-cooked cabbage, prosciutto, caraway seeds, and nutty Gruyère cheese for a robust winter supper. The flavor will remind you of a Reuben sandwich.

  1 **cup low-sodium chicken broth**
  1 **head green cabbage (about 1½ lbs.), finely shredded**
 12 **ounces dry whole wheat spaghetti**
1½ **teaspoons caraway seeds**
  2 **ounces Gruyère cheese, grated**
  4 **ounces thinly sliced prosciutto, fat trimmed, cut into slivers**

In a 4- to 5-quart pan, combine chicken broth and cabbage. Cover and bring to a boil over high heat; reduce heat and simmer, stirring occasionally, until cabbage is very tender (about 15 minutes). Uncover, increase heat to high, and continue cooking, stirring often, until most of the liquid is absorbed (3 to 5 more minutes).

Meanwhile, cook pasta in 6 quarts boiling water in an 8- to 10-quart pan until al dente (9 to 12 minutes or according to package directions).

Drain pasta and place in a large, warm bowl. Add cabbage mixture, caraway seeds, Gruyère, and prosciutto; mix well. Makes 4 servings.

PERCIATELLI WITH TURKEY MARINARA

Per serving: 497 calories, 25 g protein, 73 g carbohydrates, 13 g total fat (3 g saturated fat), 33 mg cholesterol, 809 mg sodium

Preparation time: About 20 minutes
Cooking time: About 1 hour and 40 minutes

For lean results, take a classic, chunky tomato sauce and prepare it with ground turkey. Serve it over perciatelli or bucatini (long, hollow noodles).

  2 **tablespoons olive oil**
  1 **medium-size onion, finely chopped**
  1 **medium-size green bell pepper (about 6 oz.), stemmed, seeded, and finely chopped**
  1 **large carrot (about 6 oz.), finely shredded**
 ¼ **pound mushrooms, thinly sliced**
  2 **tablespoons chopped parsley**
  1 **clove garlic, minced or pressed**
  2 **teaspoons dry basil leaves**
  1 **teaspoon *each* dry rosemary and dry oregano leaves**
  1 **pound fresh ground turkey**
  2 **cans (28 oz. *each*) peeled tomatoes**
  1 **can (12 oz.) tomato paste**
 ¼ **cup dry red wine**
  1 **bay leaf**
  1 **pound perciatelli, bucatini, or other dry pasta noodles**
     Grated Parmesan cheese

Heat oil in a 4- to 5-quart pan over medium-high heat. Add onion, bell pepper, carrot, mushrooms, parsley, garlic, basil, rosemary, and oregano. Cook, stirring often, until vegetables are tender (about 15 minutes). Lift out and set aside.

Crumble turkey into pan; cook over medium-high heat, stirring constantly, until lightly browned (about 7 minutes). Pour off fat. Return vegetables to pan. Stir in tomatoes (break up with a spoon) and their liquid, tomato paste, wine, and bay leaf. Bring to a boil; reduce heat, cover, and simmer, stirring occasionally, for 30 minutes. Uncover and continue cooking, stirring occasionally, until sauce is thickened (about 45 more minutes).

About 10 minutes before sauce is done, cook pasta in 6 quarts boiling water in an 8- to 10-quart pan until al dente (7 to 9 minutes or according to package directions).

Drain pasta and place in a large, warm bowl. Add sauce and mix lightly. Offer with Parmesan. Makes 6 to 8 servings.

TORTELLINI & PEAS IN CREAMY LEMON SAUCE

Per serving: 333 calories, 18 g protein, 46 g carbohydrates, 9 g total fat (2 g saturated fat), 45 mg cholesterol, 424 mg sodium

Preparation time: About 15 minutes
Cooking time: About 20 minutes

Give up rich pasta sauces? Not necessarily. Although those made with cream should be reserved for special occasions, you can regularly enjoy this lightened-up version made with milk. Fresh lemon adds zing.

   1   large lemon (about 5 oz.)
   1   tablespoon margarine
   ¼   cup minced shallots or onion
   2   tablespoons all-purpose flour
   1½ cups lowfat (2%) milk
   1   cup fresh or frozen peas
   1   package (9 oz.) fresh cheese-filled tortellini
   2   tablespoons grated Parmesan cheese, plus additional cheese to taste

Grate 1 tablespoon zest (colored part of peel) from lemon. Squeeze juice. Combine in a small bowl; set aside.

In a 3- to 4-quart pan, melt margarine over medium heat. Add shallots and cook, stirring, until soft (about 3 minutes). Add flour and cook, stirring, for 1 minute. Add milk, increase heat to medium-high, and cook, stirring often, until sauce is thickened (about 10 minutes). Stir about ½ cup of the sauce into lemon mixture; return mixture to pan and stir well. Remove from heat and set aside.

In a 5- to 6-quart pan, cook peas and pasta in 3 quarts boiling water until peas are tender and pasta is al dente (4 to 5 minutes or according to package directions). Drain; add to pan with lemon sauce. Cook over low heat, stirring, for 2 minutes.

Stir in the 2 tablespoons Parmesan and offer with additional Parmesan. Makes 4 servings.

SEAFOOD LINGUINE

Per serving: 342 calories, 25 g protein, 35 g carbohydrates, 11 g total fat (2 g saturated fat), 147 mg cholesterol, 410 mg sodium

Preparation time: About 25 minutes
Cooking time: About 25 minutes

Bathe seafood in a garlicky white wine sauce to make this pasta classic. If you like, substitute clams for the mussels.

   2   pounds mussels or small hard-shell clams in shells, scrubbed
   1   bottle (8 oz.) clam juice
   4   tablespoons margarine
   ¾   cup sliced green onions (including tops)
   2   large cloves garlic, minced or pressed
   ½   cup dry white wine
   1   pound medium-size shrimp (about 35 *total*), shelled and deveined
   12 ounces fresh linguine
   ½   cup chopped parsley

If using mussels, discard any that don't close when lightly tapped. With a swift tug, pull beard (clump of fibers along side of shell) off each mussel.

Pour clam juice into a 5- to 6-quart pan and bring to a boil over high heat. Add mussels; reduce heat to medium, cover, and cook until shells open (about 8 minutes). Discard any unopened shells. Drain, reserving liquid. Set mussels aside and keep warm. Strain cooking liquid to remove grit; reserve 1 cup of the liquid.

In a wide frying pan, melt 2 tablespoons of the margarine over medium-high heat. Add onions and garlic and cook, stirring often, until onions are soft (about 3 minutes). Stir in wine and reserved cooking liquid. Increase heat to high and bring to a boil; cook until reduced by about half (about 5 minutes). Stir in remaining margarine. Add shrimp, cover, and remove from heat; let stand until shrimp are opaque in center; cut to test (about 8 minutes).

Meanwhile, cook pasta in 6 quarts boiling water in an 8- to 10-quart pan until al dente (3 to 4 minutes or according to package directions). Drain.

Add pasta and parsley to shrimp mixture and mix lightly, lifting pasta with 2 forks. Mound on a warm platter; add mussels. Makes 6 servings.

With two all-time favorites—seafood and pasta—on the menu, rave reviews are sure to follow. Whether served as a first course or a main dish, Cool Pasta Shells with Scallops (recipe on facing page) mean light eating at its best. Garnish, if you wish, with a lemon wedge and a basil sprig.

CHILLED ORIENTAL PASTA WITH SHRIMP

Per serving: 487 calories, 35 g protein, 59 g carbohydrates, 14 g total fat (2 g saturated fat), 168 mg cholesterol, 647 mg sodium

Preparation time: About 30 minutes
Chilling time: At least 1 hour
Cooking time: About 18 minutes

Spoon shrimp over crisp watercress and soy- and ginger-dressed noodles for this stunning entrée.

- 3 tablespoons salad oil
- 3 cloves garlic, minced or pressed
- ⅓ cup thinly sliced green onions (including tops)
- ⅛ teaspoon ground red pepper (cayenne)
- 1½ pounds medium-size shrimp (about 35 per lb.), shelled and deveined
- 3 tablespoons *each* dry sherry and white wine vinegar
- 1 tablespoon Dijon mustard
- 1 tablespoon finely chopped fresh tarragon leaves or 1 teaspoon dry tarragon leaves
  Oriental Dressing (recipe follows)
- 12 ounces dry whole wheat spaghetti
- 2 quarts watercress sprigs, rinsed and crisped

Heat oil in a wide frying pan over medium-high heat. Add garlic, onions, and pepper; cook, stirring often, until onions are soft (about 3 minutes). Add shrimp and cook, stirring, until opaque in center; cut to test (about 5 minutes). Add sherry, vinegar, mustard, and tarragon; bring to a boil, stirring. Transfer mixture to a bowl and let cool; then cover and refrigerate for at least 1 hour or up to 8 hours.

Prepare Oriental Dressing and set aside.

In an 8- to 10-quart pan, cook pasta in 6 quarts boiling water until al dente (about 10 minutes or according to package directions). Drain, rinse with cold water until cool, and drain again. Mix lightly with dressing. (At this point, you may cover and refrigerate for up to 8 hours.)

Arrange watercress on a platter. Spoon pasta over watercress and top with shrimp mixture. Makes 4 to 6 servings.

Oriental Dressing. Mix ⅓ cup **lemon juice**, 3 tablespoons **reduced-sodium soy sauce**, 1 tablespoon *each* **sesame oil** and finely chopped **fresh ginger**, and 2 teaspoons **sugar.**

Pictured on facing page

COOL PASTA SHELLS WITH SCALLOPS

Per serving: 402 calories, 26 g protein, 47 g carbohydrates, 13 g total fat (2 g saturated fat), 30 mg cholesterol, 182 mg sodium

Preparation time: About 20 minutes
Cooking time: About 15 minutes
Chilling time: At least 2 hours

Tender scallops, fresh basil, and broccoli flowerets look especially festive with shell-shaped pasta in this elegant first course or light entrée.

- 8 ounces medium-size dry pasta shells
- 4 cups broccoli flowerets, cut into bite-size pieces
- 1 pound sea scallops, rinsed, drained, and cut in half horizontally
- ¼ cup *each* lemon juice, white wine vinegar, and olive oil
- 1 teaspoon *each* dry mustard and sugar
- 1 clove garlic, minced or pressed
- 1 cup finely chopped fresh basil leaves
  Small inner leaves from 2 large heads romaine lettuce (about 30 *total*), rinsed and crisped

In a 5- to 6-quart pan, cook pasta in 3 quarts boiling water until al dente (7 to 9 minutes or according to package directions). Drain, rinse with cold water until cool, and drain again. Set aside.

In a wide frying pan, cook broccoli, covered, in ¼ inch boiling water until tender-crisp (about 4 minutes). Drain, immerse in ice water until cool, and drain again. Set aside. In same pan, cook scallops, covered, in ¼ inch boiling water until opaque in center; cut to test (about 3 minutes). Drain; set aside.

In a large bowl, mix lemon juice, vinegar, oil, mustard, sugar, garlic, and basil. Add pasta, broccoli, and scallops; mix gently. Cover and refrigerate for at least 2 hours or until next day.

Arrange lettuce on individual plates; top with pasta mixture. Makes 4 to 6 servings.

Grains & Legumes

Fruited Rice Pilaf ■ Saffron Risotto ■ Baked
Lemon Rice ■ Kasha with Fruit ■ Confetti Wild
Rice ■ Spiced Bulgur with Apple ■ Quinoa with
Mushrooms & Broccoli ■ Barley-Onion Pilaf ■
Grits Cake with Corn & Asparagus ■ Cannellini
with Kale ■ Brown Rice & Beans ■ Lebanese
Lentils with Bulgur ■ Black Bean Tacos
■ California Hoppin' John

Although grains and legumes have been food staples for centuries, only recently have we begun to appreciate their nutritional benefits. Natural culinary partners that form the basis of so many delicious dishes, they're also two pieces of an interlocking nutritional puzzle. On their own, most of these members of the plant kingdom contain substantial, but incomplete, proteins (they lack some essential amino acids). Eaten in combination, however, they supply complete protein in an economical, lowfat, cholesterol-free package. Or you can match grains or legumes with eggs or dairy products, or legumes with nuts or seeds, to make the protein complete. In fact, many culinary mainstays—tortillas and beans, red beans and rice, and macaroni and cheese, for example—arose from the need for readily available, nonmeat protein. You'll get other nutritional benefits from eating grains and legumes, too: they're superb sources of dietary fiber, vitamins, and minerals. Best of all, they taste good and blend well with a variety of other foods.

FRUITED RICE PILAF

Per serving: 260 calories, 6 g protein, 47 g carbohydrates, 6 g total fat (1 g saturated fat), 0 mg cholesterol, 37 mg sodium

Preparation time: About 10 minutes
Cooking time: About 35 minutes

This chewy, high-fiber blend of brown rice, dried fruit, and peanuts produces a symphony of flavor. Offer with turkey as part of a holiday meal.

- 2¼ **cups low-sodium chicken broth**
- 1 **cup long-grain brown rice**
- 1 **teaspoon margarine**
- ¼ **cup dry-roasted peanuts**
- ¼ **cup *each* water, raisins, coarsely chopped dried apricots, and chopped pitted dates**

In a 2- to 3-quart pan, bring chicken broth to a boil over high heat. Add rice; reduce heat, cover, and simmer until rice is tender and liquid is absorbed (about 35 minutes).

About 5 minutes before rice is done, melt margarine in a small frying pan over medium heat. Add peanuts and cook, stirring, until golden (about 3 minutes). Remove from pan and set aside. Add water, raisins, apricots, and dates to pan and cook, stirring, until fruit is soft (about 2 minutes). Add fruit mixture and nuts to rice; stir well. Makes 4 to 6 servings.

Pictured on facing page

SAFFRON RISOTTO

Per serving: 296 calories, 8 g protein, 43 g carbohydrates, 10 g total fat (2 g saturated fat), 5 mg cholesterol, 195 mg sodium

Preparation time: About 10 minutes
Cooking time: About 35 minutes (plus 2 minutes standing time)

Can one of the most elegant first courses in Italy possibly be good for you? Yes, if it's this golden-hued rice dish made with less butter and cheese than traditionally used. Look for *arborio*, the stubby rice that distinguishes risotto, in Italian delicatessens or specialty food stores. Or substitute regular (not converted) white rice.

- **About 3½ cups low-sodium chicken broth**
- ⅛ **teaspoon saffron powder or a pinch of saffron threads**
- 1 **tablespoon *each* margarine and olive oil**
- 1 **medium-size onion, finely chopped**
- 1 **cup arborio, short-grain, or long-grain white rice**
- ¼ **cup grated Parmesan cheese**

In a 2-quart pan, bring 3½ cups of the chicken broth to a simmer over medium heat; add saffron. Reduce heat to low.

Heat margarine and oil in a 2- to 3-quart pan over medium heat. Add onion and cook, stirring, until soft (about 5 minutes). Add rice and cook, stirring, until opaque (about 2 more minutes).

Add ½ cup of the broth to rice mixture and cook, stirring, until absorbed. Continue cooking, adding broth ½ cup at a time and stirring constantly after each addition until absorbed, just until rice is tender but not starchy (about 25 minutes); if necessary, add more broth, ¼ cup at a time.

Remove risotto from heat and stir in Parmesan; let stand for 2 minutes. Makes 4 servings.

Golden-hued Saffron Risotto (recipe on facing page) tastes rich and creamy; its carbohydrate content contributes to good nutrition, too. Serve solo as an elegant first course or as a partner to meat or poultry.

151

Grains are the basic foodstuff for much of the world's population. Many cultures, in fact, subsist on diets of these starchy foods, adding meat and vegetables only as garnish. This is virtually the opposite of the way we eat; to us, rice, barley, and other grains are mostly side-dish accompaniments.

Yet a diet based on grains is healthy and sensible. Rich in fiber and complex carbohydrates, these edible seeds of various grasses provide lots of B vitamins, a host of minerals, and only a trace of fat. Most importantly, they're a good source of non-animal protein; when combined with legumes or with small amounts of meat or dairy products, they contain all the essential amino acids. Furthermore, grains are economical, easy to store, and capable of endless flavor combinations.

A Look at Grains

With all the positive attributes of grains, it's worthwhile to explore the different ones available today. Both familiar and less common types, as well as two "rediscovered" grains from ancient cultures, amaranth and quinoa, are profiled here. Look for these grains in large supermarkets and health food stores.

For optimum nutrition, buy grains in their whole, unrefined form; refining totally or partially removes both the outer bran, which contains most of the fiber, and the nutrient-rich germ. However, each grain has its own nutritional makeup. To reap the maximum benefits, consume a variety of grains instead of just one or two types.

Enjoying Grains

Cook the whole and cracked grains listed here in the same way that you cook rice. Stir into boiling liquid; then reduce the heat, cover, and simmer until all the liquid is absorbed (for quantities and approximate cooking times, see the chart on the facing page). Use grain flours in baking.

Serve grains hot as a breakfast porridge, with milk and fruit. Or prepare them as pilafs, toasting the grain first in a dry skillet (or with a small amount of oil, if you like) to enhance the nutty taste. Cooking the grain in broth instead of water and adding onions, garlic, and herbs boost the flavor, too. All grains can be incorporated into casseroles, soups, stews, stir-fries, salads, stuffings, and breads. The more often you put them on the table, the better.

Amaranth. Although it's often referred to as a new grain, amaranth has been a staple in New World diets for centuries. It features an uncommonly high protein content that includes essential amino acids rarely found in the vegetable kingdom. It's also high in calcium.

Amaranth flour can be combined with wheat and used in baked goods. Whole grain amaranth can be simmered and served as a side dish. Or pop the grains in a dry skillet, stirring constantly, for a unique snack. Rinse before cooking.

Barley. One of the oldest cultivated grains, barley is found today mostly in "pearled" form (milled to remove the hull). Although some nutritive value is lost in the process, pearl barley still provides protein and significant amounts of thiamine, niacin, and potassium, as well as soluble fiber. The taste is mild and nutty, the texture plump and chewy. Both regular and quick-cooking varieties are available.

Buckwheat. The most common form of buckwheat (a plant that's not technically a grain) is roasted groats, or kasha. Distinctively nutty in flavor, kasha contains ample fiber and protein along with iron, phosphorus, and potassium. Ground buckwheat flour can be used together with regular flour in baking or alone in pancakes.

Bulgur (cracked wheat). This whole grain product is made from wheat berries that have been steamed, dried, and cracked. Easy to prepare and widely available, bulgur is an excellent source of insoluble fiber, the kind that adds bulk to your diet. It also provides all the nutritional benefits of whole wheat, including high-quality protein and numerous vitamins and minerals.

Millet. Although millet is a common ingredient in birdseed, people in Africa and India have eaten it in its hulled form for ages. Able to grow under adverse climatic conditions, it supplies a more complete protein than most other common grains; it also provides B vitamins, iron, and other minerals. The tiny, yellow grains cook up fluffy and chewy.

Oats. Although oat bran has garnered more attention lately than almost any other grain, all forms of oats are very nutritious, simply because they aren't refined. Whole oats that have been dried, toasted, and hulled are called groats. Groats can be cut up to make steel-cut oats (also called Scottish or Irish oatmeal); or they can be steamed and flattened to make rolled oats (regular, quick-cooking, or instant), commonly used in oatmeal and in baking.

Oats contain lots of soluble fiber, which may have a cholesterol-reducing effect when eaten in conjunction with a lowfat diet.

Quinoa. Quinoa (pronounced KEEN-wah), the so-called super grain, is notable for its high protein content—16% to 17% compared with 12% to 14% for hard wheat. Like amaranth (see facing page), it contains more essential amino acids than other grains. Before cooking, quinoa must be rinsed to remove its slightly bitter coating.

Rice. The grain that supports approximately half the world's population, rice is available in numerous varieties. Brown rice contains more nutrients and fiber than polished white rice.

Rice bran, which is milled off the grain to make white rice, is available in some health food stores. Although its culinary use is limited, it may be appearing in commercial products in the future if, as some studies show, it really does help to reduce blood cholesterol levels.

Rye and triticale. Although rye flour is a familiar ingredient in bread, rye berries are not well known. Chewy and tangy when cooked, they're high in protein, phosphorus, iron, potassium, and B vitamins. Use them as you would wheat berries.

Triticale, a manmade hybrid of wheat and rye, contains more protein than either parent. Triticale berries have a slightly resilient texture when cooked. Although triticale enjoyed a flurry of attention some years ago, low crop yields have limited its distribution.

Wheat berries. These whole grain berries yield the full nutrients of wheat because the germ, bran, and endosperm are all present. They're also an excellent source of insoluble fiber. When cooked, they have a chewy texture and a pronounced, nutty flavor.

■ Grains Cooking Chart

Amounts of liquid (water or broth) and cooking times may vary, depending on brand and age of grain; check package directions. Rinse amaranth and quinoa before cooking; rinse other grains if desired.

Grain	Quantity	Simmering Time
Amaranth	1 part grain to 3 parts liquid	About 25 minutes
Barley, pearl (regular)	1 part grain to 2 parts liquid	About 35 minutes
Buckwheat groats (kasha)	1 part grain to 2 parts liquid	About 20 minutes
Bulgur	1 part grain to 2 parts liquid	About 15 minutes; or let stand, covered, in boiling water for 1 hour
Millet	1 part grain to 2–2½ parts liquid	About 30 minutes
Oat groats	1 part grain to 2¼ parts liquid	About 40 minutes
Oats, steel-cut	1 part grain to 2 parts liquid	About 20 minutes
Quinoa	1 part grain to 2 parts liquid	15 minutes
Rice, brown	1 part grain to 2¼ parts liquid	About 35 minutes
Rye berries	1 part grain to 3 parts liquid	1½ hours
Triticale berries	1 part grain to 3 parts liquid	1 hour
Wheat berries	1 part grain to 2–2½ parts liquid	1½ hours

Expand your grains repertoire with buckwheat groats,
also known as kasha. Dressed with honey and fresh
orange juice and studded with raisins, dried apricots,
and apple, Kasha with Fruit (recipe on facing page)
provides plentiful nutrition and a nutty taste.

154

BAKED LEMON RICE

Per serving: 213 calories, 5 g protein, 39 g carbohydrates, 4 g total fat (0.7 g saturated fat), 0 mg cholesterol, 64 mg sodium

Preparation time: About 5 minutes
Baking time: About 50 minutes

Whenever you need an easy side dish that goes with almost everything, look to this citrus-scented pilaf. Because it's baked, the rice cooks perfectly every time.

- 2 **cups low-sodium chicken broth**
- 1 **cup long-grain white rice**
- 2 **teaspoons grated lemon peel**
- 2 **tablespoons lemon juice**
- ¼ **cup chopped green onions (including tops)**
- 1 **tablespoon margarine, melted**
  Lemon slices and slivered green onion tops (optional)

In a deep 1½- to 2-quart baking dish, mix chicken broth, rice, lemon peel, lemon juice, chopped onions, and margarine. Cover and bake in a 350° oven until rice is tender (about 50 minutes).

Spoon onto individual plates. Garnish with lemon slices and slivered onions, if desired. Makes 4 servings.

Pictured on facing page

KASHA WITH FRUIT

Per serving: 318 calories, 6 g protein, 50 g carbohydrates, 13 g total fat (2 g saturated fat), 0 mg cholesterol, 18 mg sodium

Preparation time: About 15 minutes
Cooking time: About 17 minutes (plus 30 minutes standing time)

Kasha, or buckwheat groats, was once a mainstay in American diets. Although not technically a grain (groats are actually the edible fruit of the plant), kasha is worth rediscovering for its distinctive flavor and high nutritive value.

- ¼ **cup sliced almonds**
- 1 **tablespoon salad oil**
- 1 **cup roasted kasha**
- 1½ **cups low-sodium chicken broth**
  Orange Dressing (recipe follows)
- 1 **medium-size red apple (about 6 oz.)**
- ¾ **cup chopped dried apricots**
- ½ **cup golden raisins**
- 6 **butterhead lettuce leaves, rinsed and crisped**
  Orange slices (optional)

In a small frying pan, toast almonds over medium heat, shaking pan often, until golden (about 4 minutes). Remove from pan and set aside.

Heat oil in a 2- to 3-quart pan over medium heat. Add kasha and cook, stirring, for 3 minutes. Add chicken broth. Reduce heat, cover, and simmer just until kasha is softened and liquid is absorbed (about 10 minutes); do not stir. Uncover and let stand until cool (about 30 minutes); do not stir.

Meanwhile, prepare Orange Dressing.

Dice apple. In a large bowl, gently mix kasha, apple, apricots, almonds, raisins, and dressing. Line a platter or individual plates with lettuce leaves and top with kasha mixture. Garnish with orange, if desired. Makes 6 servings.

Orange Dressing. Mix 1 teaspoon **grated orange peel,** ¾ cup **orange juice,** 3 tablespoons **salad oil,** 1 tablespoon **cider vinegar,** and 1 teaspoon **honey.**

■ *Pictured on page 214*

CONFETTI WILD RICE

Per serving: 205 calories, 8 g protein, 38 g carbohydrates, 3 g total fat (0.4 g saturated fat), 0 mg cholesterol, 28 mg sodium

Preparation time: About 10 minutes
Cooking time: About 50 minutes

Wild rice, actually the seed of a native grass and not a rice, is a popular side dish worth bringing to the table often. Because farmers are growing wild rice more extensively than in the past, this once scarce commodity is now widely available.

- 1 **cup wild rice, rinsed and drained**
- 1 **tablespoon mustard seeds**
- 2 **teaspoons margarine**
- ½ **cup freshly squeezed orange juice**
- 1 **large red bell pepper (about ½ lb.), stemmed, seeded, and finely diced**
- ¾ **cup thinly sliced green onions (including tops)**
- ½ **cup chopped fresh mint leaves**
  Salt and pepper

In a 3- to 4-quart pan, bring 6 cups water to a boil over high heat. Stir in rice and mustard seeds; reduce heat, cover, and simmer until rice is tender (about 50 minutes). Drain well and return to pan.

Reduce heat to low, add margarine, and mix well. Stir in orange juice, bell pepper, onions, and mint. Season to taste with salt and pepper. Makes 4 servings.

SPICED BULGUR WITH APPLE

Per serving: 201 calories, 5 g protein, 34 g carbohydrates, 6 g total fat (0.9 g saturated fat), 0 mg cholesterol, 22 mg sodium

Preparation time: About 10 minutes
Cooking time: About 25 minutes

Bulgur, or cracked wheat, is a versatile, high-fiber addition to your repertoire of side dishes. Its wholesome flavor combines well with a myriad of ingredients, such as the spicy, fruity additions used here.

- 2 **tablespoons salad oil**
- 1 **medium-size onion, chopped**
- 1 **clove garlic, minced or pressed**
- 2 **teaspoons minced fresh ginger**
- 1 **cup bulgur**
- ¼ **teaspoon ground cinnamon**
- 1½ **cups low-sodium chicken broth**
- 1 **medium-size red apple (about 6 oz.)**
- ¼ **cup golden raisins**

Heat oil in a 3- to 4-quart pan over medium heat. Add onion, garlic, and ginger. Cook, stirring, until onion is soft (about 5 minutes). Add bulgur and cook, stirring, until toasted (about 3 minutes). Stir in cinnamon and chicken broth and bring to a boil; reduce heat, cover, and simmer until bulgur is tender and liquid is absorbed (about 15 minutes).

Meanwhile, finely dice apple. Stir apple and raisins into bulgur mixture; cover and continue cooking for 2 more minutes. Makes 4 to 6 servings.

QUINOA WITH MUSHROOMS & BROCCOLI

Preparation time: About 15 minutes
Cooking time: About 30 minutes

An ancient grain from South America, quinoa (pronounced KEEN-wah) is a culinary hit on today's dining tables. One of the most complete protein sources of any grain, it has an unusually delicious nutty flavor.

- 2 tablespoons margarine
- 1 pound mushrooms, sliced
- 1 small onion, chopped
- 1½ cups low-sodium beef or chicken broth
- 1 cup quinoa, rinsed and drained
- ¾ pound broccoli flowerets, cut into bite-size pieces
- 2 tablespoons grated Parmesan cheese (optional)

In a wide frying pan, melt margarine over medium heat. Add mushrooms and onion and cook, stirring occasionally, until liquid has evaporated and vegetables are soft (about 15 minutes). Add broth and bring to a boil. Stir in quinoa and broccoli; reduce

Per serving: 218 calories, 9 g protein, 33 g carbohydrates, 7 g total fat (1 g saturated fat), 0 mg cholesterol, 95 mg sodium

heat, cover, and simmer until quinoa is tender (about 15 minutes).

Transfer to a serving bowl and sprinkle with Parmesan, if desired. Makes 4 to 6 servings.

BARLEY-ONION PILAF

Per serving: 194 calories, 5 g protein, 33 g carbohydrates, 5 g total fat (0.9 g saturated fat), 0 mg cholesterol, 60 mg sodium

Preparation time: About 5 minutes
Cooking time: About 55 minutes

Instead of rice, feature plump, chewy barley in an onion-flavored pilaf. Simple to prepare, this dish complements almost any meal.

- 1 tablespoon margarine
- 1 teaspoon salad oil
- 1 large onion, halved lengthwise and thinly sliced
- ¾ cup pearl barley
- 1⅔ cups low-sodium chicken broth
  Chopped parsley (optional)
  Freshly ground pepper

Heat margarine and oil in a 3- to 4-quart pan over medium-high heat. Add onion and cook, stirring often, until limp and golden (about 15 minutes). Add barley and cook, stirring, until lightly toasted (about 3 minutes). Add chicken broth and bring to a boil over high heat; reduce heat, cover, and simmer until barley is tender and liquid is absorbed (about 35 minutes).

Stir in parsley, if desired, and season to taste with pepper. Makes 4 servings.

■ *Pictured on page 202*

GRITS CAKE WITH CORN & ASPARAGUS

Preparation time: About 20 minutes
Baking time: About 30 minutes

A staple in the American South, grits are ground from starchy field corn, a grain full of important nutrients. Baked into a golden casserole with its more familiar cousin, sweet corn, and fresh asparagus, grits are equally good for dinner or breakfast.

  1 **pound asparagus, tough ends snapped off**
  2 **cups low-sodium chicken broth**
1½ **cups water**
  1 **cup quick-cooking yellow or white hominy grits**
  1 **cup fresh or frozen corn kernels**
  ½ **cup lowfat (2%) milk**
  3 **ounces (about ¾ cup) grated extra-sharp Cheddar cheese**
     Nonstick cooking spray or salad oil

■ *Per serving: 200 calories, 9 g protein, 28 g carbohydrates, 6 g total fat (3 g saturated fat), 17 mg cholesterol, 121 mg sodium*

Cut tips off asparagus spears; then cut spears diagonally into ½-inch pieces. Set aside separately.

In a 4- to 5-quart pan, bring chicken broth and water to a boil over high heat. Add asparagus tips; reduce heat and simmer just until tender when pierced (about 4 minutes). With a slotted spoon, lift out and immerse in ice water until cool; drain and set aside.

Slowly stir grits into broth. Add corn and asparagus pieces, increase heat to high, and cook, stirring, until thickened (about 3 minutes). Remove from heat and stir in milk and Cheddar. Lightly coat a shallow 2-quart casserole with cooking spray and pour in grits mixture. (At this point, you may cool, cover, and refrigerate casserole and asparagus tips separately until next day; bring to room temperature before continuing.)

Bake in a 350° oven until firm (about 30 minutes). Halve asparagus tips lengthwise and arrange over grits cake. Makes 6 servings.

■ *Pictured on facing page*

CANNELLINI WITH KALE

Preparation time: About 10 minutes
Cooking time: About 20 minutes

Mild, creamy cannellini (white kidney beans) are the perfect foil for robust kale. Often overlooked, kale is extremely high in carotenoids, vegetable compounds believed to be beneficial in preventing certain cancers.

  4 **slices bacon, chopped**
  2 **large onions, cut into thin rings**
1½ **pounds kale, tough ends discarded, coarsely chopped**
     Freshly ground pepper
  2 **cans (about 15 oz. *each*) cannellini (white kidney beans), drained and rinsed**

■ *Per serving: 207 calories, 12 g protein, 32 g carbohydrates, 5 g total fat (1 g saturated fat), 5 mg cholesterol, 601 mg sodium*

In a wide frying pan, cook bacon over medium-high heat, stirring, until crisp (about 7 minutes). Lift out and drain on paper towels; set aside. Discard all but 1 tablespoon of the drippings from pan.

Add onions to pan and cook, stirring, until soft (about 5 minutes). Add kale and cook, stirring, until wilted (about 4 minutes). Season to taste with pepper. Arrange around edge of a serving dish and keep warm.

Add beans to pan, reduce heat to medium, and cook, stirring, until hot (about 4 minutes). Arrange beans in center of dish and sprinkle with bacon. Makes 6 servings.

Cannellini with Kale (recipe on facing page)
teams up with crispy Oven-fried Chicken (recipe on page
98) for a Southern-style meal. It's a protein-packed
menu that's easy on the cook.

159

Feature BASIC LEGUME COOKERY

Legumes—dried beans and peas—play an important role in a light and healthy diet. An excellent source of protein, legumes contain no cholesterol and only a trace of fat. They have a conveniently long shelf life, they're economical, and their varied flavors allow for endless culinary combinations.

Despite their simplicity, legumes require proper preparation to ensure good texture and digestibility. Rinse them in a colander, sorting through and discarding any foreign material or imperfect legumes; drain. Then soak, if necessary, and cook as directed below. (Add salt, if you wish, *after* cooking; otherwise, the legumes may become tough.)

Substitute home-cooked beans in any recipe calling for canned beans. Use 2 cups cooked beans (about 1 cup dried) for each 15- to 16-ounce can.

Soaking Legumes

All legumes except lentils, split peas, and black-eyed peas should be soaked. Use the first method if you're in a hurry; otherwise, soak overnight.

Quick soaking. For each pound dried legumes, bring 8 cups water to a boil in a 4- to 5-quart pan over high heat. Add rinsed legumes and boil for 2 minutes. Remove from heat, cover, and let stand for 1 hour. Drain, discarding water, and rinse.

Overnight soaking. For each pound dried legumes, place 8 cups water in a large bowl. Add rinsed legumes; let soak at room temperature until next day. Drain, discarding water, and rinse.

Cooking Legumes

Cooking times differ, depending on the type of legume and the length of time it has been stored. The older the legume, the longer the cooking time—a good reason not to combine newly purchased legumes with those already on your shelf.

For each pound dried legumes (unsoaked weight), place 8 cups cold water in a 3- to 4-quart pan. Add legumes. Cover and bring to a boil over high heat; reduce heat and simmer until tender (see at right for cooking times, or cook according to package directions); add water, if necessary, to keep legumes moist. After minimum recommended time, start tasting; legumes should be tender, but not mushy. Season to taste with salt.

Black beans (turtle beans). Popular in Caribbean and Latin American cuisines, black beans have a rich, mellow flavor. Soak first. Cook for 1½ to 2 hours.

Black-eyed peas. Beige ovals with distinctive black spots, black-eyed peas are a traditional favorite in the American South. They have an earthy flavor. Do not soak. Cook for about 50 minutes.

Garbanzo beans (chick-peas, ceci beans). These beans, with their distinctive, nutty flavor and toothsome texture, are a natural for soups and salads. Soak first. Cook for 2 to 2½ hours.

Great Northern beans. These medium-size white beans, similar in shape to kidney beans, have a mild flavor. You can substitute them for canned cannellini. Soak first. Cook for 1 to 1½ hours.

Kidney beans. Kidney beans have firm texture and meaty flavor; they're widely available canned. Dried red are more common than dried white (if you can't find the white ones, substitute Great Northerns). Soak first. Cook for 1 to 1½ hours.

Lentils. The mild, earthy flavor of lentils blends well with many foods. Lentils are disc shaped and come in brown, green, and pink varieties. Decorticated (skinless) lentils can get mushy if overcooked. Do not soak. Cook for about 40 minutes.

Lima beans. Limas cook up softer than other legumes. Serve as a side dish or in casseroles and soups. Soak first. Cook for about 1 hour.

Pinto, pink, red, cranberry, and other speckled beans. These varieties may be mottled or solid in color. All work well in casseroles and soups. Soak first. Cook for about 1½ hours.

Soybeans. Exceptionally high in protein, soybeans are used to make soybean curd (tofu). Soak in your refrigerator overnight. Cook for 3 to 3½ hours.

Split peas. These green or yellow halved peas have a distinctive flavor and a soft texture; use them in soups and side dishes. Do not soak. Cook for 35 to 45 minutes.

White navy beans. Distinguished by their small size and creamy color, navy beans are the classic for baked beans. Soak first. Cook for about 1 hour.

BROWN RICE & BEANS

Per serving: 227 calories, 11 g protein, 42 g carbohydrates, 3 g total fat (0.5 g saturated fat), 0.6 mg cholesterol, 269 mg sodium

Preparation time: About 15 minutes
Cooking time: About 1¼ hours

Rice and beans go together like hand and glove. Not only do they form a complete protein, but they also taste great together. Toasting the rice before cooking brings out its nutty flavor.

- 1 cup long-grain brown rice
- 1 teaspoon salad oil
- 3 cups low-sodium chicken broth
- 2 medium-size onions, diced
- 1 pound mushrooms, thinly sliced
- 2 cloves garlic, minced or pressed
- 1 tablespoon *each* dry basil, dry oregano, and dry marjoram leaves
- 2 bay leaves
- 1 can (about 15 oz.) cannellini (white kidney beans) or red kidney beans, drained and rinsed
- ⅓ cup chopped green onions (including tops)
- 2 large tomatoes (about 1 lb. *total*), diced
- 1 cup plain nonfat yogurt
- 12 corn tortillas (6-inch diameter), warmed (optional)

Place rice in a 9- to 10-inch square baking pan and bake in a 350° oven until golden brown (about 40 minutes), shaking pan occasionally.

Meanwhile, combine oil, ½ cup of the chicken broth, diced onions, mushrooms, garlic, basil, oregano, marjoram, and bay leaves in a 4- to 6-quart pan. Cover and cook over medium heat until vegetables are soft (about 15 minutes). Uncover and continue cooking, stirring often, until liquid has evaporated (about 5 more minutes).

Add rice and remaining broth to pan. Bring to a boil over high heat; reduce heat, cover, and simmer until rice is tender (about 35 minutes). Stir in beans and green onions.

Offer with tomatoes and yogurt. Spoon into tortillas, if desired. Makes 6 to 8 servings.

LEBANESE LENTILS WITH BULGUR

Per serving: 318 calories, 15 g protein, 47 g carbohydrates, 10 g total fat (2 g saturated fat), 53 mg cholesterol, 310 mg sodium

Preparation time: About 15 minutes
Cooking time: About 1¼ hours

Feature this Middle Eastern dish as an entrée on meatless menu nights. For a nutritionally balanced meal, all you need alongside is a cooked vegetable.

- ½ cup lentils
- 1 tablespoon salad oil
- 1 medium-size onion, finely chopped
- 1 large green bell pepper (about ½ lb.), stemmed, seeded, and chopped
- ½ teaspoon *each* ground allspice and ground cumin
- 2 cloves garlic, minced or pressed
- 1 cup bulgur
- ½ teaspoon salt
- 1 teaspoon grated lemon peel
- 2 tablespoons sesame tahini
- 2 cups boiling water
- 2 tablespoons lemon juice
- 1 hard-cooked egg, sieved
  Minced parsley

Rinse lentils and sort through, discarding any debris; drain. Place in a 3- to 4-quart pan with 2½ cups water. Bring to a boil over high heat; reduce heat, cover, and simmer until tender (about 40 minutes). Drain, rinse, and set aside. (At this point, you may cool, cover, and refrigerate until next day.)

Heat oil in pan over medium-high heat. Add onion, bell pepper, allspice, and cumin and cook, stirring, until vegetables are limp (about 10 minutes). Add garlic, bulgur, and salt; continue cooking, stirring, until bulgur is toasted (about 5 more minutes).

In a bowl, mix lemon peel, tahini, and boiling water; stir into bulgur mixture. Reduce heat, cover, and simmer until bulgur is tender and liquid is absorbed (about 15 minutes). Stir in lentils and lemon juice and cook until hot (about 5 minutes).

Spoon onto a warm platter. Sprinkle with egg and parsley. Makes 4 servings.

■ *Pictured on facing page*

BLACK BEAN TACOS

Per serving: 484 calories, 19 g protein, 80 g carbohydrates, 10 g total fat (2 g saturated fat), 6 mg cholesterol, 858 mg sodium

Preparation time: About 15 minutes
Soaking time: 1 hour
Cooking time: About 2½ hours

Elevate the humble black bean to new heights in these zesty whole-meal tacos.

Cooked Black Beans (recipe follows)
12 flour tortillas (7- to 9-inch diameter)
1 head romaine lettuce (about 1 lb.), shredded
1 large tomato (about ½ lb.), chopped
1 large red bell pepper (about ½ lb.), stemmed, seeded, and cut into strips
6 green onions (including tops), thinly sliced
¼ cup red wine vinegar
1 large clove garlic, minced or pressed
1 teaspoon chili powder
½ teaspoon *each* ground cumin and salt
¼ teaspoon pepper
2 tablespoons salad oil
¼ cup shredded extra-sharp Cheddar cheese
1 cup plain nonfat yogurt
Sliced black olives (optional)

Prepare Cooked Black Beans; keep warm.

Stack tortillas, wrap in foil, and place in a 350° oven until hot (about 15 minutes).

Meanwhile, place lettuce, tomato, bell pepper, and onions in a large bowl. In a small bowl, stir together vinegar, garlic, chili powder, cumin, salt, and pepper; add oil and whisk until blended. Pour over vegetables and toss well.

Spoon about ¼ cup of the bean mixture into each tortilla; add about ½ cup of the lettuce mixture, 1 teaspoon of the Cheddar, and 1⅓ tablespoons of the yogurt. Sprinkle with olives, if desired. Fold tortilla over filling. Makes 6 servings (2 tacos *each*).

Cooked Black Beans. Rinse 1 cup **dried black beans** and sort through, discarding any debris; drain. In a 3- to 4-quart pan, bring 4 cups **water** to a boil over high heat. Add beans; cook for 2 minutes. Remove from heat, cover, and let stand for 1 hour. Drain and rinse.

Heat 1 tablespoon **salad oil** in pan over medium heat. Add 1 large **onion,** chopped, and cook, stirring occasionally, until limp (about 10 minutes). Add beans; 1 clove **garlic,** minced or pressed; 1 **small dried hot red chile,** crushed; ½ teaspoon **salt;** and 2½ cups **water.** Bring to a boil over high heat; reduce heat, cover, and simmer until beans are tender and liquid is absorbed (about 2 hours).

CALIFORNIA HOPPIN' JOHN

Per serving: 292 calories, 13 g protein, 45 g carbohydrates, 8 g total fat (1 g saturated fat), 0 mg cholesterol, 293 mg sodium

Preparation time: About 15 minutes
Cooking time: About 1 hour and 35 minutes

The Western version of this Southern classic livens things up with cumin and chiles.

1 cup dried black-eyed peas
2 tablespoons salad oil
1 medium-size onion, chopped
2 cloves garlic, minced or pressed
1 teaspoon ground cumin
1 can (7 oz.) diced green chiles
2 jalapeño or other small hot chiles, stemmed, seeded, and halved
½ cup long-grain brown rice
3 cups low-sodium chicken broth
3 large tomatoes (about 1½ lbs. *total*), peeled and chopped

In a 4- to 5-quart pan, bring 2 quarts water to a boil over high heat. Add peas; reduce heat, cover, and simmer until tender (about 50 minutes). Drain, rinse, and set aside. (At this point, you may cool, cover, and refrigerate until next day.)

Heat oil in pan over medium-high heat. Add onion and garlic and cook, stirring, until onion is limp (about 10 minutes). Add cumin and cook, stirring, for 1 more minute. Add peas, diced chiles, jalapeños, rice, and chicken broth. Bring to a boil; reduce heat, cover, and simmer for 25 minutes.

Add tomatoes, cover, and continue cooking until rice is tender (about 10 more minutes). Discard jalapeños. Makes 4 to 6 servings.

Who can resist spicy Black Bean Tacos (recipe on facing page) with all the trimmings? Perfect for eating out of hand, they're a wonderful way to get high-protein legumes on the menu. Accompany with a cool drink and fresh fruit.

163

Vegetables

Oven Ratatouille ■ Vegetable Curry Stir-fry ■

Burgundy-braised Cabbage with Chestnuts ■

Green Bean & Tomato Casserole ■ Gingered

Asparagus ■ Lemon-Garlic Swiss Chard ■

Sweet & Bitter Mustard Greens ■ Mashed

Potatoes & Broccoli ■ Roasted Red & Yellow

Potatoes ■ Potato & Carrot Oven-fries

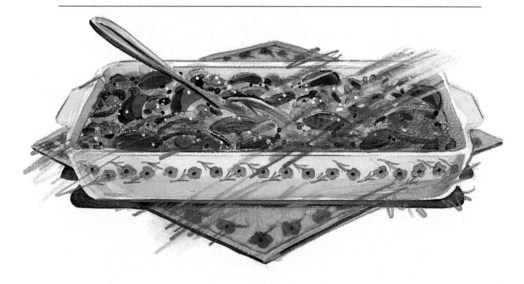

Mom was right—vegetables are good for you. But for years, few people realized just how delicious vegetables could be when properly prepared. Today's cooks are discovering that steaming or quickly stir-frying vegetables just until tender-crisp preserves not only their crunchy, natural texture but also the valuable vitamins and minerals lost by overcooking. All that's needed to enhance the flavor of such vegetables is a light sprinkling of fresh herbs, spices, lemon juice, or, for added enrichment, a bold oil, such as extra-virgin olive or sesame. So it's no surprise that exquisitely fresh vegetables, many available year-round, are taking center stage in a light and healthy diet. Even humble cruciferous vegetables, such as broccoli, cauliflower, Brussels sprouts, cabbage, mustard greens, turnips, and kale, have moved to the forefront of nutritional interest because of recent studies linking them to the prevention of certain cancers. No matter how you present them, you just can't lose by putting fresh vegetables on the table as often as possible.

Pictured on facing page

OVEN RATATOUILLE

Per serving: 100 calories, 4 g protein, 18 g carbohydrates, 3 g total fat (0.4 g saturated fat), 0 mg cholesterol, 17 mg sodium

Preparation time: About 15 minutes
Baking time: About 1 hour and 20 minutes

When you blend certain vegetables and herbs, you achieve the harmony of tastes unique to ratatouille. When you bake it, you can use just a whisper of oil and achieve its distinct texture. Serve warm or at room temperature.

- 1 **medium-size eggplant (about 1 lb.), cut into ½- by 2-inch sticks**
- 1 **pound zucchini, sliced ½ inch thick**
- 1½ **pounds firm-ripe pear-shaped tomatoes, quartered**
- 1 *each* **large red and yellow bell pepper (about 1 lb. *total*), stemmed, seeded, and thinly sliced**
- 1 **large onion, chopped**
- 1 **cup finely chopped fresh basil leaves or 3 tablespoons dry basil leaves**
- 1 **tablespoon olive oil**
  Freshly ground pepper
  Basil sprigs (optional)

In a 3- to 4-quart baking dish, mix eggplant, zucchini, tomatoes, bell peppers, onion, chopped basil, and oil. Cover and bake in a 400° oven for 1 hour. Uncover and continue baking, stirring once or twice, until eggplant is very soft and only a thin layer of liquid remains in bottom of dish (about 20 more minutes). Season to taste with pepper. If made ahead, cool, cover, and refrigerate for up to 1 week; bring to room temperature before serving.

Garnish with basil sprigs, if desired. Makes 6 servings.

VEGETABLE CURRY STIR-FRY

Per serving: 280 calories, 9 g protein, 48 g carbohydrates, 7 g total fat (0.8 g saturated fat), 0 mg cholesterol, 300 mg sodium

Preparation time: About 15 minutes
Cooking time: About 27 minutes

Quickly stir-frying vegetables in a wok or frying pan preserves nutrients and requires very little oil. A subtle tomato-curry sauce enlivens this potpourri of produce.

- ¾ **pound red thin-skinned potatoes, cut into chunks**
- 2 **tablespoons salad oil**
- 1 **large onion, chopped**
- 1 **medium-size head cauliflower (about 1 lb.), cut into flowerets**
- ½ **pound green beans, cut into 2-inch pieces**
- 2 **medium-size carrots (about 6 oz. *total*), sliced**
- 2 **tablespoons curry powder**
- ½ **cup water**
- 1 **can (8 oz.) no-salt-added tomato sauce**
- 1 **can (about 15½ oz.) garbanzo beans, drained and rinsed**
  Chopped cilantro (coriander), optional

Place potatoes on a rack in a pan above 1 inch boiling water. Cover and steam over high heat until slightly tender when pierced (about 10 minutes). Lift out and set aside.

Heat oil in a wok or wide frying pan over high heat. Add onion and cook, stirring, for 2 minutes. Add cauliflower, green beans, and carrots and cook, stirring, for 5 minutes. Add curry powder and water, stirring until vegetables are well coated. Stir in tomato sauce, garbanzo beans, and potatoes. Reduce heat, cover, and simmer until vegetables are tender (about 10 minutes).

Transfer to a serving dish and sprinkle with cilantro, if desired. Makes 4 to 6 servings.

Savor the robust flavors of Provence with
Oven Ratatouille (recipe on facing page). This colorful
medley of eggplant, zucchini, tomatoes, onion, and
bell peppers slow-cooks in the oven, allowing you to use
far less oil than usual.

Man discovered salt ages ago, and it wasn't long before it became almost indispensable to the palate. Today, we know that some sodium (the chief component in salt) is essential to balanced nutrition, but most of us consume much more than we need, primarily because of the large amounts present in processed foods. (For recommendations on daily sodium intake, see page 11.)

One of the easiest places to cut back on salt is at the table. By reaching less for the salt shaker and more for other natural food enhancers, you'll unleash a whole new spectrum of tastes. Carefully blended herb and spice combinations, such as the ones offered on these pages, distinctively flavor meats, seafood, sauces, and soups. Home-brewed vinegar infusions (see facing page) add a crisp acidity to salads and other dishes, compensating for less salt.

Other nonsalt accents you may want to try include fresh lemon, orange, or lime juice squeezed over vegetables, fish, or grilled meat; grated citrus peel, chopped fresh ginger, or chopped fresh herbs; and, of course, freshly ground pepper.

Italian Seasoning Mix

Use this herb blend in spaghetti sauce, on pizza, or in vegetable and bean soups. Or sprinkle it onto lightly oiled poultry or fish before cooking.

- 2 tablespoons dry rosemary
- ¾ teaspoon fennel seeds
- ¼ cup *each* dry oregano leaves and dry basil leaves
- 1 tablespoon *each* garlic powder and dry thyme leaves

In a blender, whirl rosemary and fennel seeds until powdery (or finely crush with a mortar and pestle). Transfer to a small jar and stir in oregano, basil, garlic powder, and thyme. Store airtight for up to 6 months. Makes about ¾ cup.

Per tablespoon: 14 calories, 0.5 g protein, 3 g carbohydrates, 0.3 g total fat (0 g saturated fat), 0 mg cholesterol, 1 mg sodium

Mexican Seasoning Mix

Stir this mixture into cooked beans, chili, tomato soup, scrambled eggs, or rice pilaf; add to salad dressings; or pat onto lean beef or pork before grilling.

- ¼ cup chili powder
- 2 tablespoons *each* ground cumin, ground coriander, dry oregano leaves, and dry basil leaves
- 1 tablespoon *each* dry thyme leaves and garlic powder
- ¾ teaspoon ground red pepper (cayenne)

Stir together chili powder, cumin, coriander, oregano, basil, thyme, garlic powder, and red pepper. Store airtight for up to 6 months. Makes about 1 cup.

Per tablespoon: 15 calories, 0.6 g protein, 3 g carbohydrates, 0.6 g total fat (0 g saturated fat), 0 mg cholesterol, 21 mg sodium

Scandinavian Seasoning Mix

Stir this seasoning combination into cottage cheese for a quick vegetable dip, add to salad dressings and seafood soups, sprinkle onto lightly oiled fish or chicken before cooking, or use on steamed vegetables.

- 6 tablespoons dry dill weed
- ⅓ cup ground lemon peel
- ¼ cup onion powder

Stir together dill weed, lemon peel, and onion powder. Store airtight for up to 6 months. Makes about 1 cup.

Per tablespoon: 10 calories, 0.4 g protein, 2 g carbohydrates, 0.1 g total fat (0 g saturated fat), 0 mg cholesterol, 3 mg sodium

Barbecue Seasoning Mix

Stir this mixture into marinades for meat or poultry, or drop onto hot coals to create an aromatic smoke.

- 1½ tablespoons *each* dry basil leaves and dry oregano leaves
- ¼ cup *each* crushed bay leaves, juniper berries, dry rosemary, and dry savory leaves

In a blender, whirl basil, oregano, bay leaves, juniper, rosemary, and savory until coarsely ground. Store airtight for up to 4 months. Makes about ¾ cup.

Per tablespoon: 13 calories, 0.3 g protein, 3 g carbohydrates, 0.4 g total fat (0 g saturated fat), 0 mg cholesterol, 1 mg sodium

Pictured on page 170

Herb Vinegar

Aromatic with fresh herbs and spices, this easy-to-make vinegar and its variations can accent much more than just salad. Use on cooked potatoes or other vegetables; in fish, vegetable, or bean soups; or on cooked meat, fish, or poultry. Any of these vinegars can be bottled attractively and presented to family or friends as a health-minded gift.

- 4 fresh rosemary sprigs (about 5 inches long *each*)
- 2 fresh lemon thyme sprigs (optional)
- 1 teaspoon whole black peppercorns
  White wine vinegar

Poke rosemary sprigs and, if desired, lemon thyme sprigs into a 3½-cup bottle. Add peppercorns and fill with vinegar. Cork bottle and let stand in a cool, dark place for 3 weeks to develop flavor. Store for up to 4 months. Makes about 3½ cups.

Per tablespoon: 2 calories, 0 g protein, 0.5 g carbohydrates, 0 g total fat (0 g saturated fat), 0 mg cholesterol, 0 mg sodium

Garlic–Green Onion Vinegar

Follow directions for Herb Vinegar (above), substituting 4 cloves garlic (impale on a thin bamboo skewer, if desired) and 2 green onions (about 6 inches long *each*) for rosemary, thyme, and peppercorns. Makes about 3½ cups.

Per tablespoon: 2 calories, 0 g protein, 0.5 g carbohydrates, 0 g total fat (0 g saturated fat), 0 mg cholesterol, 0 mg sodium

Basil-Oregano-Peppercorn Vinegar

Follow directions for Herb Vinegar (at left), substituting 2 fresh basil sprigs and 4 fresh oregano sprigs (about 5 inches long *each*) for rosemary and thyme. Substitute red wine vinegar for white wine vinegar, if desired. Makes about 3½ cups.

Per tablespoon: 2 calories, 0 g protein, 0.5 g carbohydrates, 0 g total fat (0 g saturated fat), 0 mg cholesterol, 0 mg sodium

Spicy Chile Vinegar

Follow directions for Herb Vinegar (at left), substituting 4 bay leaves, 6 small dried hot red chiles, and 4 large cloves garlic for rosemary, thyme, and peppercorns. Makes about 3½ cups.

Per tablespoon: 3 calories, 0 g protein, 0.6 g carbohydrates, 0 g total fat (0 g saturated fat), 0 mg cholesterol, 0 mg sodium

Pictured on page 170

Rose Petal Vinegar

This very special vinegar infusion is a subtle addition to fresh fruit salads. Start with any variety of rose petal, as long as it has *never* been treated with any pesticide or fungicide.

- 2 cups lightly packed fresh unsprayed rose petals, rinsed and drained
- 3 cups white wine vinegar

Place rose petals in a wide-mouthed 4-cup jar with a tight-fitting lid. Add vinegar. Cover and let stand at room temperature until next day. Uncover and push petals down into vinegar; cover and let stand for 3 days or until petals are bleached and vinegar tastes of roses. Strain, discarding petals, and pour vinegar into a clean bottle. Cork bottle and store for up to 4 months. Makes about 3 cups.

Per tablespoon: 2 calories, 0 g protein, 0.5 g carbohydrates, 0 g total fat (0 g saturated fat), 0 mg cholesterol, 0 mg sodium

*Give a gift from the heart. Herb Vinegar with its
variations and Rose Petal Vinegar (recipes on page 169)
are a delicate way to flavor foods without adding salt.
Present them in charming glass bottles, decorated with
ribbons, hand-lettered labels, and sealing wax.*

BURGUNDY-BRAISED CABBAGE WITH CHESTNUTS

Per serving: 202 calories, 3 g protein, 41 g carbohydrates, 4 g total fat (0.7 g saturated fat), 0 mg cholesterol, 72 mg sodium

Preparation time: About 15 minutes
Cooking time: About 1¼ hours

Celebrate autumn's bounty with this ruby-hued side dish. Perfect for holiday menus, it features fiber-rich cabbage and apples with chestnuts, the leanest of nuts.

- 1 large head red cabbage (about 2½ lbs.), thinly sliced
- 2 cups burgundy or other dry red wine
- ⅓ cup lemon juice
- ½ cup firmly packed brown sugar
- 1 pound Red Delicious apples, thinly sliced
- 2 tablespoons margarine
- 1 large onion, finely chopped
- 1 bay leaf
- 1 cup low-sodium chicken broth
- 1 can (10 oz. drained weight) chestnuts in water, drained, or 10 ounces roasted peeled chestnuts
  Ground white pepper

Stir together cabbage, wine, lemon juice, sugar, and apples. (At this point, you may cover and let stand until next day.)

In a 6- to 8-quart pan, melt margarine over medium-high heat. Add onion and cook, stirring, until soft (about 5 minutes). Add cabbage mixture, bay leaf, and chicken broth. Bring to a boil; reduce heat, cover, and simmer until cabbage is wilted (about 15 minutes). Uncover and continue cooking, stirring occasionally, until cabbage is very tender when pierced (about 50 more minutes); if any liquid remains in pan, increase heat to high and boil, stirring occasionally, until evaporated.

Stir in chestnuts and cook until hot (about 5 minutes). Season to taste with pepper. Makes 8 servings.

GREEN BEAN & TOMATO CASSEROLE

Per serving: 95 calories, 4 g protein, 15 g carbohydrates, 3 g total fat (0.7 g saturated fat), 1 mg cholesterol, 87 mg sodium

Preparation time: About 30 minutes
Baking time: About 35 minutes

Need to feed a crowd? Here's a wholesome side dish that serves a dozen. Because you can make it ahead, it's a good choice for entertaining.

- 2½ pounds green beans, cut into 2-inch pieces
- 1 tablespoon salad oil
- 1 large onion, chopped
- 3 cloves garlic, minced or pressed
- ½ pound mushrooms, thinly sliced
- 2 pounds tomatoes, cut into wedges
- ¼ teaspoon ground red pepper (cayenne)
- 1½ teaspoons *each* dry basil leaves and dry oregano leaves
- 1 tablespoon margarine
- 1½ cups soft whole wheat bread crumbs
- ¼ cup grated Parmesan cheese

Place beans on a rack in a pan above 1 inch boiling water. Cover and steam over high heat until tender-crisp (about 10 minutes). Lift out and immerse in ice water until cool. Drain and set aside.

Heat oil in a wide frying pan over medium-high heat. Add onion, about two-thirds of the garlic, and mushrooms. Cook, stirring, until liquid has evaporated (about 10 minutes). Remove from heat and stir in beans, tomatoes, red pepper, and 1 teaspoon *each* of the basil and oregano. Spread mixture in a 9- by 13-inch baking pan and set aside.

Reduce heat to medium and melt margarine in frying pan. Add bread crumbs and remaining garlic, basil, and oregano; cook, stirring, until golden brown. (At this point, you may cool, cover, and refrigerate vegetables and topping separately for up to 2 days.)

Scatter bread crumb mixture over vegetables; sprinkle with Parmesan. Cover and bake in a 400° oven for 20 minutes (30 minutes if refrigerated). Uncover and continue baking until tomatoes are soft (about 15 more minutes). Makes 12 servings.

■ *Pictured on page 214*

GINGERED ASPARAGUS

■ *Per serving: 37 calories, 2 g protein, 3 g carbohydrates, 2 g total fat (0.4 g saturated fat), 0 mg cholesterol, 4 mg sodium*

Preparation time: About 10 minutes
Cooking time: 5 to 7 minutes

This dish demonstrates how fresh, bright season-ings can transform a simple vegetable into a mas-terpiece. Offer the asparagus warm or at room temperature.

- **1 pound asparagus, tough ends snapped off, cut diagonally into 2-inch pieces**
- **1 tablespoon minced fresh ginger**
- **3 tablespoons lemon juice**
- **2 teaspoons sesame oil**

Place asparagus on a rack in a pan above 1 inch boiling water. Cover and steam over high heat until tender-crisp (5 to 7 minutes).

Transfer to a bowl and add ginger, lemon juice, and oil. Stir well. Serve warm or at room tempera-ture. Makes 4 servings.

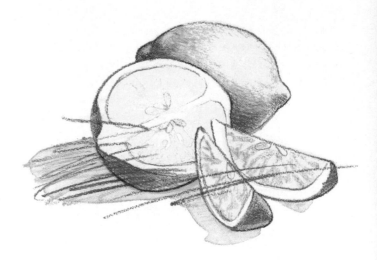

LEMON-GARLIC SWISS CHARD

■ *Per serving: 55 calories, 3 g protein, 7 g carbohydrates, 3 g total fat (0.3 g saturated fat), 0 mg cholesterol, 334 mg sodium*

Preparation time: About 10 minutes
Cooking time: About 20 minutes

Swiss chard is anointed with lemon juice and olive oil in this simple dish, inspired by Italian cuisine. Chard, a dark, leafy green, provides vitamins A and C, as well as potassium, iron, and calcium.

- **1½ pounds Swiss chard, rinsed and drained**
- **¼ cup lemon juice**
- **1 clove garlic, minced or pressed**
- **2 teaspoons olive oil**
  Freshly ground pepper
- **4 teaspoons grated Parmesan cheese (optional)**

Trim off and discard discolored ends of Swiss chard stems. Cut white stalks from leaves and coarsely chop; set aside. Shred leaves.

Place chopped stalks on a rack in a pan above 1 inch boiling water. Cover and steam over high heat for 5 minutes. Add leaves and continue steaming, covered, until leaves are tender and bright green (about 15 more minutes).

Transfer chard to a bowl and add lemon juice, garlic, and oil; season to taste with pepper. Toss well. Sprinkle with Parmesan, if desired. Makes 4 servings.

SWEET & BITTER MUSTARD GREENS

■

Per serving: 99 calories, 2 g protein, 19 g carbohydrates, 3 g total fat (0.4 g saturated fat), 0 mg cholesterol, 19 mg sodium

Preparation time: About 10 minutes
Cooking time: About 18 minutes

Never judge a book by its cover—or a vegetable by its humble appearance. Unassuming mustard greens conceal a wealth of vitamin A, as well as the possible cancer-fighting properties associated with cruciferous vegetables. A mellow blend of slow-cooked onion and raisins tempers the greens' natural bitterness.

- ¾ **pound mustard greens, tough stems trimmed, rinsed and drained**
- 1 **tablespoon olive oil**
- 1 **large onion, thinly sliced**
- 1 **tablespoon minced fresh marjoram leaves or 1 teaspoon dry marjoram leaves**
- ¾ **cup golden raisins**
- ⅓ **cup low-sodium chicken broth**
  Salt and pepper

Set aside 6 large mustard green leaves. Finely chop remaining leaves.

Place whole leaves on a rack in a pan above 1 inch boiling water. Cover and steam over high heat just until slightly limp (about 30 seconds). Remove from pan and set aside.

Heat oil in a wide frying pan over medium-low heat. Add onion and marjoram and cook, stirring often, until onion is golden (about 15 minutes). Stir in raisins and cook for 30 seconds. Add chopped leaves and chicken broth and cook, stirring, until leaves are wilted (about 2 minutes).

Place a whole leaf on each plate and mound greens mixture on top. Season to taste with salt and pepper. Makes 6 servings.

MASHED POTATOES & BROCCOLI

■

Per serving: 258 calories, 7 g protein, 42 g carbohydrates, 8 g total fat (1 g saturated fat), 1 mg cholesterol, 127 mg sodium

Preparation time: About 10 minutes
Cooking time: About 25 minutes

When you add broccoli to classic mashed potatoes, you add fiber, calcium, iron, and vitamins to the high-potassium tubers. For the best texture, use a potato masher to blend the vegetables.

- 1 **pound broccoli**
- 2½ **pounds russet potatoes**
- 3 **tablespoons margarine**
  About ¼ cup lowfat (2%) milk
  Salt and pepper

Cut off broccoli flowerets; peel stalks. Finely chop stalks and all but a few small flowerets; set aside. Peel potatoes and cut into ½-inch cubes.

In a 6-quart pan, bring 3 quarts water to a boil over high heat. Add potatoes; cover and cook until tender when pierced (about 15 minutes). Add broccoli and cook, covered, until tender (about 10 minutes). Drain well. Remove whole flowerets and set aside.

Return potatoes and remaining broccoli to pan. Reduce heat to low, add margarine and ¼ cup of the milk, and cook, stirring, until margarine has melted. Remove from heat. With a potato masher, mash vegetables smoothly, adding more milk, a tablespoon at a time, if mixture is too thick. Season to taste with salt and pepper. Transfer to a serving dish and top with reserved flowerets. Makes 4 to 6 servings.

Dig in! Because crispy Potato & Carrot Oven-fries (recipe on facing page) roast in a hot oven, they come out golden brown and delectable, with only a fraction of the fat of traditional fries. A sprinkling of cider vinegar provides delicious contrast.

ROASTED RED & YELLOW POTATOES

Preparation time: About 10 minutes
Baking time: About 55 minutes

Put some extra vitamins on the menu by teaming up golden sweet potatoes with their red-jacketed cousins. Roasting the vegetables at a high temperature crisps the skins and renders the flesh creamy and soft. Onions add a touch of sweetness. For contrast, sprinkle with sherry vinegar, if you wish.

- 2 **pounds medium-size red thin-skinned potatoes, quartered**
- 3 **small sweet potatoes or yams (about 1½ lbs. *total*), cut lengthwise into 1-inch wedges**
- 3 **medium-size onions, quartered**
- 3 **tablespoons olive oil**
    Salt and pepper
    Sherry vinegar or cider vinegar (optional)

Per serving: 315 calories, 5 g protein, 58 g carbohydrates, 7 g total fat (1 g saturated fat), 0 mg cholesterol, 27 mg sodium

Mix red potatoes, sweet potatoes, onions, and oil. Spread mixture evenly on a large rimmed baking sheet. Bake in a 425° oven until vegetables are tender and browned (about 55 minutes).

Transfer to a serving dish and season to taste with salt and pepper. Sprinkle with vinegar, if desired. Makes 6 servings.

■ *Pictured on facing page*

POTATO & CARROT OVEN-FRIES

Preparation time: About 10 minutes
Baking time: About 45 minutes

Enjoy crunchy french fries with much less fat by baking them in the oven. Carrots add extra color, flavor, and nutrients. Offer the oven-fries in a napkin-lined basket for a diner-style presentation.

- 3 **large white thin-skinned potatoes (about 2 lbs. *total*), cut into ½- by 4-inch sticks**
- 2 **pounds carrots, cut into ½- by 4-inch sticks**
- 2 **tablespoons salad oil**
    Salt and pepper
    Cider vinegar (optional)

Per serving: 341 calories, 7 g protein, 64 g carbohydrates, 8 g total fat (0.9 g saturated fat), 0 mg cholesterol, 97 mg sodium

Mix potatoes, carrots, and 1½ tablespoons of the oil; set aside.

Grease 2 large rimmed baking sheets with remaining oil and place in a 425° oven for 5 minutes. Spread vegetable mixture evenly on hot baking sheets and bake, turning once with a spatula, until vegetables are lightly browned and tender when pierced (about 45 minutes *total*); switch pan positions halfway through baking.

Transfer vegetables to a napkin-lined basket. Season to taste with salt and pepper. Sprinkle with vinegar, if desired. Makes 4 servings.

Breads

Dilled Bread ■ Bulgur Wheat Rolls

■ Mini-Calzones ■ Cornmeal-Oat Muffins

■ Herb-Cheese Muffins ■ Applesauce Raisin

Bread ■ Irish Soda Bread ■ Apricot–Oat

Bran Scones

Few foods are as comforting as a loaf of bread emerging golden brown and crusty from the oven, and few pleasures can match that first bite into the bread's warm, soft interior. If you've always thought that baking bread at home from scratch takes too much time and effort, the recipes in this chapter will surely change your mind. The yeast doughs are easy to prepare, and you can do other things while the bread is rising. The muffins and calzones can be made ahead, and the quick breads and scones need no rising. And with the satisfaction of making your own bread comes the knowledge that you're serving healthy fare. Because they're augmented with whole wheat flour, bulgur, oats, or cornmeal, these breads have extra fiber. Herbs and spices, vegetables, dried fruits, and nuts contribute hearty goodness and flavor. It's hard to imagine a more delicious way to help fill your family's carbohydrate and fiber quotas than with wholesome, homemade bread. Why not put a freshly baked loaf on your table tonight?

■ *Pictured on facing page*

DILLED BREAD

Per slice: 180 calories, 6 g protein, 36 g carbohydrates, 1 g total fat (0.5 g saturated fat), 3 mg cholesterol, 130 mg sodium

Preparation time: About 30 minutes
Rising time: About 2 hours
Baking time: About 40 minutes

Because it's so simple to make, this fragrant loaf is a good choice for a novice baker. Milk in the dough ensures a richly browned crust.

    1½ cups lowfat (2%) milk
    1   package active dry yeast
    1   tablespoon sugar
    1   cup whole wheat flour
        About 2½ cups all-purpose flour
    ½   teaspoon salt
    1   tablespoon dry dill weed
        Cornmeal

In a small pan, warm milk over low heat to about 110°F. Pour into a small bowl and sprinkle with yeast and sugar; let stand until foamy (about 10 minutes).

In a large bowl or heavy-duty mixer, combine whole wheat flour, 2 cups of the all-purpose flour, salt, and dill weed. Beat in yeast mixture until it forms a stiff dough.

Turn dough out onto a lightly floured surface and knead until smooth and elastic (about 15 minutes), adding more all-purpose flour as needed to prevent sticking. Place in an oiled bowl; turn over to grease top. Cover and let rise in a warm place until doubled (about 1 hour).

Punch dough down and knead briefly. Shape into a round loaf. Sprinkle a baking sheet with cornmeal and place loaf on top. Cover and let rise until doubled (about 1 hour); slash top with a sharp knife. Bake in a 375° oven until bread is well browned and sounds hollow when tapped (about 40 minutes). Let cool briefly on a rack. Makes 1 loaf (about 10 slices).

BULGUR WHEAT ROLLS

Per roll: 215 calories, 6 g protein, 40 g carbohydrates, 3 g total fat (0.9 g saturated fat), 21 mg cholesterol, 131 mg sodium

Preparation time: About 30 minutes (plus 1 hour standing time)
Rising time: About 1½ hours
Baking time: About 20 minutes

Bulgur adds chewy goodness and extra fiber to these wholesome rolls; milk and egg make the dough tender.

    ½   cup *each* bulgur and boiling water
    1   cup milk
    1   package active dry yeast
    ¼   cup sugar
    ½   teaspoon salt
    2   tablespoons margarine, cut into small
        pieces
    1   egg
        About 3¾ cups all-purpose flour

In a small bowl, combine bulgur and water; cover with foil and let stand until bulgur is soft and liquid is absorbed (about 1 hour).

In a small pan, warm milk over low heat to about 110°F. Pour into a large bowl or heavy-duty mixer and sprinkle with yeast; let stand until foamy (about 10 minutes). Add sugar, salt, margarine, egg, and bulgur mixture. Beat in about 3½ cups of the flour or enough to make a stiff dough.

Turn dough out onto a lightly floured surface and knead until smooth and elastic (about 15 minutes), adding more flour as needed to prevent sticking. Place in an oiled bowl; turn over to grease top. Cover and let rise in a warm place until doubled (about 50 minutes).

Punch dough down and cut into 12 equal pieces. Shape each into a round and arrange on a lightly greased baking sheet. Cover and let rise until puffy (about 40 minutes).

Bake in a 400° oven until well browned (about 20 minutes). Let cool briefly on a rack. Makes 12 rolls.

*Straight from the hearth, savory Dilled Bread (recipe on
facing page) offers hearty sustenance and plenty of fiber.
It's so easy to make, you may want to double the recipe
and bake two loaves.*

179

■ *Pictured on page 62*

MINI-CALZONES

■

Per calzone: 38 calories, 2 g protein, 6 g carbohydrates, 1 g total fat (0.2 g saturated fat), 1 mg cholesterol, 88 mg sodium

Preparation time: About 30 minutes
Rising time: About 1 hour
Baking time: About 15 minutes

Whether they're served as appetizers, at lunch, or for snacks, these bite-size turnovers will delight the palate. They can be baked ahead and reheated just before serving.

> Whole Wheat Dough (recipe follows)
> 2 tablespoons olive oil
> 2 tablespoons minced shallots
> 2 ounces Black Forest ham, chopped
> 4 cups coarsely chopped, lightly packed spinach
> ¼ cup part-skim ricotta cheese
> ½ teaspoon ground nutmeg
> Cornmeal

Prepare Whole Wheat Dough. While dough is rising, heat 1 tablespoon of the oil in a wide frying pan over medium-high heat. Add shallots and ham and cook, stirring occasionally, until shallots are soft (about 7 minutes). Add spinach and cook until liquid has evaporated (about 5 minutes). Remove from heat. Add ricotta and nutmeg and mix well. Let cool.

Punch dough down and shape into a ball. On a lightly floured surface, roll into a circle ⅛ inch thick. Using a 3-inch cookie cutter, cut out circles.

Place about 1 teaspoon of the spinach filling on each circle. Fold dough over, pinching edges together.

Sprinkle a lightly greased baking sheet with cornmeal. Arrange calzones on top and brush lightly with remaining oil; prick tops with a fork. Bake in a 425° oven until lightly browned (about 15 minutes).

If made ahead, cool, cover, and refrigerate until next day. To reheat, place on a baking sheet and heat in a 425° oven until warm (about 10 minutes). Makes 3 dozen calzones.

Whole Wheat Dough. Pour ¾ cup warm **water** (about 110°F) into a large bowl or heavy-duty mixer. Sprinkle with 1 package **active dry yeast;** let stand until foamy (about 10 minutes). Add 1 teaspoon *each* **salt** and **sugar** and 1 cup **all-purpose flour;** beat until smooth. Beat in about 1 cup **whole wheat flour** or enough to make a stiff dough.

Turn dough out onto a lightly floured surface and knead until smooth and elastic (about 5 minutes), adding more all-purpose flour as needed to prevent sticking. Place in an oiled bowl; turn over to grease top. Cover and let rise in a warm place until doubled (about 1 hour).

CORNMEAL-OAT MUFFINS

■

Per muffin: 207 calories, 5 g protein, 34 g carbohydrates, 6 g total fat (0.9 g saturated fat), 19 mg cholesterol, 283 mg sodium

Preparation time: About 15 minutes
Baking time: About 20 minutes

An unexpected combination of two favorite grains—cornmeal and oats—gives these muffins a nutritional boost. They go equally well with coffee at breakfast and with milk at snack time.

> 1½ cups all-purpose flour
> 1 cup yellow cornmeal
> ½ cup plus 2 tablespoons rolled oats
> 2 tablespoons baking powder
> ½ teaspoon baking soda
> ½ cup firmly packed brown sugar
> 1¼ cups lowfat buttermilk
> ¼ cup salad oil
> 1 egg

In a large bowl, stir together flour, cornmeal, ½ cup of the oats, baking powder, baking soda, and sugar. In another bowl, beat buttermilk, oil, and egg until blended. Add to flour mixture, stirring just until moistened.

Spoon batter equally into 12 paper-lined or greased 2½-inch muffin cups. Sprinkle with remaining oats. Bake in a 350° oven until a pick inserted in center comes out clean (about 20 minutes).

If made ahead, cool, wrap airtight, and store at room temperature until next day; freeze for longer storage (thaw unwrapped). To reheat, place in a baking pan, cover with foil, and heat in a 350° oven until warm (15 to 18 minutes). Makes 12 muffins.

HERB-CHEESE MUFFINS

Per muffin: 145 calories, 5 g protein, 22 g carbohydrates, 4 g total fat (1 g saturated fat), 22 mg cholesterol, 157 mg sodium

Preparation time: About 25 minutes
Baking time: About 20 minutes

Brimming with such savory accents as bell pepper, herbs, onion, and cheese, these muffins stand in for bread at lunch or dinner.

- 2 tablespoons salad oil
- 1 large onion, minced
- 1 large green bell pepper (about ½ lb.), stemmed, seeded, and finely chopped
- 2 tablespoons honey
- 1 tablespoon Dijon mustard
- 1 cup nonfat milk
- 1 egg
- 2 egg whites
- 6 tablespoons shredded Cheddar cheese
- 1 cup whole wheat flour
- ½ cup *each* all-purpose flour and yellow cornmeal
- 2 teaspoons baking powder
- 1 teaspoon dry thyme leaves
- ⅛ teaspoon ground red pepper (cayenne)

Heat 1 tablespoon of the oil in a wide frying pan over medium heat. Add onion and bell pepper and cook, stirring often, until limp (about 10 minutes). Let cool briefly.

In a large bowl, mix remaining oil, honey, mustard, milk, egg, egg whites, and 4 tablespoons of the Cheddar; stir in onion mixture. In another bowl, stir together whole wheat flour, all-purpose flour, cornmeal, baking powder, thyme, and red pepper. Add egg mixture, stirring just until moistened. Spoon batter equally into 12 paper-lined or greased 2½-inch muffin cups. Sprinkle with remaining Cheddar. Bake in a 375° oven until a pick inserted in center comes out clean (about 20 minutes).

If made ahead, cool, wrap airtight, and store at room temperature until next day; freeze for longer storage (thaw unwrapped). To reheat, place in a baking pan, cover with foil, and heat in a 350° oven until warm (15 to 18 minutes). Makes 12 muffins.

■ *Pictured on page 183*

APPLESAUCE RAISIN BREAD

Per slice: 234 calories, 4 g protein, 43 g carbohydrates, 6 g total fat (0.8 g saturated fat), 18 mg cholesterol, 115 mg sodium

Preparation time: About 15 minutes
Baking time: About 1 hour

This moist, fragrantly spiced bread is so good, it will disappear in a flash. Try to save a few slices for the next day; it makes wonderful toast.

- 1 egg
- 1 jar (about 14 oz.) unsweetened applesauce
- 2 tablespoons salad oil
- ½ cup granulated sugar
- ¼ cup firmly packed brown sugar
- 1½ cups all-purpose flour
- ½ cup whole wheat flour
- 2 teaspoons baking powder
- ½ teaspoon *each* baking soda and ground cinnamon
- 1 teaspoon ground nutmeg
- 1 cup raisins
- ½ cup chopped walnuts

In a large bowl, beat egg lightly. Stir in applesauce and oil and mix well. Stir in granulated sugar and brown sugar until smooth. Add all-purpose flour, whole wheat flour, baking powder, baking soda, cinnamon, and nutmeg; mix well. Stir in raisins and nuts.

Pour batter into a lightly greased 5- by 9-inch loaf pan. Bake in a 350° oven until crust is richly browned and a pick inserted in center comes out clean (about 1 hour). Let cool in pan for 10 minutes; then turn out onto a rack to cool completely. Makes 1 loaf (about 12 slices).

■ *Pictured on facing page*

IRISH SODA BREAD

■ Per slice: 263 calories, 8 g protein, 52 g carbohydrates, 4 g total fat (2 g saturated fat), 10 mg cholesterol, 452 mg sodium

Preparation time: About 15 minutes
Baking time: About 40 minutes

This hearty loaf is studded with currants and caraway seeds. As in the Apricot–Oat Bran Scones (below), a modicum of butter enriches the dough.

    1 cup all-purpose flour
    2 cups whole wheat flour
    2 tablespoons brown sugar
    1 teaspoon *each* salt and baking soda
    2 tablespoons cold butter or margarine, cut into small pieces
    1 cup currants
    1 teaspoon caraway seeds
 1¼ cups lowfat buttermilk
    1 tablespoon milk

In a large bowl or food processor, mix all-purpose flour, whole wheat flour, sugar, salt, and baking soda. With a pastry blender or steel blade, cut in butter until mixture resembles coarse crumbs. Stir in currants and caraway seeds. Add buttermilk, stirring just until moistened.

Turn dough out onto a lightly floured surface and knead briefly. Pat into a round about 7 inches in diameter and place on a lightly greased baking sheet. Brush with milk. With a sharp knife or scissors, cut a ½-inch-deep cross in top of dough.

Bake in a 375° oven until crust is golden and bread sounds hollow when tapped (about 40 minutes). Let cool on a rack; slice thickly. Makes 1 loaf (about 8 slices).

■ *Pictured on facing page*

APRICOT–OAT BRAN SCONES

■ Per scone: 121 calories, 3 g protein, 20 g carbohydrates, 3 g total fat (2 g saturated fat), 19 mg cholesterol, 187 mg sodium

Preparation time: About 15 minutes
Baking time: About 15 minutes

Fiber—both soluble and insoluble—adds substance to these updated scones. Split them horizontally and spread with honey or preserves for a morning treat or for afternoon tea.

    1 cup *each* all-purpose flour and whole wheat flour
  ¼ cup sugar
    4 teaspoons baking powder
    2 cups oat bran flake cereal
  ¼ cup cold butter or margarine, cut into small pieces
    1 egg
  ⅔ cup lowfat (2%) milk
  ½ cup chopped moist-pack dried apricots or pitted prunes

In a large bowl or food processor, mix all-purpose flour, whole wheat flour, sugar, baking powder, and cereal. With a pastry blender or steel blade, cut in butter until mixture resembles coarse crumbs. Mix in egg and milk. Stir in apricots.

Turn dough out onto a lightly floured surface and knead briefly. Divide into thirds. Pat each portion into a 5-inch circle about ½ inch thick. With a floured knife, cut each round into 6 wedges.

Arrange wedges on a lightly greased baking sheet and bake in a 400° oven until lightly browned (about 15 minutes). Transfer scones to a rack and let cool briefly. Makes 18 scones.

Linger with friends over hot tea and servings of (from top) high-fiber Applesauce Raisin Bread (recipe on page 181), Irish Soda Bread (recipe on facing page), and Apricot–Oat Bran Scones (recipe on facing page). Spread the breads with preserves and honey instead of butter.

Desserts

Minted Poached Pears ■ Wine & Berry

Compote ■ Creamy Peach-Yogurt Pie ■ Sherry-

Plum Crisp ■ Oatie Peach Crumble ■ Angel

Food Cake ■ Crazy Cocoa Cake ■ Old-fashioned

Apple Cake ■ Spiced Pumpkin Roll ■ Baked

Apples & Figs with Cassis ■ Quick Macaroons

■ Oatmeal Raisin Cookies

Who doesn't love dessert? That sweet fillip at the end of a meal is so delicious and rewarding that even the most health-conscious among us find it hard to give up. Now you won't have to. The recipes in this chapter showcase desserts you can enjoy because they're prepared with a light touch. Even "sinful" treats have been adapted. Substituting unsweetened cocoa for chocolate, for example, gives the same intensity of flavor without the saturated fat; reducing the amount of sugar in a recipe means fewer calories and a cleaner taste. Still, you'll find enough temptations on the pages ahead to please even the most stubborn sweet tooth. Splurge on moist and tender cakes, baked fruit crisps, and creamy frozen confections. Bite into a lightened-up oatmeal cookie and you'll have a hard time closing the cookie jar. For an incomparable low-calorie cheesecake, see page 26. Of course, you can end any meal with delicious fresh fruit selected at its peak of flavor; we've devoted a special section to recipes that celebrate fruit's natural goodness and infinite variety.

■ *Pictured on facing page*

MINTED POACHED PEARS

Per serving: 229 calories, 1 g protein, 53 g carbohydrates, 0.8 g total fat (0 g saturated fat), 0 mg cholesterol, 2 mg sodium

Preparation time: About 10 minutes
Cooking time: About 30 minutes

Enlivened with unsweetened pineapple juice and a touch of mint, this cooked fruit dessert is an unbeatably light finish to any meal. You can serve it hot or cold.

>   2 **cans (12 oz.** *each***) unsweetened pineapple juice**
>   4 **medium-size firm-ripe Bosc, d'Anjou, or Comice pears (about 1½ lbs.** *total***)**
>   2 **tablespoons crème de menthe or ¼ teaspoon mint extract**
>   **Mint sprigs**

Pour juice into a 3-quart pan and place over medium heat. Peel pears, leaving some peel around stems; do not remove stems. With an apple corer, cut out blossom end and core from each pear. Place pears in juice and bring to a boil; reduce heat, cover, and simmer until pears are tender when pierced (about 20 minutes).

With a slotted spoon, lift out pears and place in a serving dish. Increase heat to high and boil juice, uncovered, stirring often, until reduced to about 1 cup (about 10 minutes). Stir in crème de menthe. Pour over pears. Serve warm; or cool, cover, and refrigerate until chilled and serve cold. Garnish with mint sprigs. Makes 4 servings.

WINE & BERRY COMPOTE

Per serving: 134 calories, 0.8 g protein, 34 g carbohydrates, 0.4 g total fat (0 g saturated fat), 0 mg cholesterol, 7 mg sodium

Preparation time: About 10 minutes
Cooking time: About 15 minutes

For an elegant, low-calorie dessert, spoon this berry compote into goblets and top with vanilla yogurt. Or use the compote as a sauce for frozen yogurt, sponge cake, or angel food cake.

>   1 **cup each dry red wine and water**
>   ¾ **cup sugar**
>   6 **tablespoons lemon juice**
>   1 **teaspoon vanilla extract**
>   1½ **pounds mixed berries, such as strawberries, raspberries, blackberries, or blueberries**
>   **Vanilla lowfat yogurt (optional)**

In a 4- to 5-quart pan, combine wine, water, sugar, and lemon juice. Boil over high heat, stirring, until sugar is dissolved. Continue boiling until mixture is reduced by about half (about 15 minutes). Stir in vanilla extract. (At this point, you may cool, cover, and refrigerate for up to 3 weeks; reheat to a simmer before continuing.)

Hull berries, if necessary. Rinse and drain. Gently stir berries into hot syrup; let cool briefly. Spoon into individual goblets and top each serving with a dollop of yogurt, if desired. Makes 6 to 8 servings.

Utterly simple and totally delicious, Minted
Poached Pears (recipe on facing page) require no fancy
embellishments. Pineapple juice and a touch of crème de
menthe give the poaching liquid special flavor.

187

Feature FRESH FRUIT FINALES

For superb nutrition, endless variety, and dazzling color and taste, fresh fruit is your best bet for dessert. A naturally light counterpoint to any menu, fruit satisfies a sweet tooth without lots of added sugar. Moreover, it contains an impressive checklist of vitamins and minerals, relatively few calories, and lots of fiber.

To maximize flavor and minimize cost, serve fresh fruit in season (see guidelines for selecting and buying fresh fruit beginning on page 219).

Here's a sampling of recipes that rely on uncooked fruits in all their natural glory. You'll be surprised at how easy it is to make nutritious fresh fruit a part of your diet.

Strawberries with Gingered Vanilla Yogurt

If you can't find strawberries with stems attached, hull the berries before serving.

> **About ¾ pound large strawberries with stems, rinsed and drained**
> **¾ cup vanilla lowfat yogurt**
> **¼ teaspoon ground ginger**

Arrange berries on a serving platter. In a small bowl, stir together yogurt and ginger. Offer with berries for dipping. Makes 2 servings.

Per serving: 121 calories, 5 g protein, 23 g carbohydrates, 2 g total fat (0.7 g saturated fat), 4 mg cholesterol, 58 mg sodium

Frosted Corinth Grapes

Clusters of these tiny grapes appear in markets in midsummer. You'll need a helper to assist with the frosting.

> **4 clusters (about 1½ lbs. *total*) Black Corinth grapes (also called champagne grapes), rinsed**
> **1 egg white, lightly beaten**
> **¾ cup sugar**
> **Lemon sorbet (optional)**

Lay clusters of grapes flat. Turning fruit with stem, gently brush all over with egg white. With a helper holding each cluster horizontally by stem and fruit ends, sprinkle with sugar, having helper turn fruit as you work.

Clip stems with a clothespin to a rack in freezer, being sure nothing touches grapes (put plastic wrap beneath to catch any drips). Freeze until solid (about 3 hours). If made ahead, seal in a plastic bag and freeze for up to 2 months.

Offer with sorbet, if desired. Makes 4 servings.

Per serving: 247 calories, 2 g protein, 64 g carbohydrates, 0.5 g total fat (0.2 g saturated fat), 0 mg cholesterol, 17 mg sodium

Island Fruit Platter with Mango Velvet

Simple yet elegant, this fruit offering is perfect for breakfast or brunch, or for dessert at dinner.

> **1 small pineapple (about 3 lbs.), peeled and cored**
> **1 large ripe papaya (about 1¼ lbs.), peeled, halved, and seeded**
> **About 2-pound piece honeydew melon, seeded and rind removed**
> **Mint sprigs (optional)**
> **Mango Velvet (recipe follows)**

Slice pineapple crosswise ½ inch thick. Thinly slice papaya halves crosswise. Cut melon into thin wedges. Arrange pineapple slices, overlapping, down center of a large platter. Arrange papaya and melon on either side. Garnish with mint sprigs, if desired.

Prepare Mango Velvet. Offer with fruit. Makes 6 servings.

Mango Velvet. Peel 1 ripe **mango** (about 1 lb.) and cut fruit from pit in chunks. Whirl fruit in a food processor or blender until puréed. Add ¼ cup **frozen orange juice concentrate** and 2 tablespoons **lime juice.** Whirl until blended. Spoon into a small bowl.

Per serving: 161 calories, 2 g protein, 41 g carbohydrates, 0.8 g total fat (0.1 g saturated fat), 0 mg cholesterol, 12 mg sodium

Cantaloupe in Raspberry Purée

Sliced strawberries can be substituted for the raspberries, if you wish.

- 1½ cups raspberries, rinsed and drained
- 3 tablespoons sugar
- ¼ cup cream sherry
- 1 medium-size cantaloupe (about 2½ lbs.), quartered, seeded, and rind removed

In a blender or food processor, whirl raspberries until puréed; press through a fine sieve to remove seeds.

In a 1-quart pan, combine raspberry purée, sugar, and sherry. Cook over medium-high heat, stirring, until sugar is dissolved and mixture is boiling. Boil for 30 more seconds. Remove from heat and let cool. (At this point, you may cover and let stand for up to 1 hour.)

Thinly slice cantaloupe. Spoon raspberry purée onto individual dessert plates; arrange cantaloupe decoratively over sauce. Makes 4 servings.

Per serving: 131 calories, 2 g protein, 28 g carbohydrates, 0.6 g total fat (0 g saturated fat), 0 mg cholesterol, 14 mg sodium

Ricotta-Pear Parfaits

Here's a light alternative to fruit and whipped cream.

- 3 very ripe pears (about 1½ lbs. *total*)
- 2 tablespoons lemon juice
- 2 cups part-skim ricotta cheese
- 5 tablespoons lowfat (2%) milk
- 3 tablespoons powdered sugar
- 2 tablespoons grated orange peel
- 2 teaspoons vanilla
- ¼ teaspoon ground cinnamon

Cut pears into bite-size chunks. Mix with lemon juice and set aside.

In small bowl of an electric mixer, beat ricotta, milk, sugar, orange peel, and vanilla until fluffy. Spoon a heaping tablespoonful of the ricotta mixture into each of 4 parfait glasses or small bowls; top each with a large spoonful of the pears. Repeat layers. Top with remaining ricotta and dust with cinnamon. Makes 4 servings.

Per serving: 283 calories, 13 g protein, 38 g carbohydrates, 9 g total fat (5 g saturated fat), 34 mg cholesterol, 144 mg sodium

Papaya Snow

After a spicy meal, what could be better than this super-cooling finish?

- 1 large ripe papaya (about 1¼ lbs.), peeled, halved, and seeded
- 4 lime wedges

Wrap each papaya half in plastic wrap and freeze until solid (about 3 hours). About 1 hour before serving, transfer papaya to refrigerator. Just before serving, unwrap each half and coarsely shred. Spoon into chilled dessert goblets or small bowls. Offer with lime. Makes 4 servings.

Per serving: 40 calories, 0.6 g protein, 10 g carbohydrates, 0.1 g total fat (0 g saturated fat), 0 mg cholesterol, 3 mg sodium

Oranges in Ginger Champagne

Part beverage and part dessert, this stylish offering is well suited to elegant occasions.

- ¾ cup *each* sugar and water
- 2 tablespoons minced candied ginger
- 4 medium-size oranges (about 2 lbs. *total*)
- 1 bottle (750 ml.) dry champagne or 4 cups ginger ale

In a 2- to 3-quart pan, combine sugar, water, and ginger. Cook over medium heat, stirring, until sugar is dissolved. Increase heat to high and boil, without stirring, for 5 minutes. Transfer to a bowl; cool, cover, and refrigerate until cold or until next day.

Peel oranges and remove white membrane. Holding oranges over bowl of ginger syrup, cut between segments to release fruit; stir. Cover and refrigerate for 3 hours.

Spoon orange mixture into champagne or wine glasses. Fill with champagne. Makes 8 servings.

Per serving: 188 calories, 0.7 g protein, 33 g carbohydrates, 0.2 g total fat (0 g saturated fat), 0 mg cholesterol, 7 mg sodium

*Show off summer's bounty in Sherry-Plum Crisp
(recipe on facing page). Rosy-hued plums bake to juicy
perfection beneath a crunchy topping; allspice and
nutmeg add spicy aroma and taste.*

CREAMY PEACH-YOGURT PIE

Per serving: 255 calories, 7 g protein, 43 g carbohydrates, 7 g total fat (5 g saturated fat), 24 mg cholesterol, 166 mg sodium

Preparation time: About 30 minutes
Baking time: About 50 minutes
Freezing time: About 8 hours

This creamy frozen pie in a crunchy meringue shell is a summertime treat. Offer it when peaches are at their best.

- ½ teaspoon margarine
- 2 egg whites, at room temperature
- ½ teaspoon cream of tartar
- ½ cup sugar
- 1 package (8 oz.) Neufchâtel cheese, at room temperature
- 1 cup plain lowfat yogurt
- ⅓ cup instant nonfat dry milk
- ½ cup honey
- 1 teaspoon almond extract
- 1½ cups coarsely chopped peeled peaches
- 2 medium-size firm-ripe peaches (about ¾ lb. *total*)
- 1 tablespoon lemon juice

Coat bottom and sides of a 9-inch pie pan with margarine. Set aside.

In large bowl of an electric mixer, beat egg whites and cream of tartar on high speed until frothy. Add sugar, 1 tablespoon at a time, beating well after each addition, until meringue holds stiff, glossy peaks.

Spread meringue in pan, pushing it up pan sides to resemble a pie shell and smoothing with a spatula dipped in cold water. Bake in a 275° oven until lightly browned and dry to the touch (about 50 minutes). Let cool completely.

In a food processor or blender, whirl Neufchâtel, yogurt, dry milk, honey, and almond extract until smooth. Add chopped peaches and whirl just until blended. Spread mixture in crust, wrap airtight, and freeze until firm (about 8 hours).

To serve, let pie stand at room temperature for 15 minutes. Slice whole peaches (you should have about 2 cups) and arrange on pie. Brush with lemon juice. Makes 8 servings.

Pictured on facing page

SHERRY-PLUM CRISP

Per serving: 333 calories, 4 g protein, 63 g carbohydrates, 9 g total fat (1 g saturated fat), 0 mg cholesterol, 122 mg sodium

Preparation time: About 20 minutes (plus 20 minutes standing time)
Baking time: About 45 minutes

Tender fruit and a crunchy topping blend irresistibly in this warming dessert. Tapioca thickens the fruit juices.

- ¼ teaspoon *each* ground allspice and ground nutmeg
- ¼ cup *each* quick-cooking tapioca and cream sherry
- 12 large firm-ripe plums (about 3½ lbs. *total*), sliced
- ½ cup firmly packed brown sugar
- ½ cup *each* all-purpose flour and granulated sugar
- ¼ cup cold margarine, cut into small pieces
- ¾ cup crunchy wheat and barley cereal
- ⅓ cup finely chopped walnuts

In a 9- by 13-inch baking pan, mix allspice, nutmeg, tapioca, sherry, plums, and brown sugar. Let stand, stirring occasionally, until tapioca is softened (about 20 minutes).

In a small bowl or food processor, combine flour and granulated sugar. With a pastry blender or steel blade, cut in margarine until mixture resembles fine crumbs. Stir in cereal and nuts. Squeeze mixture into large lumps and coarsely crumble over plum mixture.

Bake in a 350° oven until fruit is bubbling and topping is golden brown (about 45 minutes). Serve warm or at room temperature. Makes 8 to 10 servings.

OATIE PEACH CRUMBLE

Per serving: 314 calories, 3 g protein, 59 g carbohydrates, 8 g total fat (1 g saturated fat), 0 mg cholesterol, 93 mg sodium

Preparation time: About 20 minutes
Baking time: About 40 minutes

Simple, homey desserts like this baked crumble have long been popular, and with good reason: they're easy to make and they taste great. Leave the fruit unpeeled for added fiber and vitamins.

■ *Pictured on page 214*

6 cups sliced unpeeled peaches or nectarines
½ cup sugar
1½ tablespoons cornstarch
½ teaspoon *each* ground nutmeg and vanilla
1 tablespoon lemon juice
Oat Topping (recipe follows)

Gently stir together peaches, sugar, cornstarch, nutmeg, vanilla, and lemon juice. Spoon into a 2-quart baking pan.

Prepare Oat Topping and sprinkle over peach mixture. Bake on middle rack of a 375° oven until fruit is bubbling and topping is golden (about 40 minutes). Serve warm or at room temperature. Makes 6 servings.

Oat Topping. Stir together ½ cup *each* **rolled oats** and **all-purpose flour** and ¼ cup firmly packed **brown sugar.** With a pastry blender or 2 knives, cut in ¼ cup cold **margarine,** cut into small pieces, until mixture resembles coarse crumbs.

ANGEL FOOD CAKE

Per serving: 128 calories, 4 g protein, 27 g carbohydrates, 0.1 g total fat (0 g saturated fat), 0 mg cholesterol, 146 mg sodium

Preparation time: About 20 minutes
Baking time: About 35 minutes

Tender, snowy white, and cholesterol-free—no wonder angel food cake is so popular.

1 cup sifted cake flour
1¼ cups granulated sugar
12 egg whites, at room temperature
½ teaspoon salt
2 teaspoons cream of tartar
1½ teaspoons vanilla or almond extract
Powdered sugar and sliced fresh strawberries (optional)

Sift together flour and ½ cup of the granulated sugar; sift again and set aside.

In large bowl of an electric mixer, beat egg whites on high speed until foamy. Add salt and cream of tartar and continue beating until mixture holds soft peaks. Add remaining sugar, 2 tablespoons at a time, beating well after each addition, until mixture holds stiff, glossy peaks.

With a rubber spatula, fold in vanilla. Sprinkle in flour mixture, about ¼ cup at a time, gently folding in each addition just until blended. Turn batter into an ungreased 10-inch tube pan with a removable bottom; gently smooth top. Slide spatula down outside edge of batter and run around pan to eliminate large air bubbles.

Bake in a 375° oven until cake is golden and springs back when lightly pressed (about 35 minutes). Invert pan on a funnel or pop bottle to keep cake from shrinking; let cool completely. Remove from pan and place on a cake plate or platter. Dust with powdered sugar and decorate with strawberries, if desired. Slice with an angel food cake knife or serrated knife. Makes 12 servings.

CRAZY COCOA CAKE

Per serving: 264 calories, 3 g protein, 44 g carbohydrates, 9 g total fat (1 g saturated fat), 0 mg cholesterol, 240 mg sodium

Preparation time: About 10 minutes
Baking time: About 30 minutes

A kitchen standard for years, this fluffy, moist chocolate cake fits right in with today's lighter menus. It's also one of the easiest cakes you'll ever make.

- 1½ **cups all-purpose flour**
- 1 **cup granulated sugar**
- 3 **tablespoons unsweetened cocoa**
- 1 **teaspoon baking soda**
- ½ **teaspoon salt**
- 5 **tablespoons salad oil**
- 1 **tablespoon vinegar**
- 1 **teaspoon vanilla**
- 1 **cup cold water**
  Whipped Topping (recipe follows) or powdered sugar (optional)

Sift flour, granulated sugar, cocoa, baking soda, and salt into a 9-inch square baking pan. Make 3 depressions in flour mixture and evenly distribute oil, vinegar, and vanilla among them. Pour cold water over all.

With a rubber spatula, combine ingredients, scraping sides and bottom of pan to mix thoroughly. (A few lumps may remain in batter.)

Bake in a 350° oven until a pick inserted in center comes out clean (about 30 minutes). Let cool on a rack. Prepare Whipped Topping, if desired, and offer with cake. Or sprinkle with powdered sugar, if desired. Makes 8 servings.

Whipped Topping. Pour ½ cup **canned evaporated skimmed milk** into bowl of an electric mixer. Cover and refrigerate milk and beaters for 1 hour.

Beat milk on high speed until fluffy. Add 4 teaspoons **sugar** and ½ teaspoon **vanilla;** continue beating until mixture forms soft peaks. Serve immediately.

OLD-FASHIONED APPLE CAKE

Per serving: 279 calories, 4 g protein, 52 g carbohydrates, 7 g total fat (0.9 g saturated fat), 14 mg cholesterol, 190 mg sodium

Preparation time: About 20 minutes (plus 15 minutes standing time)
Baking time: About 50 minutes

Crisp apples and spicy cinnamon enliven this buttermilk-enriched cake. Serve with hot cider for a midday snack or a satisfying dessert.

- 1½ **pounds tart green apples, such as Granny Smith or Newtown Pippin, coarsely grated**
- 1½ **cups sugar**
- 2½ **cups all-purpose flour**
- 1½ **teaspoons baking soda**
- 1 **tablespoon baking powder**
- 2 **teaspoons cinnamon**
- 1 **egg**
- 2 **egg whites**
- ¼ **cup salad oil**
- ½ **cup lowfat buttermilk**
- 2 **teaspoons vanilla**
- 1 **cup raisins**
- ½ **cup chopped walnuts**
  Nonstick cooking spray or salad oil

Place apples in a large bowl. Add sugar and mix well; let stand for 15 minutes.

Sift together flour, baking soda, baking powder, and cinnamon; add to apple mixture. In another bowl, stir together egg, egg whites, oil, buttermilk, and vanilla. Add to apple mixture and stir well. Fold in raisins and nuts.

Lightly coat a 9- by 13-inch baking dish with cooking spray. Pour in batter and bake in a 350° oven until a knife inserted in center comes out clean (about 50 minutes). Let cool on a rack. Makes 15 servings.

*Be indulgent—yet virtuous—by serving Spiced
Pumpkin Roll (recipe on facing page), a perfect choice for
an autumn menu. Creamy frozen yogurt fills moist
pumpkin cake for low-calorie results.*

194

■ *Pictured on facing page*

SPICED PUMPKIN ROLL

Per serving: 177 calories, 4 g protein, 37 g carbohydrates, 2 g total fat (0.4 g saturated fat), 48 mg cholesterol, 123 mg sodium

Preparation time: About 1 hour
Baking time: About 15 minutes
Freezing time: About 3 hours

This frozen cake roll boasts the flavors of pumpkin pie à la mode, but with a fraction of the calories. Its elegant appearance makes it a fitting finale for a holiday meal.

Nonstick cooking spray or salad oil
¾ cup all-purpose flour
2 teaspoons ground cinnamon
1 teaspoon *each* baking powder and ground ginger
½ teaspoon *each* ground nutmeg and salt
3 eggs
1 cup granulated sugar
⅔ cup canned solid-pack pumpkin
⅓ cup powdered sugar
1 quart vanilla frozen yogurt, slightly softened
Shredded orange peel (optional)

Lightly coat a 10- by 15-inch rimmed baking pan with cooking spray; line with wax paper and spray again. Set aside.

In a small bowl, stir together flour, cinnamon, baking powder, ginger, nutmeg, and salt; set aside.

In large bowl of an electric mixer, beat eggs on high speed until thick and lemon colored. Gradually add granulated sugar and continue beating, scraping bowl often, until creamy and pale in color. With mixer on low, beat in pumpkin and flour mixture. Pour batter into pan, spreading evenly.

Bake in a 375° oven until top springs back when lightly pressed (about 15 minutes). Immediately invert onto a dish towel sprinkled with 3 tablespoons of the powdered sugar. Peel off wax paper and, starting with a long side, immediately roll cake and towel into a cylinder. Let cool completely on a rack. Unroll cake, remove towel, and spread cake with frozen yogurt; reroll. Wrap in plastic wrap and freeze until firm (about 3 hours).

To serve, unwrap cake and place on a platter. Let stand at room temperature for about 10 minutes. Sift remaining powdered sugar over top, slice, and, if desired, garnish each serving with orange peel. Makes 14 servings.

BAKED APPLES & FIGS WITH CASSIS

Per serving: 172 calories, 0.9 g protein, 40 g carbohydrates, 3 g total fat (0.4 g saturated fat), 0 mg cholesterol, 24 mg sodium

Preparation time: About 15 minutes
Baking time: About 15 minutes

End a special meal with tart apples and plump, supple figs baked in liqueur. This dessert's sophisticated flavor belies its simple preparation.

2 medium-size Granny Smith or Gravenstein apples (about 1 lb. *total*)
1 tablespoon lemon juice
6 large ripe figs (about ¾ lb. *total*)
¼ cup cassis (currant-flavored liqueur) or black raspberry–flavored liqueur
1 tablespoon sugar
2 teaspoons margarine
Vanilla lowfat yogurt

Peel and thinly slice apples. Overlap slices in a 9-inch pie dish and drizzle with lemon juice. Thinly slice figs crosswise and arrange over apples. Pour liqueur over fruit, sprinkle with sugar, and dot with margarine.

Bake in a 400° oven until bubbling (about 15 minutes). Spoon onto individual dessert plates and top each serving with a dollop of yogurt. Makes 4 servings.

Beverages are an important, but often overlooked, component of a healthy diet. Some drinks tease the palate, others cool you off or warm you up, and still others are calorie-rich indulgences.

On these pages we offer a variety of refreshing beverages that fill many roles, but with a light profile. The fruit-based spritzers and the cooler are designed for cocktail time. The sorbet-based sodas, the smoothies, and the cappuccino satisfy the urge for something cold and creamy. The steamy milk and honey concoction and the heated apricot nectar warm the soul. For the best and simplest thirst quencher, just drink water—and lots of it!

Pictured on page 198

Citrus Spritzers

5 medium-size oranges (about 2½ lbs. *total*)
3 large limes (about 10 oz. *total*)
1 bottle (24 oz.) white grape juice
Ice cubes
About 3 cups sparkling mineral water

With a vegetable peeler, cut 3 strips zest (orange part only) from 1 orange. Cut 2 strips zest (green part only) from 1 lime. Place in a pitcher and bruise with a wooden spoon.

Squeeze enough of the oranges to make 2 cups juice. From 1 lime, cut 10 thin slices and reserve. Squeeze enough of the remaining limes to make ¼ cup juice. Add orange juice, lime juice, and grape juice to pitcher; stir. (At this point, you may cover and refrigerate until next day.)

For each serving, fill a tall glass with ice, juice blend, and mineral water, using about 2 parts juice to 1 part water. Garnish with lime slices. Makes 10 servings (about ¾ cup *each*).

Per serving: 72 calories, 0.4 g protein, 18 g carbohydrates, 0.1 g total fat (0 g saturated fat), 0 mg cholesterol, 7 mg sodium

Pictured on page 198

Chilled Apple-Ginger Spritzers

2 cups apple juice
½ cup chopped preserved ginger in syrup (including syrup)
8 cinnamon sticks (about 3 inches long *each*)
Ice cubes
2 bottles (750 ml. *each*) chilled brut-style dry sparkling wine or 5 small bottles (10 oz. *each*) chilled sparkling mineral water

In a 1- to 2-quart pan, bring apple juice, ginger, and cinnamon sticks to a boil over high heat. Cook, stirring occasionally, until reduced to 1 cup (about 15 minutes). Let cool. Pour into a small bowl, cover, and refrigerate for at least 1 hour or until next day.

For each serving, spoon about 2 tablespoons of the juice mixture into a large wine glass. Add ice and fill with wine. Garnish with a cinnamon stick, if desired. Makes 8 servings (about 1 cup *each*).

Per serving: 177 calories, 0.3 g protein, 14 g carbohydrates, 0.1 g total fat (0 g saturated fat), 0 mg cholesterol, 16 mg sodium

Pictured on page 198

Banana-Citrus Coolers

2 large ripe bananas (about 1 lb. *total*), diced
½ cup lime juice
1 can (12 oz.) frozen pineapple-orange-banana juice concentrate
1 bottle (28 oz.) chilled sparkling mineral water
Ice cubes
1 lime, thinly sliced (optional)

In a blender or food processor, combine bananas, lime juice, and juice concentrate. Whirl until smooth. Pour into a 3-quart pitcher and add mineral water. Stir down foam. Fill glasses with ice and add juice mixture. Garnish with lime slices, if desired. Makes 10 servings (about 1 cup *each*).

Per serving: 102 calories, 0.3 g protein, 26 g carbohydrates, 0.2 g total fat (0.1 g saturated fat), 0 mg cholesterol, 6 mg sodium

Pictured on page 198

Fruit Sorbet Sodas

About 1 pint fruit sorbet (use your favorite flavor)
About 1 bottle (28 oz.) chilled sparkling mineral water
Fresh strawberries (optional)

Place 1 or 2 scoops of sorbet in each of 4 large chilled glasses. Slowly pour mineral water into each glass and garnish with strawberries, if desired. Makes 4 servings (about 1¼ cups *each*).

Per serving: 110 calories, 0.5 g protein, 28 g carbohydrates, 0.1 g total fat (0 g saturated fat), 0 mg cholesterol, 11 mg sodium

Pictured on page 21

Fruit Smoothies

2 cups plain nonfat or lowfat yogurt
½ cup lowfat (2%) milk
1 medium-size very ripe banana (about 6 oz.), diced
1 cup unsweetened frozen berries; or 1 cup rinsed and hulled fresh berries or chopped peaches and ½ cup crushed ice
1 teaspoon vanilla
Honey

In a blender, combine yogurt, milk, banana, berries, and vanilla; whirl until smooth and frothy. Sweeten to taste with honey; then whirl again. Pour into glasses. Makes 4 servings (about 1 cup *each*).

Per serving: 121 calories, 8 g protein, 20 g carbohydrates, 1 g total fat (0.6 g saturated fat), 5 mg cholesterol, 102 mg sodium

Pictured on page 198

Frozen Cappuccino

1 cup lowfat (2%) milk
1½ cups chilled strong regular or decaffeinated coffee
Sugar
Unsweetened cocoa and ground cinnamon (optional)

Pour milk into an ice-cube tray and freeze until solid (about 4 hours).

In a blender or food processor, combine coffee and frozen milk cubes. Whirl with short bursts to break up cubes; then whirl until smooth. Pour into chilled glasses or mugs. Add sugar to taste. Sprinkle with cocoa and cinnamon, if desired. Makes 2 servings (about 1½ cups *each*).

Per serving: 68 calories, 4 g protein, 7 g carbohydrates, 2 g total fat (1 g saturated fat), 10 mg cholesterol, 68 mg sodium

Pictured on page 198

Steaming Honey-spiced Milk

6 cups lowfat (2%) milk
¼ cup honey
2 or 3 cinnamon sticks (about 3 inches long *each*)
2 teaspoons whole cloves

In a 2- to 3-quart pan, bring milk, honey, cinnamon sticks, and cloves to a gentle boil over medium heat, stirring. Reduce heat and simmer gently for 10 minutes. Strain to remove cinnamon sticks and cloves. Pour into tall heatproof glasses or mugs. Makes 4 to 6 servings (1 to 1½ cups *each*).

Per serving: 200 calories, 10 g protein, 28 g carbohydrates, 6 g total fat (4 g saturated fat), 23 mg cholesterol, 148 mg sodium

Pictured on page 198

Warm Apricot Jewel

½ cup firmly packed dried apricots
1½ cups water
1 can (46 oz.) apricot nectar
¼ cup frozen tangerine juice concentrate
3 tablespoons lemon juice
½ cup brandy (optional)

In a blender, combine dried apricots and water. Whirl until smooth. Rub through a fine strainer into a 3- to 4-quart pan. Add apricot nectar, tangerine juice concentrate, and lemon juice. Cook over high heat, stirring, until steaming. Add brandy, if desired, and pour into mugs. Makes 6 to 8 servings (1 to 1¼ cups *each*).

Per serving: 155 calories, 1 g protein, 40 g carbohydrates, 0.3 g total fat (0 g saturated fat), 0 mg cholesterol, 9 mg sodium

Here's a rainbow of deliciously light beverages (from left): Warm Apricot Jewel, Chilled Apple-Ginger Spritzers, Banana-Citrus Coolers, Fruit Sorbet Sodas, Steaming Honey-spiced Milk, Citrus Spritzers, and Frozen Cappuccino (recipes on pages 196–197).

QUICK MACAROONS

Per cookie: 67 calories, 1 g protein, 12 g carbohydrates, 2 g total fat (2 g saturated fat), 0 mg cholesterol, 30 mg sodium

Preparation time: About 15 minutes
Baking time: About 30 minutes

Coconut lovers will applaud these simple cookies. Because they tend to be very sticky, bake them in paper muffin cups.

      3 **egg whites, at room temperature**
         Pinch of cream of tartar
      ½ **cup sugar**
      1 **teaspoon lemon juice**
     1½ **teaspoons all-purpose flour**
      1 **cup sweetened flaked dry coconut**

In small bowl of an electric mixer, beat egg whites and cream of tartar on high speed until foamy. Add sugar, 1 tablespoon at a time, beating well after each addition, until mixture holds stiff, glossy peaks. With a rubber spatula, gently fold in lemon juice and flour until blended. Fold in coconut.

Spoon batter equally into 12 paper-lined 2½-inch muffin cups. Bake in a 300° oven until golden brown (about 30 minutes). Remove from pan and let cool thoroughly on a rack. Makes 12 cookies.

OATMEAL RAISIN COOKIES

Per cookie: 79 calories, 2 g protein, 13 g carbohydrates, 3 g total fat (0.3 g saturated fat), 0.1 mg cholesterol, 23 mg sodium

Preparation time: About 15 minutes
Baking time: About 10 minutes

Who says cookies are just for kids? Spicy, cakelike, and full of plump raisins, these treats will delight all ages.

      1 **cup all-purpose flour**
      ½ **cup oat bran**
      ½ **teaspoon ground allspice**
      1 **teaspoon baking soda**
      ½ **teaspoon salt (optional)**
      1 **cup firmly packed brown sugar**
      ½ **cup salad oil**
      ½ **cup nonfat milk**
      2 **egg whites**
      1 **teaspoon vanilla**
      3 **cups rolled oats**
      1 **cup raisins**

In a small bowl, stir together flour, oat bran, allspice, baking soda, and, if desired, salt. Set aside.

In large bowl of an electric mixer, beat sugar and oil until creamy. Add milk, egg whites, and vanilla; beat until well combined. Gradually add flour mixture, beating until well blended. Stir in oats and raisins.

Drop rounded tablespoonfuls of dough about 2 inches apart on baking sheets. Bake in a 375° oven until light golden (about 10 minutes). Let cool briefly on baking sheets; then transfer cookies to racks to cool completely. Store airtight. Makes 4 dozen cookies.

Food, Fun & Exercise

Getting together with groups of people—family, friends, or co-workers—is always fun. Often, the focus of such gatherings is a meal. Why not add physical activity to the schedule? In this chapter, you'll find ideas for combining exercise with a nutritious meal for both convivial, athletic weekend excursions and workday breaks. Read the general guidelines for exercise beginning on page 20; then turn to the menus here and enjoy a breakfast workout with friends, a beach picnic or a refreshing hike with family, or a fast-walk lunch with co-workers.

Or create your own way to make food, fun, and exercise part of your everyday life. (For information on how many calories various physical activities burn per hour, see page 209.)

■ BEACH PICNIC

Because a day at the beach offers so much variety, there's something for all ages. Games and exercise can continue throughout the day, with people eating at a casual pace. You'll need food that can be served cold (transport it in an ice chest) and that holds up well. If you don't live near the ocean, tote your picnic to a park, a pool, or a lake. Just get outdoors and enjoy!

Fun and games in the sun. When you arrive at your destination, involve everyone in setting up; this will warm up muscles and get energy flowing.

Check to be sure that the water is safe for swimming. An excellent aerobic conditioner for the whole body, swimming can be done at a variety of speeds; beach balls, goggles, and rafts make it more fun. Be sure to watch small children and nonswimmers while they're near or in the water.

Other good activities at the beach include volleyball (bring a net and ball), jogging or walking, and, if you have a boat, rowing (good for conditioning the upper body and back) or canoeing. Don't be afraid to play "camp counselor," encouraging everyone to participate; remember, the point is to get exercise while you're having fun!

A flexible feast. The picnic menu suggested here can be made in advance and modified to suit the group. Carry the celery, feta cheese, dip, and shrimp and artichokes (or sandwiches), tightly wrapped, in an ice chest; pack plenty of cold beverages in there, too. Bring a cutting board and serrated knife for the bread, and don't forget paper plates, napkins, plastic utensils, cups, and a trash bag for removing the debris when you leave.

Menu

Celery Sticks Stuffed with Feta Cheese or Peanut Butter

Dry-roasted Potato Chips (page 40) with Curried Spinach Dip (page 41)

Steeped Shrimp with Artichokes (recipe at right) and Whole Wheat Bread, Dilly Salmon on Dark Rye (page 54), or Roasted Turkey Breast Sandwiches on Whole Wheat Bread

Oatmeal Raisin Cookies (page 199)

Fresh Fruit

Assorted Fruit Juices

Steeped Shrimp with Artichokes

- ⅓ cup vinegar
- 1 tablespoon *each* mustard seeds and cumin seeds
- 2 teaspoons black peppercorns
- 8 thin slices fresh ginger (*each* about the size of a quarter)
- 10 cilantro (coriander) sprigs
- 10 mint sprigs or 2 tablespoons dry mint leaves
- 1 tablespoon olive oil
- 8 large artichokes (about ¾ lb. *each*)
- 2 pounds medium-size shrimp (about 35 per lb.)
- Mint-Ginger Vinegar (recipe follows)

In a 10- to 12-quart pan, combine 5 quarts water, vinegar, mustard seeds, cumin seeds, peppercorns, ginger, cilantro, mint, and oil. Cover and bring to a boil over high heat.

Meanwhile, remove coarse outer leaves from artichokes; trim stems even with bases. Cut off top third of artichokes and trim thorny tips from remaining leaves. Rinse well and place in pan. Reduce heat, cover, and simmer until bottoms are tender when pierced (35 to 40 minutes).

Meanwhile, devein shrimp by inserting a wooden pick between shell joints and under vein running down shrimp's back; gently pull out vein. If vein breaks, repeat at another shell joint.

Lift out artichokes and drain. Return water in pan to boiling and add shrimp. Cover pan tightly and remove from heat. Let shrimp stand until opaque in center; cut to test (3 to 5 minutes). Lift out. Cover and refrigerate shrimp and artichokes separately until chilled or until next day.

Prepare Mint-Ginger Vinegar and transfer to a container with a tight-fitting lid. Offer with shrimp and artichokes. Makes 8 servings.

Mint-Ginger Vinegar. Mix 1½ cups **unseasoned rice vinegar** or cider vinegar, 3 tablespoons **sugar,** and 2 tablespoons minced **fresh ginger** until sugar is dissolved. Add 2 tablespoons *each* minced **cilantro (coriander)** and **fresh or dry mint leaves.**

Per serving: 202 calories, 22 g protein, 25 g carbohydrates, 3 g total fat (0.4 g saturated fat), 140 mg cholesterol, 247 mg sodium

After a vigorous workout with friends, bring the gang over for a super-nutritious brunch. Ginger-Peach Smoothies (recipe on facing page), Blueberry Muffins (page 32), Grits Cake with Corn & Asparagus (page 158), and Tropical Ham Plate with Basil Honey (page 33) replenish appetites.

■ BREAKFAST WORKOUT

Start the weekend with a whole new party idea: invite friends to join in a morning workout followed by a fabulous breakfast. Not only is it the perfect way to set the course for an energetic day, but it's also a great entertainment alternative for early risers too tired for late-night events. For late risers, just push the schedule back and have everyone arrive later in the morning. Whatever hour you choose, you'll find that the breakfast workout is a great way to spend time with friends.

Rise-and-shine sports. The physical activity you choose to start the day depends on the weather and your guests. On a sunny day, everyone will want to be outdoors. Bicycling is fun; if done vigorously, it's a superb lower-body conditioner. Jogging is also a popular morning activity; it's a very efficient toner that can be done almost anywhere. For those who prefer less strenuous exercise, a fast-paced walk with friends is particularly enjoyable.

If it's cold and wet, you'll need to choose an indoor sport, such as racquetball, aerobics (either a class or a video in your living room), or another gym sport.

Choose an exercise that all will enjoy and plan to exercise for whatever length of time is comfortable for everyone. The chart on page 209 indicates how many calories various physical activities burn per hour. Use this information to motivate your guests.

A well-balanced breakfast. After working out and winding down, your guests will be ravenous. Treat them to a balanced breakfast that features energy-restoring carbohydrates and lots of replenishing fluids. This menu, which serves six, is easy on the host. After all, why should you be so busy that you can't work out, too?

Prepare the Blueberry Muffins and Grits Cake with Corn & Asparagus the day before the party. Early the next morning, cut up the fruit for the Tropical Ham Plate with Basil Honey and refrigerate; take the grits cake out of the refrigerator so it can come to room temperature before baking.

As soon as you return home from your workout, put the grits cake in the oven; reheat the muffins, too. Whip up Ginger-Peach Smoothies and offer them to your guests while you—and any helpers—set the table and prepare the ham plate. Make another batch of smoothies to serve with breakfast, or offer fruit juice, tea, or coffee; just be sure there are plenty of liquids available. For convenience, serve buffet style and don't be fussy about decorations or presentation; the idea is to make it casual and comfortable.

Pictured on facing page
Menu

Ginger-Peach Smoothies (recipe below)

Blueberry Muffins (page 32)

Grits Cake with Corn & Asparagus (page 158)

Tropical Ham Plate with Basil Honey (page 33; make a double recipe)

Fruit Juice, Tea, or Coffee (optional)

Ginger-Peach Smoothies

- 3 cups lowfat buttermilk
- 3 tablespoons honey
- 2 ripe peaches (about 10 oz. *total*), sliced
- 2 large pieces crystallized ginger
- ¾ cup crushed ice

In a blender, combine buttermilk, honey, peaches, and ginger; whirl until blended. Add ice and whirl until smooth and frothy. Makes 6 servings (about 1 cup *each*).

Per serving: 106 calories, 4 g protein, 21 g carbohydrates, 1 g total fat (0.7 g saturated fat), 5 mg cholesterol, 131 mg sodium

Treat yourself to a mini-holiday with a day of hiking. There's no better way to get away from it all, enjoy a change of scenery, and achieve gentle conditioning all at the same time.

To turn your hike into an adventure, seek out a new and interesting destination. Whether you choose a nearby park, a local forest, or just some hills you've always wanted to conquer, hiking is a great opportunity to explore your environment. For families, it's a special way to introduce children to the wonders of nature while parents renew their appreciation of the great outdoors. During the winter, you can substitute cross-country skiing for the hike.

Over the hills or through the woods. The more challenging the hike, the greater the cardiovascular workout. Uphill walking with a pack is the most invigorating; be careful, however, not to weigh yourself down with more than is comfortable or you risk injuring your back. All you'll need are comfortable shoes with durable soles and a good backpack. Dress in layers so you can cool down while you're hiking and warm up when you're resting.

By including a lunch stop, you can benefit from a rest in the middle of your hike. If possible, choose a time that comes after the most vigorous part of the hike so that the remaining part is at a gentler pace; you'll have less weight to carry once lunch is eaten, too. Don't try to lug a picnic basket along or you'll overtax your arm muscles and be thrown off balance.

As with any exercise, it's essential to drink fluids while you're hiking so you don't become dehydrated. Carry plenty of water in a canteen or plastic water bottle; pack fruit juices or other drinks for lunch as well.

The chart on page 209 shows how many calories are burned for each hour of climbing hills or hiking over either easy or difficult terrain.

Carry-it-anywhere lunch. For any all-day hike, you'll need a substantial lunch. The menu suggested here is easy to carry and offers balanced nutrition to maintain energy. Prepare the soup ahead of time; it stays warm in a thermos for up to 3 hours. The well-seasoned sandwich filling can be made ahead, too, and doesn't need to be kept cold while you travel; just place it in a leakproof container. Pack the pita bread and sauce separately. Nibble cucumber spears and cherry tomatoes with the sandwiches. For a quick snack or dessert, bring along a chunk of halvah (a sweet-tasting ground sesame confection) to eat on dried apricot halves. (Look for halvah in a Middle Eastern delicatessen or in the international section of a well-stocked supermarket. If you can't find it, substitute another sesame or nut candy.)

Pictured on facing page

Menu

Cucumber Spears & Cherry Tomatoes

Clear Vegetable Soup (recipe below)

Spiced Lentil Pockets (page 52)

Halvah with Dried Apricots

Sparkling Lemonade or Mineral Water

Clear Vegetable Soup

    7   cups low-sodium beef broth
    1½ cups small cauliflowerets
    1   medium-size red or green bell pepper
        (about 6 oz.), stemmed, seeded, and
        chopped
    1   medium-size onion, chopped
    ¼   cup tiny alphabet-shaped pasta
        Freshly ground pepper

In a 3- to 4-quart pan, bring beef broth, cauliflower, bell pepper, onion, and pasta to a boil over high heat. Reduce heat, cover, and simmer until cauliflower is tender (about 10 minutes). Season to taste with pepper. If made ahead, cover and refrigerate for up to 2 days. To reheat, bring to a boil over high heat, stirring.

Ladle into a wide-mouthed thermos (at least 2½-quart size); serve within 3 hours. Makes 4 servings.

Per serving: 79 calories, 3 g protein, 15 g carbohydrates, 2 g total fat (0 g saturated fat), 0 mg cholesterol, 16 mg sodium

When hunger strikes during a hike, unpack this portable
picnic: Clear Vegetable Soup (recipe on facing page), Spiced
Lentil Pockets (recipe on page 52), cucumber spears and cherry
tomatoes, and halvah with dried apricots for dessert. A
strap-on water bottle is good for carrying liquids.

■ FAST-WALK LUNCH

Too busy to exercise before work and too tired to do it afterward? If so, you're not alone. Yet exercising on a regular basis is too important an activity to forgo, especially for people who have sedentary desk jobs.

There's an easy—and very enjoyable—way to put exercise into your busy work schedule: take a walk during your lunch break. Then eat a healthy meal that you've brought from home, purchased on your walking route, or prepared at work.

Fast-walking for exercise. Walking for exercise has become increasingly popular in recent years; millions of people now walk regularly to keep fit and trim. It's easy, fun, inexpensive, accessible, and safe, and it requires no special facility, training, or equipment. When performed at a challenging pace, walking for 30 to 60 minutes at least three times a week will improve your cardiovascular endurance and enhance your general health, with very little risk of injury. Moreover, there are great psychological rewards. Walking gives you time to clear your head, think through difficult situations, and mentally rejuvenate for the remainder of the day.

To maximize fun and motivation, ask your co-workers to join you in your fast-walk lunches. You can enjoy each other's company and get to know one another better. If anyone eager to walk with you is particularly out of shape, the person should consult a physician before participating.

To get the most out of your fast-walk lunch, you need to move at a pace that's quick enough to meet your target heart rate (see page 20 to learn how to calculate this number, which is different for each person). For the first 10 minutes or so, walk at a casual pace (2 mph) to warm up. Then increase your speed so you're walking briskly (3.5 mph). For most people in average condition, this will be sufficiently challenging to reap cardiovascular benefits.

As you improve, aim for striding (3.5 to 5 mph). To advance to this level, bend your arms at a 90° angle, swinging your elbows forward and back as you walk, and roll completely through the foot, from heel to toe, with each step. Keep the torso tall, the abdominals tensed, and the hips pressed slightly forward.

Some people carry weights while they walk to increase their exertion. Be careful, however: the extra calories burned may not be worth the added stress on your body. Ankle weights are not recom-

mended—they can alter stride, throw you off balance, and lead to injuries. It's better to carry weights in your hands, if at all.

Always cool down by walking slowly for several minutes before returning to your desk; a few gentle stretches after your walk will increase flexibility and alleviate stiffness.

The chart on page 209 lists caloric expenditures for an hour of walking at different speeds. Bear in mind that walking on a grade or hill will increase exertion.

Dressing for success. The only equipment you need for fast-walking is a comfortable pair of shoes. The ones you choose should have adequate arch support, a padded heel, plenty of toe room, laces for a snug fit, and a cushioned, flexible sole. Invest in a pair to keep in your desk drawer just for walking. That way, leaving your shoes at home can never be an excuse for not walking. Keep a pair of comfortable socks handy, too.

You don't need to change your clothes to walk, but try to wear something loose and comfortable. Layers of clothing are the wisest choice; as you warm up on the walk, you'll want to peel off sweaters or jackets so you don't become overheated. As you cool down afterward, you'll want to put the warm layers back on, especially if your office is air-conditioned. Use common sense in dressing for the seasons; there's no reason you can't enjoy fast-walking year-round, as long as you're properly prepared.

Eating a healthy lunch. After you've worked off calories by fast-walking, choose a fresh, light lunch or snack brought from home, picked up at the deli, or prepared at the office. It's handy to have a few staples, such as dry herbs, pepper, a small bottle of vinegar, and paper plates and napkins, stashed in your desk drawer for convenience. Also, keep a large glass of water at your desk and sip it throughout the day, refilling it as many times as possible.

Here are some quick and convenient workday lunch and snack ideas:

■ *Packing your own lunch.* For bringing lunch from home, invest in an insulated lunch box for storing cold food. In addition to the sandwich recipes on pages 52–54, consider the following combinations, spread on wholesome bread, bagels, crackers, or tortillas: peanut butter with apples or dried fruit; flaked cooked fish mixed with lowfat yogurt, lemon juice, and fresh herbs; chopped cooked chicken or turkey combined with fresh vegetables and cottage cheese; or leftover beans and rice mixed with salsa and grated cheese. Tuck sliced fresh vegetables and fresh or dried fruit into your lunch box for nibbling throughout the day.

■ *Deli do's and don'ts.* You may want to pick up a carry-out meal while you're on your walk. Choose sandwiches made with white meat poultry (no skin), lean meat, or baked ham on whole grain bread. Avoid pastrami, sausage meats, rich tuna salads, and egg salads. Ask for a very small amount of mayonnaise or, better yet, none at all; mustard (though high in sodium) or a thin spread of guacamole is a leaner alternative.

Use cheese as a meat alternative, not as an addition to a meat sandwich. Instead, pile sandwiches high with lettuce, tomatoes, and other fresh vegetables, limiting the amount of meat or cheese to 2 to 3 ounces per sandwich.

If you go to a salad bar, load up on greens, fresh vegetables, and beans; avoid prepared salads made with a lot of mayonnaise. To cut back on fat, squeeze a lemon over your salad or sprinkle it with vinegar and a little bit of oil. If you must have a prepared dressing, ask for it in a separate container and then dip each forkful of salad into it; you'll end up using a lot less than if you just poured the dressing over the salad.

■ *Snack managers.* When you need a between-meal nibble at work, go to your desk drawer instead of the candy machine. Nonperishable lowfat snacks you can keep on hand include rice crackers, pretzels, graham crackers, rusks and flatbread, gingersnaps, and animal cookies. Herb tea and instant low-sodium chicken broth make warm pick-me-ups.

■ *Made at the office.* Many workplaces today are equipped with small kitchens that contain a refrigerator and microwave oven. If these are available where you work, you can prepare any number of satisfying hot lunches, including Stuffed Micro Potato (recipe at right). An even simpler choice is Couscous Soup (recipe at right); it requires only boiling water and can be mixed in a disposable cup or in a coffee mug.

Pictured on page 208

Stuffed Micro Potato

Scrub the potato and chop the vegetables the night before so you don't have to rush in the morning.

　1　**russet potato (about ½ lb.), scrubbed**
　1　**small container (8 oz.) lowfat (1% or 2%) cottage cheese**
　½　**cup mixed chopped vegetables, such as celery, carrots, green or red bell peppers, and green onions (including tops)**
　1　**teaspoon dry dill weed or dry oregano leaves**
　　　Wine vinegar (optional)

Pierce potato in several places with a fork or knife. Place on a paper plate and microwave on **HIGH (100%)** for 7 minutes, turning once. Cover with a napkin and let stand for 3 minutes. Slash potato open and spoon in cottage cheese; top with vegetables and dill weed. Sprinkle with vinegar, if desired. Makes 1 serving.

Per serving: 364 calories, 33 g protein, 51 g carbohydrates, 3 g total fat (1 g saturated fat), 9 mg cholesterol, 960 mg sodium

Couscous Soup

Keep the couscous, dehydrated vegetables, and broth packets in your desk drawer.

　1　**tablespoon couscous**
　2　**teaspoons dehydrated mixed vegetable flakes**
　1　**packet instant low-sodium chicken broth**

Place couscous, vegetable flakes, and instant chicken broth in an 8-ounce heatproof cup. Fill with boiling water; cover with a lid or foil and let stand until couscous is soft (about 5 minutes). Makes 1 serving.

Per serving: 59 calories, 2 g protein, 12 g carbohydrates, 0.2 g total fat (0 g saturated fat), 0 mg cholesterol, 7 mg sodium

Take a break for exercise and good nutrition at the office.
Start with a fast-paced walk during lunch; then quickly
prepare Stuffed Micro Potato (recipe on page 207) to eat at
your desk. A large glass of water and some lowfat snacks
stowed in your desk will keep you going all afternoon.

■ Physical Activity Caloric Expenditure Chart

The figures below give the approximate number of calories burned per hour during various physical activities for different body weights. The actual number of calories burned will vary, depending on specific weight, efficiency, skill, physical condition, and the intensity of the activity.

A good goal is to try to burn at least 300 calories a day. To improve endurance, engage in activities that elevate your heart rate to between 60% and 80% of maximum, and sustain this rate for at least 20 minutes a minimum of three times a week. (For more on exercise, see page 20.)

ACTIVITY	130 lbs. Calories/Hour	150 lbs. Calories/Hour	170 lbs. Calories/Hour	190 lbs. Calories/Hour
*Aerobic dancing, medium	366	420	474	534
*Aerobic dancing, intense	474	552	624	696
Calisthenics	270	306	342	383
*Canoeing, leisure	156	180	204	228
*Climbing hills	426	492	558	624
*Climbing hills with 11-lb. load	456	528	594	666
*Cross-country skiing, level	420	486	552	612
*Cycling (5.5 mph)	228	264	294	330
*Cycling (9.4 mph)	354	408	462	516
*Gardening, raking	192	222	252	276
*Gardening, manual mowing	396	456	516	576
*Golf, without cart	300	348	390	438
Hiking, easy terrain (3 mph)	324	360	396	450
Hiking, difficult terrain (3 mph)	405	450	495	563
*Jumping rope (70 per min.)	576	660	750	834
*Racquetball	630	726	822	918
Rowing, light pace	360	400	440	500
*Running (8 min. per mile)	750	852	960	1,062
*Running (6 min. per mile)	936	1,038	1,146	1,248
*Squash	750	864	978	1,092
*Swimming, slow crawl	456	522	594	660
*Swimming, breaststroke	576	660	750	834
*Swimming, backstroke	600	690	780	870
*Tennis singles, vigorous	384	444	504	564
*Volleyball	180	204	234	258
Walking (3.5 mph)	286	318	350	398
Walking (5 mph)	498	558	618	698
*Weight lifting, free weights	300	348	396	444

* Used by permission. Fitness Technologies, Inc., P. O. Box 431, Amherst, MA 01004. From Katch, F. I. and W. D. McArdle. Nutrition, Weight Control, and Exercise. Third edition. Lea & Febiger, Philadelphia. 1988.

Menus for All Occasions

When you need to cook dinner in a flash, is there enough time to whip up something healthy? If your boss is coming to dinner, can the meal be both elegant and light? At holiday time, can you serve a meal that's festive, yet still good for your family?

The answer to all these questions is yes. On the next few pages, you'll find suggestions for make-ahead menus, quick-to-fix menus, holiday menus, and menus you can use when entertaining (adjust the quantities of each recipe as needed). But you needn't stop there. With the recipes in this book, you can construct dozens of meals without sacrificing your commitment to good nutrition and great taste.

■ MAKE-AHEAD MENUS

Rush-hour Breakfast

Make weekday breakfasts less of a hassle by mixing muffin batter and servings of high-fiber cereal during the weekend. Bake the muffins all at once and then reheat them as needed; or use the batter straight from the refrigerator to cook up fresh ones (the batter lasts for up to 2 weeks). Prepare a pot of coffee the night before and chill it; then whirl up batches of cold cappuccino at the last minute.

**Freshly Squeezed Orange or
Grapefruit Juice**

**Fruit Muesli (page 30) with Yogurt
& Fresh Fruit**

Homestead Bran Muffins (page 32)

Frozen Cappuccino (page 197)

Alfresco Luncheon

Whether offered as an elegant picnic or a simple lunch on the porch, this sandwich-and-salad menu lets you relax in warm weather. As a bonus, the flavors of the food improve from making ahead; if there are left-overs, they'll keep well, too. Fill out the menu with cheese, breadsticks, and cookies purchased at an Italian delicatessen.

Sliced Aged Asiago Cheese

Breadsticks

Summer Sandwich (page 53)

Tuscan Bean Salad (page 73)

Fresh Grapes with Biscotti

Lemonade or Iced Tea

Cool Summertime Dinner

When the weather's warm and you don't want to fuss in a hot kitchen, rely on dishes that are served cold or at room temperature.

White Gazpacho (page 56)

Cool Spiced Chicken (page 105)

Oven Ratatouille (page 166)

Crusty Whole Wheat Bread

Creamy Peach-Yogurt Pie (page 191)

**Citrus Spritzers (page 196) or Sparkling
Mineral Water with Lime & Orange Slices**

Hearthside Stew Supper

A warming meat and vegetable stew tastes even better when it's made ahead; overnight chilling also enables you to lift off and discard the fat to make it healthier. Fluffy wheat rolls, a simple salad, and a warm berry compote complete this home-style meal.

**Tossed Green Salad with Lowfat Dressing
(choices on page 77)**

**Oregon Spring Stew with Vegetables
(page 93)**

Bulgur Wheat Rolls (page 178)

Wine & Berry Compote (page 186)

Better Than Store-bought

With a little advance planning, working parents can present a nutritious, no-fuss dinner in about the same time that it takes to prepare something from a box. Simply reheat the family-style casserole when you arrive home; serve it with quick-cooking couscous and fresh spinach sautéed in a touch of olive oil and garlic. Finish with cheesecake made the day before.

Turkey & Eggplant Parmigiana (page 110)

Cooked Couscous

Sautéed Spinach

Lowfat Cheesecake (page 26)

Nonfat Milk or Cranberry Juice

Rise-and-Shine Breakfast

Even when you don't have much time in the morning, try to keep good nutrition in mind. This menu provides lots of carbohydrates and calcium, and it can be prepared in less than half an hour. Toast and a hot drink go alongside.

Couscous in Cantaloupe (page 30)

Fruit Smoothies (page 197)

Whole Wheat Toast with Cinnamon Sugar

Hot Tea or Coffee

A Light Lunch

Ideal for outdoor entertaining, this menu features a glamorous two-tone soup and a delicate chicken salad, both served cool. Finish with purchased sorbet and frozen tiny grapes that you prepare ahead of time. Make enough chicken to feed the number of guests you're expecting.

Green & Gold Melon Soup (page 56)

Chicken & Pears with Mint Vinaigrette (page 76)

Poppy Seed Breadsticks

Frosted Corinth Grapes (page 188) with Lemon Sorbet

Iced Tea or Lemonade

Stylish but Speedy

When time is short but you don't want to sacrifice sophisticated flavor, poach frozen fish in a wine-based broth and then finish with a mustard sauce. For dessert, whip up a no-cook parfait topped with fresh fruit. As a first course, offer plump tortellini in a sauce that's so rich tasting you won't believe that it's light.

Tortellini & Peas in Creamy Lemon Sauce (page 145)

Simmered Cod & Vegetables (page 117)

Warm French Bread Baguettes

Ricotta-Pear Parfaits (page 189)

South-of-the-Border Soup & Sandwich

Add spice to your life with a lunch or dinner featuring recipes with a Latin accent. Substantial enough for six, this meal takes only about 45 minutes to prepare. Accompany the tacos with a salad of crunchy jicama and apples (if pomegranates are not in season, leave them out). Finish with hollowed papaya halves cradling lime wedges to squeeze over the fruit.

Mexican Albondigas Soup (page 61)

Vegetable Taco Roll-ups (page 54)

Jicama & Apples with Pomegranate (page 68)

Papaya Boats with Lime Wedges

Mexican Beer or Fruit Juices

Dinner for Two

Elegant enough for a special occasion but simple enough for a workday evening, this meal for two can be on the table in less than an hour. Pick up a chilled bottle of white wine and some gingersnaps on your way home, if you wish. Prepare a half-recipe of the spinach salad.

Spinach Salad with Garlic Croutons (page 66)

Clam Paella for Two (page 127)

Strawberries with Gingered Vanilla Yogurt (page 188)

Gingersnaps (optional)

Chilled Sauvignon Blanc (optional)

Seafood in a Snap

A cool bisque with shrimp teams up with sea bass cooked in the microwave for a meal that's incredibly quick and utterly delicious. You can also use your microwave to cook the vegetables, or use a steamer; start simmering the rice as you sit down for soup. If you're serving only two people, save half the soup for the next night.

Cold Cucumber & Dill Bisque (page 50)

Sea Bass with Ginger (page 124)

Steamed Snow Peas

Hot Cooked Rice

Honeydew Melon Wedges with Fresh Berries

A Taste of the Tropics

Dinner doesn't have to be ordinary just because you're in a hurry. This special menu features the subtle flavors of tropical islands. Look for bok choy (Chinese chard cabbage) in the specialty produce section of your supermarket; the small heads (baby bok choy) make perfect single servings.

Curry Beef in Lettuce (page 82)

Fruited Rice Pilaf (page 150)

Steamed Baby Bok Choy

Island Fruit Platter with Mango Velvet (page 188)

Meatless Menu

It's a healthy practice to turn to lean, meatless recipes a few times a week. Here's an attractive menu that can be prepared in less than 45 minutes. And it doesn't stint on taste.

Vegetable Curry Stir-fry (page 166)

Spiced Bulgur with Apple (page 156)

Sliced Cucumbers with Vinegar and Dry Dill Weed

Minted Poached Pears (page 186)

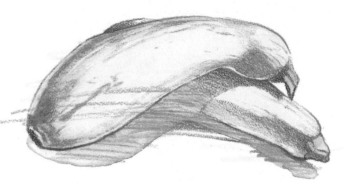

Elegance with Ease

If preparing a fancy dinner for six sounds daunting, this easy-to-cook menu will change your mind. Whip up the appetizer a little ahead of time so you can relax with your guests. Then pop the chicken in the oven and, while it bakes, prepare the pasta. Steam some asparagus just before serving. Offer a purchased frozen dessert for a carefree finish.

Mushroom Pâté with Wheat Toast Points (page 38)

Baked Chicken with Pears (page 103)

Pasta with Parsley-Lemon Pesto (page 138)

Steamed Asparagus

Chocolate Frozen Yogurt with Sliced Fresh Strawberries

Easy-on-the-Cook Menu for Four

When you invite your closest friends for dinner, you don't want to spend the evening in the kitchen. Prepare the sauce for the dessert just before your guests arrive. Let the rice bake and the swordfish marinate while you enjoy your friends. At the last minute, broil the fish and quickly sauté cherry tomatoes in a touch of olive oil.

Swordfish with Mushroom Sauce (page 120)

Baked Lemon Rice (page 155)

Sautéed Red & Yellow Cherry Tomatoes

Cantaloupe in Raspberry Purée (page 189)

*Celebrate the spring harvest with this holiday menu
of Grilled Turkey with Peaches (recipe on page 106), Gingered
Asparagus (page 172), Confetti Wild Rice (page 156), and Angel
Food Cake (page 192) adorned with fresh strawberries.*

■ HOLIDAY MENUS

Valentine's Day Brunch

Treat the ones you love to a festive Valentine's Day brunch that's as healthy as it is attractive. For a special presentation, cook the waffles in a heart-shaped waffle iron (available in many cookware and department stores); then drizzle with maple syrup and top with mixed berries. To sip alongside, offer warm apricot nectar. Lean Canadian bacon, browned in a nonstick skillet, and broiled grapefruit sprinkled with brown sugar round out the menu.

Broiled Grapefruit Halves with Brown Sugar

Orange-Yogurt Waffles (page 34) with Fresh Berries & Maple Syrup

Sautéed Canadian Bacon

Warm Apricot Jewel (page 197)

Springtime Holiday Menu

Pictured on facing page

Whatever the occasion—Easter, Mother's Day, or graduation—spring is the season to celebrate special family events. What better way than by putting fresh asparagus and plump, juicy strawberries on the menu?

Grilled Turkey with Peaches (page 106)

Confetti Wild Rice (page 156)

Gingered Asparagus (page 172)

Angel Food Cake (page 192) with Fresh Strawberries

Fourth of July Barbecue

All-American favorites—with a twist—set the theme for this summertime meal. To grill the vegetables, brush the onion halves very lightly with olive oil and cook, cut sides down, until soft; husk the corn, wrap in foil, and grill for about 20 minutes.

Chili Chicken Chunks with Blender Salsa (page 45)

Potato & Avocado Salad (page 72)

Grilled Orange-Coriander Steak (page 87)

Grilled Onion Halves & Corn on the Cob

Oatmeal Raisin Cookies (page 199) & Vanilla Frozen Yogurt

Thanksgiving for a Crowd

Lean turkey breast is the centerpiece of this menu, instead of the traditional whole bird. Present it accompanied with a parade of wholesome appetizers and side dishes. Be careful to remove all the fat from the turkey drippings before making the gravy; use whole wheat bread as a base for your favorite stuffing. To serve an even dozen, double the recipe for the roasted potatoes.

Curried Spinach Dip (page 41) with Raw Vegetable Spears

Crabby Potatoes (page 47)

Roasted Turkey Breast with Gravy & Stuffing

Green Bean & Tomato Casserole (page 171)

Roasted Red & Yellow Potatoes (page 175)

Herb-Cheese Muffins (page 181)

Spiced Pumpkin Roll (page 195)

Southern-style Christmas Dinner

Try something new this year with a Christmas feast inspired by the traditions of the American South. Nippy Texas Caviar sets the pace for this spirited meal. Serve baked yam halves sprinkled with brown sugar. Make a recipe and a half of the tenderloins to serve eight people.

Chilled Apple-Ginger Spritzers (page 196)

Texas Caviar (page 38)

Orange-Onion Salad (page 68)

Spicy Pork Tenderloins (page 90)

Burgundy-braised Cabbage with Chestnuts (page 171)

Baked Yams with Brown Sugar

Old-fashioned Apple Cake (page 193)

■ MENUS FOR ENTERTAINING

Tailgate Extravaganza

Root the home team on to victory with this tailgate feast that requires no last-minute cooking. The cool appetizers and salads, plus a selection of purchased breads and cookies from your favorite bakery, create a smorgasbord of around-the-world flavors. You'll probably want to double the rice salad and double or triple the pasta dish to feed a large crowd.

Turkey-Broccoli Bundles (page 44)

Jicama & Fresh Fruit Platter (page 43)

Corn & Black Bean Salad (page 69)

Turkey & Rice Salad (page 76)

Summertime Pasta Alfresco (page 140)

Assorted Breads & Cookies

Iced Tea & Flavored Sparkling Mineral Water

Super Bowl Chili Fest

Watching athletes perform on television sometimes motivates people to evaluate their own condition. That's all the more reason to feature healthy recipes at your Super Bowl party. Start with baskets of low-fat tortilla chips with two tangy salsas for dipping; also offer copious bowls of popcorn to nibble during the action. At halftime, present an irresistible chili and salad menu, with sweet muffins for a finish.

Water-crisped Tortilla Chips (page 40) with Salsa Fresca (page 41) & Salsa Verde (page 41)

Garlic-Herb Popcorn (page 40)

Red & Yellow Pepper Salad (page 69)

Turkey & Corn Chili (page 108)

Cornmeal-Oat Muffins (page 180)

Assorted Beers & Sparkling Mineral Water

Kids' Birthday Party

Chips, fried chicken, mashed potatoes, and chocolate cake? If that doesn't sound like good nutrition to you, look again. Each of the wholesome recipes below is made with a minimum of fat, and all feature the familiar tastes that kids love. Even fussy eaters will like the easy-to-eat texture of the vegetables; just don't tell them that they're good for them, too!

Dry-roasted Potato Chips (page 40)

Oven-fried Chicken (page 98)

Mashed Potatoes & Broccoli (page 173)

Crazy Cocoa Cake (page 193)

Lowfat Milk

Afternoon Tea

Pictured on page 183

Rediscover the gracious art of afternoon tea and bring it up to date with a wholesome selection of high-fiber breads. Set the table lavishly with steaming mugs of herbal tea and an assortment of honey, jams, and preserves (omit the butter). Send any leftover bread home with your guests.

Irish Soda Bread (page 182)

Apricot–Oat Bran Scones (page 182)

Applesauce Raisin Bread (page 181)

Honey & Assorted Fruit Jams & Preserves

Herbal Tea with Sliced Lemon

Lunch for the Calorie-Conscious

What do you do when you want to entertain, but you know your guests are trying to diet? Be thoughtful and offer a lean chef's salad, little calzones, and fizzy sorbet sodas for dessert. With two calzones each, the menu totals less than 500 calories per person.

Sweet & Sour Onion Spread (page 41) with Celery Sticks

Chef's Salad with Fruit (page 74)

Mini-Calzones (page 180)

Fruit Sorbet Sodas (page 197)

Middle Eastern Buffet

Feature an array of exotic, subtly spiced dishes from the Middle East for a memorable dinner party. For an authentic presentation, offer all the dishes at the same time, letting guests eat at their own pace. Or, if you prefer a more familiar approach, serve the hummus as an appetizer, followed by the soup and the remaining courses. To serve eight, double all the recipes except the hummus.

Hummus with Pita Crisps (page 44)

Roasted Eggplant Soup (page 57)

Souvlaki in Pitas (page 85)

Lebanese Lentils with Bulgur (page 161)

Baked Apples & Figs with Cassis (page 195)

Festa Italiana

This Italian-inspired menu for four is a guarantee for a successful evening. Start off with crostini, a favorite Tuscan appetizer. A spectacular first course of creamy risotto is followed by a main-course offering of succulent veal stew and tender garden vegetables. Conclude with a platter of fresh figs or other seasonal fresh fruit, topped with yogurt and crumbled amaretti cookies.

Crostini with Fresh Tomatoes (page 43)

Saffron Risotto (page 150)

Mediterranean Veal Ragout (page 95)

Steamed Baby Summer Squash, Zucchini & Red Bell Pepper

Fresh Figs with Vanilla Lowfat Yogurt & Crumbled Amaretti

Chianti or Varietal Grape Juice

Chinese New Year's Buffet

Oriental accents make this unique party menu especially appropriate for Chinese New Year or any other festive occasion during the year. The sandwiches are offered with a variety of condiments to suit individual tastes. For dessert, toast the New Year with a fruit and champagne concoction and serve purchased fortune cookies alongside.

Sweet Potato & Carrot Soup (page 58)

Chinese Chicken Sandwiches (page 54)

Napa Cabbage Slaw (page 66)

Oranges in Ginger Champagne (page 189) with Fortune Cookies

Shore Dinner

"Seafood lovers' delight" aptly describes this buffet-style menu. Because it's served entirely at room temperature, it's a good choice for a summer party. The salmon recipe includes ample vegetables. To serve eight, double the soup and salmon recipes.

Shrimp with Tart Dipping Sauce (page 47)

Cool Scallop Soup (page 50)

Cool Salmon with Radish Tartar (page 118)

Dilled Bread (page 178) or Crusty French Bread

Oatie Peach Crumble (page 192)

When the Company's Special

Impress important guests with a sophisticated three-course dinner that's deceptively easy to prepare. You needn't worry about preparing a vegetable dish because the lamb recipe includes an elegant cucumber side dish.

Caribbean Corn Chowder (page 57)

Lamb Chops with Papaya Chutney (page 92)

Barley-Onion Pilaf (page 157)

Sherry-Plum Crisp (page 191)

Merlot or Zinfandel Wine

Appendix

Collected in this chapter are charts and references to help you build a light and healthy diet. On the following pages you'll find the guidelines for selecting and storing fresh produce, the Recommended Dietary Allowances (RDA) for nutrients, information on how to read food labels, and the American Heart Association Diet. The personal profile information on pages 226–227 will allow you to determine how many calories and grams of protein, carbohydrates, and fat you should consume each day. Finally, to choose recipes that will enable you to create well-balanced meals, consult the extended nutritional data beginning on page 228.

■ SELECTING & STORING FRESH PRODUCE

Fruit	Season	Selection	Ripening & Storage
Apples	All year	Choose a variety suitable for intended use. Look for bright color and a smooth, blemish-free surface.	Ripen apples for a few days at room temperature, if necessary. Store ripe apples in refrigerator in a plastic bag, or in a cool (32°F to 50°F) cellar. Weed out defective apples before storing.
Apricots	Mid-May–mid-August	Look for plump fruit with as much golden orange color as possible. Avoid fruit that's pale, shriveled, very hard, or bruised.	Ripen at room temperature until fruit gives to gentle pressure. Refrigerate ripe fruit in a paper or plastic bag for up to 2 days.
Avocados	All year	For best eating, fruit should give to gentle pressure; if rock hard when purchased, ripen first. Avoid fruit that looks badly bruised or that has any soft, dark, sunken spots.	Ripen hard avocados in a loosely closed paper bag at room temperature. Refrigerate cut or whole ripe avocados in a paper or plastic bag for up to 2 days.
Bananas	All year	Depending on preference, bananas can be eaten when firm and greenish yellow to clear yellow with some black spots.	Ripen green bananas at room temperature out of direct sun. Use ripe fruit quickly. Ripe bananas can be refrigerated, but skins will turn black.
Berries	May–July, depending on variety	Select firm, plump berries with full color. Check packaged berries carefully for mold.	Berries don't ripen after picking; use within 2 days. Store unwashed berries in a pan lined with paper towels; top with towels, cover with plastic wrap, and refrigerate for up to 2 days. Rinse just before using.
Cherries	Mid-May–July	Look for plump, brightly colored fruit with light, pliable stems. Colors range from deep mahogany red to pale yellow.	Cherries are very perishable; store, unwashed, as directed for Berries (above) for up to 3 days. Rinse just before using.
Citrus	All year	Choose firm, thin-skinned fruit that's fully colored for its type and heavy for its size.	Citrus fruits are sold ripe. Store at cool room temperature for up to 1 week or refrigerate for up to 2 weeks.
Grapes	All year	Look for plump, even-colored grapes firmly attached to pliable green stems. Avoid soft or wrinkled fruit.	Grapes are sold ripe and ready to eat. Refrigerate, unwashed, in a paper or plastic bag for 2 to 5 days, depending on variety. Rinse just before using.
Kiwi fruit	All year	Choose evenly firm fruit free of mold and soft spots. Kiwis are ready to eat when as soft as a ripe peach.	Ripen firm fruit at room temperature out of direct sun. Refrigerate ripe fruit in a plastic or paper bag for up to 1 week.
Melons	Sporadically all year, depending on variety	Choose melons that are evenly ripe with no soft, water-soaked areas or mold. Most melons emit a delicate fragrance when ripe.	Ripen, if necessary, at room temperature for a few days; once cut, melons won't ripen further. Refrigerate in sealed plastic bags.
Nectarines	Mid-June–mid-September	Choose fruit with an orange yellow (not green) background between red areas. Ripe nectarines give to gentle pressure but aren't as soft as a ripe peach.	Ripen firm-ripe fruit at room temperature out of direct sun. Refrigerate ripe fruit in a plastic or paper bag for up to 1 week.
Papayas	Usually all year	Most papayas are sold firm-ripe; they should be as soft as a ripe peach when ready to eat. Look for papayas that are more yellow than green. Avoid bruised fruit.	Ripen at room temperature in a loosely closed paper bag. Refrigerate ripe fruit in a plastic or paper bag for up to 3 days.

(Continued on next page)

Fruit	Season	Selection	Ripening & Storage
Peaches	Mid-May–mid-October	Choose fruit with a creamy or yellow background color. Ripe peaches give to gentle pressure.	Ripen and store, unwashed, as directed for Papayas (page 219).
Pears	All year	Choose fruit that's well colored for its variety; minor surface blemishes don't affect quality of flesh. Use fully ripe pears immediately (best for eating out of hand). For slicing or cooking, use firm-ripe pears.	Ripen firm pears at room temperature in a loosely closed paper bag until they reach desired stage of ripeness (3 to 7 days). Refrigerate ripe pears in a plastic or paper bag for up to 3 days.
Pineapple	All year	Select large, plump, fresh-looking pineapples with fresh green leaves and a sweet fragrance. Thumping fruit or pulling a leaf from crown isn't an indication of ripeness.	Ripe pineapples deteriorate rapidly, so use soon after purchase. Store at room temperature out of direct sun for up to 2 days. Refrigerate cut pieces, wrapped in plastic, for up to 1 week.
Plums	Mid-May–mid-October	Look for full color for variety. Ripe plums are slightly soft at tip end and give when gently squeezed.	Ripen firm plums in a loosely closed paper bag, checking daily. Refrigerate ripe fruit, unwashed, in a plastic or paper bag for up to 3 days.

Vegetable	Season	Selection	Storage
Artichokes	Peak March–mid-May	Choose tight, compact heads that feel heavy for their size. Surface brown spots, caused by frost, don't affect quality.	Refrigerate, unwashed, in a plastic bag for up to 1 week.
Asparagus	Peak March–June	Choose firm, brittle spears that are bright green almost their entire length, with tightly closed tips.	Wrap ends in a damp paper towel. Refrigerate, unwashed, in a plastic bag for up to 4 days.
Beans, green and wax	All year	Choose slender, crisp beans that are bright and blemish-free. Avoid mature beans with large seeds and swollen pods.	Refrigerate, unwashed, in a plastic bag for up to 4 days.
Broccoli	All year	Look for compact clusters of tightly closed dark green flowerets.	Refrigerate, unwashed, in a plastic bag for up to 5 days.
Cabbage	All year	Choose firm heads that feel heavy for their size, with fresh-looking, blemish-free outer leaves.	Refrigerate, unwashed, in a plastic bag for up to 1 week (up to 4 days for napa cabbage).
Carrots	All year	Choose firm, clean, well-shaped carrots with bright orange gold color. Those with tops still attached are likely to be freshest.	Cut off and discard green tops, if necessary, leaving 1 to 2 inches attached. Refrigerate, unwashed, in a plastic bag for up to 2 weeks.
Cauliflower	All year	Choose firm, compact, creamy white heads with flowerets pressed tightly together. Any leaves should be crisp and bright green.	Refrigerate, unwashed, in a plastic bag for up to 1 week.
Corn	Peak May–September	For best flavor, eat corn on the day it's purchased. Choose fresh-looking ears with green husks, moist stems, and silk ends free of decay.	Wrap unhusked ears in damp paper towels. If necessary, refrigerate in a plastic bag for up to 2 days.
Eggplant	All year	Look for firm eggplant that's heavy for its size, with taut, glossy, deeply colored skin.	Refrigerate, unwashed, in a plastic bag for up to 5 days.
Jicama	Most of year; peak October–June	Choose firm, well-formed tubers that are free of blemishes. Larger jicama tends to have a coarser texture.	Store whole jicama, unwashed, in a cool (50°F), dry, dark place with good ventilation for up to 3 weeks. Wrap cut pieces in plastic and refrigerate for up to 1 week.

Vegetable	Season	Selection	Storage
Mushrooms	All year	Look for fresh, blemish-free mushrooms with no slimy spots or signs of decay. For button mushrooms, choose smooth caps that are closed around stems.	Wrap in paper towels and refrigerate, unwashed, in a paper bag for up to 4 days.
Onions	All year (October–May for leeks)	Choose *chives* with all-over green color, *green onions* and *leeks* with crisp, bright green tops and clean white bottoms. *Shallots* and *dry onions* should be firm, with brittle outer skin; avoid those with sprouting green shoots or soft spots.	*Chives:* Rinse, shake dry, and wrap in paper towels. Refrigerate in a plastic bag for up to 4 days. *Green onions and leeks:* Refrigerate, unwashed, in a plastic bag for up to 1 week. *Shallots and dry onions:* Store, unwrapped, in a cool (50°F), dry, dark place with good ventilation for up to 2 months.
Peas	April–August for green and shell peas, February–June for edible-pod peas	Choose firm, crisp, bright green pods; *green peas* should be small, plump, and well filled with medium-size peas.	Refrigerate all peas, unwashed, in a plastic bag for up to 3 days.
Peppers	All year	Choose bright, glossy peppers that are firm and well shaped; avoid those with soft spots, gashes, or shriveled skin.	Refrigerate, unwashed, in a plastic bag for up to 5 days.
Potatoes	All year	Choose firm, smooth potatoes with no wrinkles, sprouts, cracks, bruises, decay, or bitter green areas.	Buy only as many potatoes as you can use in 1 to 2 weeks. Store in a cool (50°F), dry, dark place with good ventilation; do not store in an airtight plastic bag.
Spinach	All year	Choose bunches with crisp, tender, unblemished, deep green leaves.	Discard any yellow, damaged, or wilted leaves. Refrigerate, unwashed, in a plastic bag for up to 3 days. Remove stems just before using.
Squash	Peak July–September for summer squash, September–March for winter squash	*Summer squash:* Select firm, smooth-skinned squash that feel heavy for their size. *Winter squash:* Choose hard, thick-shelled squash that feel heavy for their size.	*Summer squash:* Refrigerate, unwashed, in a plastic bag for up to 5 days. *Winter squash:* Store whole squash, unwrapped, in a cool (50°F), dry, dark place with good ventilation for up to 2 months. Wrap cut pieces in plastic wrap and refrigerate for up to 5 days.
Sweet potatoes	All year	Choose firm, well-shaped potatoes with bright, uniformly colored skin.	Store in a cool (50°F), dry, dark place with good ventilation for up to 2 months or at room temperature for up to 1 week.
Swiss chard	Most of year; peak July–October	Look for bunches with fresh, glossy leaves and heavy white or red stems.	Refrigerate, unwashed, in a plastic bag for up to 3 days.
Tomatoes	All year	Choose smooth, well-formed tomatoes that are firm (but not hard) and heavy for their size. Vine-ripened tomatoes, mostly available in summer, have better flavor than commercially ripened ones.	Store at room temperature until ready to use. Refrigerate very ripe tomatoes for up to 4 days.

■ A GUIDE TO THE RDA

First issued in 1943 and most recently updated by the National Research Council in 1989, the Recommended Dietary Allowances (RDA) suggest daily intake levels for essential nutrients for different groups of people in the United States. Because they're set well above the mean requirements of most individuals, the RDA cover almost everyone's needs by a comfortable margin.

Designed as a way for normal people to maintain their good health, the RDA can be met by eating a balanced, varied diet. It's unrealistic to try to meet each RDA every day. Instead, plan menus that allow you to meet your RDA over a week, a more reasonable span of time.

The U.S. RDA. The U.S. Recommended Daily Allowances, used on food labels, are standards set by the Food and Drug Administration (FDA). The figures are based on the highest RDA level for each nutrient, which makes the numbers very generous. The U.S. RDA weren't modified in the 1989 RDA revision.

■ Recommended Dietary Allowances

The allowances, expressed as average daily intakes over time, are intended to provide for individual variations among most normal persons as they live in the United States under usual environmental stresses. Diets should be based on a variety of common foods in order to provide other nutrients for which human requirements have been less well defined.

				Vitamins												Minerals						
Age (years)	Weight	Height	Protein	Vitamin A	Vitamin D	Vitamin E	Vitamin K	Vitamin C	Thiamin	Riboflavin	Niacin	Vitamin B6	Folacin	Vitamin B12	Calcium	Iodine	Iron	Magnesium	Phosphorus	Selenium	Zinc
	Lbs.	In.	g	RE*	µg	αTE	µg	mg	mg	mg	mg NE	mg	µg	µg	mg	µg	mg	mg	mg	µg	mg
Infants																					
0.0–0.5	13	24	13	375	7.5	3	5	30	0.3	0.4	5	0.3	25	0.3	400	40	6	40	300	10	5
0.5–1.0	20	28	14	375	10	4	10	35	0.4	0.5	6	0.6	35	0.5	600	50	10	60	500	15	5
Children																					
1–3	29	35	16	400	10	6	15	40	0.7	0.8	9	1.0	50	0.7	800	70	10	80	800	20	10
4–6	44	44	24	500	10	7	20	45	0.9	1.1	12	1.1	75	1.0	800	90	10	120	800	20	10
7–10	62	52	28	700	10	7	30	45	1.0	1.2	13	1.4	100	1.4	800	120	10	170	800	30	10
Males																					
11–14	99	62	45	1,000	10	10	45	50	1.3	1.5	17	1.7	150	2.0	1,200	150	12	270	1,200	40	15
15–18	145	69	59	1,000	10	10	65	60	1.5	1.8	20	2.0	200	2.0	1,200	150	12	400	1,200	50	15
19–24	160	70	58	1,000	10	10	70	60	1.5	1.7	19	2.0	200	2.0	1,200	150	10	350	1,200	70	15
25–50	174	70	63	1,000	5	10	80	60	1.5	1.7	19	2.0	200	2.0	800	150	10	350	800	70	15
51+	170	68	63	1,000	5	10	80	60	1.2	1.4	15	2.0	200	2.0	800	150	10	350	800	70	15
Females																					
11–14	101	62	46	800	10	8	45	50	1.1	1.3	15	1.4	150	2.0	1,200	150	15	280	1,200	45	12
15–18	120	64	44	800	10	8	55	60	1.1	1.3	15	1.5	180	2.0	1,200	150	15	300	1,200	50	12
19–24	128	65	46	800	10	8	60	60	1.1	1.3	15	1.6	180	2.0	1,200	150	15	280	1,200	55	12
25–50	138	64	50	800	5	8	65	60	1.1	1.3	15	1.6	180	2.0	800	150	15	280	800	55	12
51+	143	63	50	800	5	8	65	60	1.0	1.2	13	1.6	180	2.0	800	150	10	280	800	55	12
Pregnant			60	800	10	10	65	70	1.5	1.6	17	2.2	400	2.2	1,200	175	30	320	1,200	65	15
Lactating																					
1st 6 months			65	1,300	10	12	65	95	1.6	1.8	20	2.1	280	2.6	1,200	200	15	355	1,200	75	19
2nd 6 months			62	1,200	10	11	65	90	1.6	1.7	20	2.1	260	2.6	1,200	200	15	340	1,200	75	16

Reprinted by permission from Recommended Dietary Allowances, © 1989, by the National Academy of Sciences, National Academy Press, Washington, DC

*1 RE of Vitamin A = approximately 5 IU (see page 10)

µg = microgram. TE = tocopherol equivalents (1 mg d-α tocopherol = 1 α-TE).

NE = niacin equivalent (equal to 1 mg of niacin or 60 mg dietary tryptophan).

■ READING FOOD LABELS

Supermarket shelves are crammed with products advertising their health benefits, from vegetable oils proclaiming "No Cholesterol" to cereal boxes announcing "All Natural." How can the average consumer interpret and verify those claims? The best way is to learn how to read food labels.

Since 1975, the Food and Drug Administration (FDA) has required that foods to which nutrients have been added or those that make health claims contain nutritional information. Labeling of meat and poultry is regulated by the U.S. Department of Agriculture (USDA). Most other food labeling is voluntary; however, it's expected to become more strictly regulated in the future.

What's required on a nutrition label? If a food requires labeling, the following information must appear: serving size; number of servings; calories per serving; protein, carbohydrates, and fat in grams (g) per serving; milligrams (mg) of sodium per serving; and percentage of the U.S. Recommended Daily Allowances (U.S. RDA) for protein, several vitamins, and minerals per serving. Finally, the ingredients must be listed in descending order by weight. Amounts of cholesterol, fiber, and fat aren't required, nor is the percentage of total calories that come from protein, carbohydrates, or fat. (To calculate those percentages, use the formulas on page 227. As a rule of thumb, foods with no more than 3 grams of fat per 100 calories get 30% or less of their total calories from fat.)

Moreover, because serving sizes aren't standardized, manufacturers can make their own rules. Often, the consumer must figure out how many crackers there are in a 1-ounce serving or how much ice cream is contained in a 3-fluid-ounce serving. Trying to compare similar products with different serving sizes can be particularly difficult.

Ingredients. Always read the list of ingredients carefully. If no ingredients from animal sources are listed, it will be naturally cholesterol free, though it may still be high in saturated fat (note the types of fats used). Even if sugar isn't listed first, it still may be the principal ingredient; check the list for other types of sugars, such as corn syrup, fructose, honey, or sorbitol.

Use the ingredient list to compare a product against a similar one of another brand; this may allow you to choose the healthier product.

What do food labeling terms mean? The use of such terms as light, natural, or no cholesterol is very loosely controlled. To help you sort through the realities and myths, here's a brief glossary:

■ *Lean:* For meats and poultry, this means no more than 10% fat by weight. *Extra-lean* meat and poultry products must contain no more than 5% fat by weight. This doesn't mean that only 5% or 10% of the *calories* come from fat.

■ *Light, lite:* This very ambiguous, unregulated term can mean fewer calories, lighter color (as in the case of light olive oil), lighter density (light cream versus heavy cream), less salt, lighter flavor, or whatever the manufacturer wants. For meats and poultry, "light" products must contain 25% less fat than similar products. The term can also apply to products with reduced calories, sodium, or breading; the label must indicate what has been reduced.

■ *Low calorie:* Foods that contain no more than 40 calories per serving or no more than 0.4 calories per gram can be labeled low calorie.

■ *Lowfat:* Lowfat dairy products contain between 0.5% and 2% fat by weight (not the same as percent of total calories). For meats, "lowfat" means no more than 10% fat by weight (the same as "lean").

■ *Natural:* There is no nationally regulated definition of this term, except for meat and poultry. For these, the USDA defines "natural" as minimally processed and containing no artificial flavors, colors, or preservatives. Otherwise, it can mean whatever the manufacturer wishes.

■ *No cholesterol:* The use of this term is completely unregulated, which accounts for its appearance on products that never contained cholesterol in the first place, such as vegetable oils. Remember: Only foods of animal origin contain cholesterol.

■ *Reduced calorie:* A reduced-calorie product must contain a third fewer calories than the original, with a comparison of both versions printed on the label.

■ *Salt free, unsalted, no salt added:* Any of these terms indicates that no salt was added during processing. However, the food may contain sodium either naturally or from nonsalt sources.

■ *Sodium:* Foods that are *sodium free* must contain no more than 5 milligrams of sodium per serving, *very low sodium* no more than 35 milligrams per serving, and *low sodium* no more than 140 milligrams per serving. Products sold as *reduced sodium* must contain 75% less sodium than the original.

■ *Sugar free, sugarless:* Foods labeled this way cannot contain sucrose (table sugar), but that doesn't mean that other sweeteners aren't present. If the food isn't low in calories, the label must clarify this.

■ THE AMERICAN HEART ASSOCIATION DIET

Vegetables & Fruits

High in Vitamins, Minerals, Potassium, Fiber; Low in Fat, Calories, Sodium…Contain *no* Cholesterol

Okay Foods:

Almost all vegetables and fruits are "Okay Foods" and should be part of your daily eating plan.

Use at least 3 servings (Sv) of fruit or real fruit juice every day. (1 Sv = 1 medium-sized piece of fruit or ½ cup juice or canned fruit.) Also, use at least 3 servings of vegetables every day. (1 Sv = ½ to 1 cup, cooked or raw.)

Include *at least one serving* from the High Vitamin C list every day and *at least one serving* from the High Vitamin A list several times a week:

High Vitamin C—Asparagus, broccoli, cabbage, cantaloupe, grapefruit, greens (mustard, beet, kale, collards), green pepper, oranges, potatoes, spinach, strawberries, tangerines, tomatoes.

High Vitamin A—Broccoli, cantaloupe, carrots, greens, peaches, pumpkin, spinach, sweet potatoes, winter squash.

When you are reducing your intake of red meat and egg yolks, you can *increase your iron intake* by eating more green, leafy vegetables; peas and beans (fresh and dried); dried fruits; and whole-grain or enriched cereals. *Your body can make better use of the iron these foods provide if you eat them along with a good source of Vitamin C.*

Enjoy plenty of vegetables and fruits. If you are watching your weight, these foods will give you the most nutrition for the fewest calories.

Foods to Avoid:

Almost all fruits and vegetables are very low in fat, except:

Coconut, Coconut Oil, Palm Oil, and Palm Kernel Oil—Contain saturated fat and should be avoided.

Olives ▲ and Avocados—Also contain fat (and therefore are higher in calories). Tips for using these are included in the "Fats and Oils" section.

Milk Products

High in Protein, Calcium, Phosphorus, Niacin, Riboflavin, Vitamins A and D

Okay Foods:

Milk Products Containing Only 0–1% Milk Fat—Skim milk or fluid nonfat milk *(0% fat);* low-fat milk *(1% fat);* nonfat or low-fat dry milk; evaporated skim milk; buttermilk made from skim or low-fat milk; skim or low-fat yogurt; drinks made with skim or low-fat milk and cocoa or other low-fat drink powders; ice milk, sherbet, frozen low-fat yogurt.

Low-Fat Cheeses—Dry-curd or low-fat cottage cheese ▲; low-fat natural cheeses ▲ or processed special cheeses ▲ *labeled as containing not more than two grams of fat per ounce.*

Begin trying lower-in-fat milk products. Whole milk is 4% fat. If you use whole milk now, first try 2% fat milk…Then move along to 1% fat milk…Soon, you will enjoy the taste of skim milk.

Look for milk products labeled *fortified with vitamins A and D.* Adults and young children need 2 servings daily (1 Sv = 8 oz. low-fat or skim milk or yogurt, 2 oz. low-fat cheese, or ½ cup low-fat cottage cheese); older children, teenagers and women who are pregnant or breastfeeding need 3–4 servings.

Foods to Avoid:

Milk Products Containing More Than 1% Milk Fat—Low-fat milk with 1½–2% milk fat; whole milk; dried whole milk; buttermilk or yogurt made from whole milk; drinks made from whole milk; condensed milk; evaporated milk; ice cream.

Cream, All Kinds—Half and half, light, heavy, whipping or sour.

Nondairy Cream Substitutes—Coffee creamers, sour cream substitutes made with *coconut, palm, or palm kernel oil, which are high in saturated fat.* Look for special ones labeled *"made from poly-unsaturated fat."*

All Cheeses Containing More Than 2 Grams of Fat Per Ounce—Cream cheese ■ creamed cottage cheese ■ and most other natural and processed cheeses ■ such as American, Swiss, mozzarella and blue.

Fats & Oils

Some of these foods are high in Vitamin A or E, but *all* are high in fat and calories. The amount of food per serving (Sv) is described for each item so you can keep track of fat intake in teaspoons (tsp).

Okay Foods:

Vegetable Oils—Safflower, sunflower, corn, partially hydrogenated soybean, cottonseed, sesame, canola, olive. (1 Sv = 1 tsp)

Margarines—Stick, tub, squeeze (1 Sv = 1 tsp) or diet (1 Sv = 2 tsp)—One of the "Okay" vegetable oils should be listed as the first ingredient on the label with twice as much polyunsaturated as saturated fat.

Salad Dressing and Mayonnaise ●—Homemade or store-bought, made with "Okay" oils (1 Sv = 2 tsp). Low-calorie dressings ● can be used as desired.

Seeds and Nuts—All seeds ● (pumpkin, sesame, sunflower) and most nuts ● (except cashew and macadamia). (1 Sv = 3 tsp)

Avocados and Olives ▲—Use only in small amounts. (1 Sv = 3 tsp chopped)

Peanut Butter ●—Count as a fat (1 Sv = 2 tsp) or use as a "Meatless Main Dish." (1 Sv = 3 tsp)

Peanut Oil—This choice is not as good as the "Okay" oils. It may be used sparingly for a flavor change.

Depending upon your need for weight control, use no more than 5–8 servings of "Okay" fats and oils per day.

Remember to count the "hidden fats" (in bakery products and snack foods, in cooking, on vegetables and breads).

Use cooking styles which use little or no fat—instead of frying, try roasting, broiling, steaming.

Foods to Avoid:

Solid Fats and Shortenings—Butter ●, bacon drippings ■, ham hocks ■, lard, salt pork ■, meat fat and drippings, gravy from meat drippings, shortening, suet; margarines except those listed as "Okay."

Chocolate, Coconut, Coconut Oil, Palm Oil, or Palm Kernel Oil—These are often used in bakery products, nondairy creamers, whipped toppings, candy and commercially fried foods. *Read labels carefully.*

Breads, Cereals, Pasta & Starchy Vegetables

Low in Fat and Cholesterol; High in B Vitamins, Iron, Fiber

Okay Foods:

Low-Fat Breads—All kinds (wheat, rye, raisin, white); those with whole-grain or enriched flours are best. (1 Sv = 1 slice)

Low-Fat Rolls—English muffins, frankfurter and hamburger buns, water (not egg) bagels, pita bread, tortillas (not fried).

Low-Fat Crackers and Snacks—Animal, graham, rye, saltine●, oyster● and matzo crackers; store-bought fig bar, ginger snap and molasses cookies; bread sticks, melba toast, rusks and flatbread; pretzels ●, popcorn● (with "Okay" fat).

Hot or Cold Cereals—All kinds, except granola-type cereals with coconut or coconut oil. (1 Sv = ¼–¾ cup)

Rice and Pasta—All kinds (pasta made without egg). (1 Sv = ½ cup)

Starchy Vegetables—Potatoes, lima beans, green peas, winter squash, corn, yams or sweet potatoes. (1 Sv = ¼–½ cup)

Quick Breads—Home-made with "Okay" fats, oils and milk products—Biscuits, muffins, cornbread, banana bread, soft rolls, pancakes, French toast and waffles. Use your weekly egg yolk allowance (3 per week), or try egg whites in recipes. Use two egg whites instead of one whole egg.

Low-Fat Soups—Broth●, bouillon●, chicken noodle●, tomato-based seafood chowders●, minestrone●, onion●, split pea●, tomato●, vegetarian vegetable● Use the canned or powdered varieties, but *read labels* to choose those lowest in salt and fat. Better still, make soups at home so that you can avoid salt, fat, cream, whole milk or cheese. (1 Sv = 1 cup)

Breads, cereals, pasta and starchy vegetables (in moderate-sized portions) are not extremely high in calories. It's the fat and sauces added to them that run up the total calories.

Stretch your meat allowance and your budget by combining small portions of poultry, fish or meat with vegetables, herbs, and rice or pasta.

Foods to Avoid:

Products made with egg yolks or with "AVOID" fats, oils and whole milk products:

Butter rolls, egg breads, egg bagels, cheese breads, croissants, commercial doughnuts, muffins, sweet rolls, biscuits, waffles, pancakes; buttered popcorn■; store-bought mixes.

High-fat commercial crackers such as cheese crackers■, butter crackers■ and those made with coconut oil, palm oil, or palm kernel oil.

Pasta, rice and vegetables prepared with whole eggs, cream sauce or high-fat cheese; or fried in "AVOID" fats.

Cream soups■, vichyssoise■ and chunky-style soups■ which have large amounts of meat in them.

Meat, Poultry, Seafood, Nuts…Dried Beans & Peas…Eggs

High in Protein, B Vitamins, Iron, Other Minerals

Okay Foods:

Chicken and Turkey—Trim the skin; this is where much of the fat is found.

Lean Beef, Veal, Pork, Lamb—Trim all visible fat.

Fish and Shellfish—All kinds, but limit the use of shrimp or lobster to *no more than* one serving of one of these per week.

Meatless or "Low-Meat" Main Dishes—Try recipes with dried beans, peas, lentils, soybean curd (tofu), peanut butter● or low-fat cheese▲ instead of meat a few times a week. Also try combining small amounts of meat, fish or poultry with rice or pasta in mixed dishes or casseroles.

Egg Whites—But limit whole eggs or egg yolks to no more than three to four per week, including those used in cooking.

Wild Game—Rabbit, pheasant, venison, wild duck and other wild game animals generally have less fat than animals raised for the market.

Adults need no more than 6 ounces of meat, poultry or seafood per day (about two small servings). Examples of a 3-ounce portion:
  ½ of a chicken breast or a chicken leg and a thigh together
  ½ cup of flaked fish
  2 thin slices lean roast beef (3″ x 3″ x ¼″)
Preschool children should have about one ounce of meat, poultry or seafood per day for each year of age.

Use poultry (without the skin) and fish more often than red meat.

Instead of high-fat luncheon meats, choose low-fat processed sandwich meats with *labels showing no more than 2 grams fat per ounce* such as turkey▲ or chicken roll▲, turkey ham▲, turkey pastrami▲ or lean boiled ham▲

Buy only the leanest ground beef, *labeled as containing no more than 15% fat*. Pour off the fat after browning. Ask your butcher for the fat content, if it is not noted on the label.

Skim the fat off meat juices before adding to stews, soups and gravy. Chilling the meat juices first allows you to easily remove the hardened fat.

Foods to Avoid:

Meats—"Prime" grade and other heavily-marbled and fatty meats such as corned beef■, regular pastrami■, short ribs, spareribs, rib eye roast or steak, regular ground meat, frankfurters■, sausage■, bacon■ and high-fat luncheon meats■.

Goose and Domestic Duck

Organ Meats—Brains, chitterlings, gizzard, heart, kidney, sweetbreads, pork maws and liver are high in cholesterol. However, liver is so rich in iron and vitamins, a small serving (3 ounces) is recommended about once a month.

Desserts, Beverages & Snacks

Okay Foods:

The foods listed here are low in saturated fat and cholesterol but many are high in calories and low in nutritional value. Use the foods from the other five food lists to make your eating plan. Then occasionally choose a few of the foods listed below to add interest. For weight control, select from the first two lists. If you are at your recommended weight, add selections from the "Other Choices" list.

First Choice (low in calories or no calories)—Raw vegetables, fresh fruit, fruit canned without sugar, plain gelatin, tea, coffee and cocoa powder.

Second Choice (low in saturated fat, fairly low in calories)—Frozen or canned fruit with sugar, dried fruits; seeds; "Okay" nuts ●; plain popcorn●; pretzels●; "Okay" crackers● or cookies; sherbet, ice milk; frozen or fruited low-fat yogurt; angel food cake.

Other Choices (higher in calories)
Foods that are low in fat, also low in nutrition—Hard candy, gum drops; flavored gelatin; water ices; fruit punches, carbonated drinks; sugar, syrup, honey, jam, jelly, marmalade.

Special recipe items—Home-made desserts (cakes, pies, cookies and puddings) made with the fats and oils, low-fat milk products and egg products listed as "Okay."

Alcoholic beverages—If you drink, do so in moderation; no more than two drinks per day of wine, beer or liquor.

Foods To Avoid:

Other desserts and snacks not listed above, such as store-bought cakes, pies, cookies and mixes; coconut; high-fat snack products such as deep fried chips ■ and rich crackers■; desserts and snacks containing cheese■, cream or whole milk, and ice cream.

Be Salt-Wise

The following codes used in the food lists identify store-bought foods which are usually very high in salt or fat.

▲ means that although the food is okay for occasional use, it has a high salt content which cannot be removed.

● means the food usually contains salt, but good low-salt products are available.

■ means the food is high in *both* salt and dietary fat and cholesterol, making it a very poor food choice.

■ PERSONAL PROFILE & WEIGHT CHARTS

Good nutrition depends on the right distribution of nutrients, both caloric and noncaloric (see pages 8–11). The recommended daily intake of the caloric nutrients—protein, carbohydrates, and fat—is usually expressed as percentages: ideally, about 15% of total calories should come from protein, about 55% from carbohydrates, and 30% or less from fat.

But recipe analyses and food labels generally list protein, carbohydrates, and fat content in grams. How can you determine how many grams of each you should consume? First, you need to find your desirable body weight and, using that number, calculate your daily intake of calories. Then, based on your calorie level, you can figure how many grams of each nutrient you should eat in a day.

Determining desirable body weight. Your daily intake of protein, carbohydrates, and fat is based on your daily caloric intake, which, in turn, is predicated on your desirable body weight. To determine that number, you'll need to know whether your frame size is small, medium, or large.

Perform this simple test: Extend your arm; then bend the forearm up at a 90° angle. Keeping your fingers straight, turn the inside of your wrist toward your body. Place the thumb and index finger of your other hand on the two prominent bones on either side of your elbow. Measure the space between your fingers against a ruler or tape measure.

Compare this figure with the measurements for a medium frame given in the chart below. Measurements lower than those listed mean you have a small frame; higher measurements indicate a large frame. Once you've determined your frame size, use the second chart to find your desirable weight range.

Medium Frame Size

Men

Height (without shoes)	Elbow Breadth
5'1"–5'2"	2½"–2⅞"
5'3"–5'6"	2⅝"–2⅞"
5'7"–5'10"	2¾"–3"
5'11"–6'2"	2¾"–3⅛"
6'3"	2⅞"–3¼"

Women

Height (without shoes)	Elbow Breadth
4'9"–4'10"	2¼"–2½"
4'11"–5'2"	2¼"–2½"
5'3"–5'6"	2⅜"–2⅝"
5'7"–5'10"	2⅜"–2⅝"

Desirable Body Weight Ranges

Men

Height (without shoes)	Small Frame (lbs.)	Medium Frame (lbs.)	Large Frame (lbs.)
5'2"	108–116	114–126	122–137
5'3"	111–119	117–129	125–141
5'4"	114–122	120–132	128–145
5'5"	117–126	123–136	131–149
5'6"	121–130	127–140	135–154
5'7"	125–134	131–145	140–159
5'8"	129–138	135–149	144–163
5'9"	133–143	139–153	148–167
5'10"	137–147	143–158	152–172
5'11"	141–151	147–163	157–177
6'0"	145–155	151–168	161–182
6'1"	149–160	155–173	166–187
6'2"	153–164	160–178	171–192
6'3"	157–168	165–183	175–197

Women

Height (without shoes)	Small Frame (lbs.)	Medium Frame (lbs.)	Large Frame (lbs.)
4'9"	90–97	94–106	102–118
4'10"	92–100	97–109	105–121
4'11"	95–103	100–112	108–124
5'0"	98–106	103–115	111–127
5'1"	101–109	106–118	114–130
5'2"	104–112	109–122	117–134
5'3"	107–115	112–126	121–138
5'4"	110–119	116–131	125–142
5'5"	114–123	120–135	129–146
5'6"	118–127	124–139	133–150
5'7"	122–131	128–143	137–154
5'8"	126–136	132–147	141–159
5'9"	130–140	136–151	145–164
5'10"	134–144	140–155	149–169

Source: 1959 Metropolitan Desirable Weight Table, courtesy of Metropolitan Life Insurance Company

Daily calorie consumption. With your desirable body weight determined, you can now calculate how many calories you should eat each day simply by multiplying that number by 14 if you're male and by 12 if you're female. For example, a 6'0" male with a large frame who weighs 165 pounds can consume about 2,300 calories a day. A 5'4" female with a medium-size frame who weighs 125 pounds should plan on eating about 1,500 calories each day. (Note that the recommendations are for the moderately active person; if you exercise at a higher level, your caloric intake will be higher.)

Grams of protein, carbohydrates, and fat.
Once you know the number of calories you can consume each day, you can determine how many grams of protein, carbohydrates, and fat you should eat. As mentioned earlier, an ideal breakdown is about 15% of total calories from protein, about 55% from carbohydrates, and 30% or less from fat.

To convert those percentages into grams, use the formulas below; or refer to the chart at right. Use the figures as guidelines, not as absolutes.

■ *Protein:* Multiply the total number of calories in your daily intake by 15%, or .15, to arrive at total protein calories per day. Divide this number by 4 (the number of calories in 1 gram of protein). The result is the number of grams of protein you should consume per day. For example, if your total caloric intake is about 2,000 calories a day, multiply 2,000 by .15 to get 300 calories a day from protein. Then divide by 4 to get 75 grams of protein per day.

Note that there is also an RDA for protein (see page 222). While most people consuming 15% of their daily calories in protein will generously meet the RDA, persons on restricted-calorie diets may have to slightly increase the percentage of protein in their diet to meet the RDA. Conversely, those consuming lots of calories may want to reduce their protein intake to less than 15% (and increase consumption of carbohydrates) to stay closer to the RDA for protein.

■ *Carbohydrates:* Multiply the total number of calories in your daily intake by 55% (.55) to arrive at total carbohydrate calories per day. Divide this number by 4 (the number of calories in 1 gram of carbohydrates). The result is the number of grams of carbohydrates you should consume per day. For example, if your total caloric intake is about 2,000 calories a day, multiply 2,000 by .55 to get 1,100 calories a day from carbohydrates. Then divide by 4 to get 275 grams of carbohydrates per day.

■ *Fat:* Multiply the total number of calories in your daily intake by 30% (.30) to arrive at total fat calories per day. Divide this number by 9 (the number of calories in 1 gram of fat). The result is

the number of grams of fat you should consume per day. For example, if your total caloric intake is about 2,000 calories a day, multiply 2,000 by .30 to get 600 calories a day from fat. Then divide by 9 to get 67 grams of fat per day.

Daily Caloric Intake (per day)	Protein (g) 15%/Cals.	Carbohydrates (g) 55%/Cals.	Total Fat (g) 30%/Cals.
1,200	45	165	40
1,500	56	206	50
1,800	68*	248	60
2,000	75*	275	67
2,200	83*	303	73
2,400	90*	330	80
2,600	98*	358	87

Note that these figures are higher than the adult male RDA for protein.

Counting grams. Once you know how many total grams of protein, carbohydrates, and fat you should be consuming each day, you can keep track of your intake by adding up the grams of protein, carbohydrates, and fat in the foods you're eating. Packaged foods usually list this information on the label (see page 223). For the recipes in this book, see the nutritional analysis following each recipe or refer to the data beginning on page 228.

Figuring percentages of total calories. Just as it's important to know how to convert percentages of nutrients into grams, it's also helpful to know how to convert grams of nutrients into percentages. You may want to use this information when comparing one packaged food or recipe to another. To do this, you simply work the formulas in reverse.

The following example shows how to calculate the percentages of nutrients in 1 cup of milk, which contains 149 calories. Note: Because the percentages have been rounded off, the total does not equal 100%.

■ *Protein:* A cup of milk contains 8 grams of protein. Multiply that number by 4 (the number of calories in 1 gram of protein) and then divide by total calories: $8 \times 4 = 32 \div 149 = .21$. The milk gets 21% of its total calories from protein.

■ *Carbohydrates:* A cup of milk contains 11 grams of carbohydrates. Use the same formula as for protein: $11 \times 4 = 44 \div 149 = .30$. The milk gets 30% of its total calories from carbohydrates.

■ *Fat:* A cup of milk contains 8 grams of fat. Multiply that number by 9 (the number of calories in 1 gram of fat) and divide by total calories: $8 \times 9 = 72 \div 149 = .48$. The milk gets 48% of its total calories from fat.

■ EXTENDED NUTRITIONAL DATA

On the following pages, you'll find nutritional analyses for recipes in this book, presented alphabetically by chapter. Use this chart as a reference guide in choosing recipes and composing menus that meet your dietary goals.

Each recipe lists nutritional data per serving for calories, protein, carbohydrates, total fat, saturated fat, cholesterol, and sodium. Below you'll find additional data for dietary fiber, calcium, iron, vitamin A, and vitamin C.

Recipe	Calories	Protein (g)	Carbs. (g)	Total Fat (g)	Sat. Fat (g)	Chol. (mg)	Sodium (mg)	Fiber (g)	Calcium (mg)	Iron (mg)	Vit. A (IU)	Vit. C (mg)
BREAKFASTS												
Banana-Oatmeal Pancakes (page 34)	252	8	39	8	2	45	247	4	135	1	137	19
Blueberry Muffins (page 32)	265	6	48	6	1	37	331	3	145	2	89	4
Couscous in Cantaloupe (page 30)	302	12	49	8	2	3	80	3*	139	1	6,984	92
Fruit Muesli (page 30)	127	3	28	1	0.2	0	2	3	20	1	348	3
Homestead Bran Muffins (page 32)	213	5	37	7	0.9	19	211	5	45	2	516	9
Joe's Morning Special (page 33)	151	12	14	6	1	54	187	4	135	4	6,109	142
Orange-Yogurt Waffles (page 34)	264	12	38	7	2	76	488	2	209	1	345	6
Tropical Ham Plate (page 33)	303	11	53	8	1	21	608	5	50	2	206	91
APPETIZERS												
Chili Chicken Chunks (page 45)	128	19	9	1	0.3	43	116	1	22	1	808	11
Crabby Potatoes (page 47)	83	4	11	3	0.6	12	69	1	33	0.5	65	10
Crostini with Fresh Tomatoes (page 43)	188	5	31	5	0.6	0.5	282	2	31	2	850	13
Hummus with Pita Crisps (page 44)	175	6	32	3	0.3	0	354	4	43	2	66	4
Jicama & Fresh Fruit Platter (page 43)	88	2	21	0.6	0	0	155	3	47	0.6	1,130	71
Lamb Shish Kebabs (page 45)	238	25	19	7	2	76	164	0	12	3	24	1
Mushroom Pâté (page 38)	99	4	16	3	2	7	149	3	32	1	2,216	3
Shrimp with Tart Dipping Sauce (page 47)	57	10	1	0.8	0.2	70	69	0.2	29	1	304	4
Texas Caviar (page 38)	104	7	19	0.4	0.1	0	130	8	36	3	578	15
Turkey-Broccoli Bundles (page 44)	88	12	4	3	1	27	62	0.8	87	0.8	512	26
SNACKS (pages 40–41)												
Curried Spinach Dip	12	2	1	0.2	0.1	0.8	47	0.2	17	0.2	562	2
Dry-roasted Potato Chips	91	2	20	0.3	0	0	7	2	8	0.9	0	22
Garlic-Herb Popcorn	43	1	7	1	0.2	0	12	0*	16	0.7	89	0.2
Salsa Fresca	11	0.1	0.8	0.9	0.1	0	1	0.2	2	0.1	155	4
Salsa Verde	4	0.2	0.6	0.1	0	0	1	0	1	0	46	1

Recipe	Calories	Protein (g)	Carbs. (g)	Total Fat (g)	Sat. Fat (g)	Chol. (mg)	Sodium (mg)	Fiber (g)	Calcium (mg)	Iron (mg)	Vit. A (IU)	Vit. C (mg)
Sweet & Sour Onion Spread	19	0.7	2	0.9	0.1	0.1	6	0.3	19	0.1	0.5	2
Water-crisped Tortilla Chips	100	3	19	2	0	0	80	2	63	2	0	0.2
SOUPS												
Caribbean Corn Chowder (page 57)	159	6	26	5	0.9	0	67	4	19	2	2,259	135
Clear Vegetable Soup (page 204)	79	3	15	2	0	0	16	2	19	1	1,994	95
Cold Cucumber & Dill Bisque (page 50)	132	17	12	2	0.8	114	196	1	180	3	39	22
Cool Scallop Soup (page 50)	178	24	17	2	0.7	41	240	3	173	1	1,218	32
Couscous Soup (page 207)	59	2	12	0.2	0	0	7	0	6	0.2	73	1
Creamy Garbanzo Soup with Barley (page 60)	322	12	46	11	1	0	485**	5	123	4	792	13
Green & Gold Melon Soup (page 56)	115	2	29	0.5	0	0	27	2	23	0.4	3,749	82
Jamaican Black Bean & Rice Soup (page 60)	280	15	45	5	1	2	46	8	131	4	380	6
Lemony Lentil Soup (page 61)	295	19	41	7	1	0	303	6	90	8	3,505	43
Mexican Albondigas Soup (page 61)	265	18	29	9	2	33	266	6	128	5	31,277	40
Roasted Eggplant Soup (page 57)	71	4	13	1	0.4	0	49	3	57	2	1,779	60
Shrimp & Rice Chowder (page 63)	282	23	31	7	1	148	292	3	61	5	877	35
Sweet Potato & Carrot Soup (page 58)	234	8	45	3	0.7	0	447	8	65	3	55,453	40
Tortellini & Chicken Soup (page 63)	201	19	21	4	0.8	37	247	1*	96	4	2,866	34
White Gazpacho (page 56)	111	8	14	3	1	7	111	2	241	1	1,422	20
Winter Minestrone (page 58)	241	9	41	5	0.8	0	314**	8	61	3	14,423	32
SANDWICHES (pages 52–54)												
Chinese Chicken Sandwiches	282	32	28	5	0.9	68	648	4	75	3	26	2
Cottage Cheese & Tomato Breakfast Stack	118	11	16	2	0.8	5	355	2	65	1	682	10
Dilly Salmon on Dark Rye	183	20	15	5	2	31	527	2	251	0.9	58	4
Eggplant, Radish & Cucumber Sandwiches	194	7	30	7	1	1	244	6	107	2	69	16
Greek Salad Pockets	262	9	38	10	3	13	571	6	129	3	1,849	27
Spiced Lentil Pockets	488	23	69	15	2	1	397	10	182	7	957	12
Summer Sandwich	277	10	36	11	2	13	591	3	86	4	5,057	160
Vegetable Taco Roll-ups	329	13	57	6	3	15	731	6	229	3	2,886	168

*Some fiber data not available; actual fiber content may be higher.

**Sodium data doesn't account for draining beans; actual sodium content may be lower.

Recipe	Calories	Protein (g)	Carbs. (g)	Total Fat (g)	Sat. Fat (g)	Chol. (mg)	Sodium (mg)	Fiber (g)	Calcium (mg)	Iron (mg)	Vit. A (IU)	Vit. C (mg)
SALADS												
Bulgur & Vegetables (page 72)	327	8	53	10	1	0	316	10	55	3	1,028	25
Chef's Salad with Fruit (page 74)	286	12	40	11	3	21	110	7	211	3	16,497	76
Chicken & Pears (page 76)	350	35	44	4	1	91	76	6	55	2	634	13
Corn & Black Bean Salad (page 69)	183	8	29	5	0.7	0	388**	5	41	2	662	15
Crab & Cucumber Salad (page 79)	124	18	9	2	0.2	85	243	1	109	1	239	10
Jicama & Apples (page 68)	40	0.6	10	0.2	0	0	5	1	9	0.3	16	10
Mixed Greens (page 71)	32	0.8	2	2	0.3	0	31	0.8	20	0.4	827	9
Napa Cabbage Slaw (page 66)	76	2	18	0.3	0.1	0	44	4	71	0.7	15,868	24
Orange-Onion Salad (page 68)	117	2	21	4	0.5	0	5	3*	32	0.4	972	42
Orzo with Spinach & Pine Nuts (page 73)	226	8	32	7	3	13	177	2	108	2	1,657	13
Panzanella (page 79)	239	16	30	7	1	15	367	5	111	4	1,417	24
Pepper, Pasta & Orange Salad (page 74)	331	8	53	11	1	0	5	5	71	3	7,285	275
Potato & Avocado Salad (page 72)	185	4	37	3	0.4	0	20	4	11	2	649	46
Red & Yellow Pepper Salad (page 69)	59	1	10	2	0.3	0	4	2	27	1	2,139	96
Spinach Salad (page 66)	255	10	38	8	3	11	471	5	192	5	8,722	114
Turkey & Rice Salad (page 76)	290	30	20	9	2	64	81	1	36	2	306	10
Tuscan Bean Salad (page 73)	215	8	31	8	1	0	434**	9	44	2	849	29
DRESSINGS (page 77)												
Creamy Blue Cheese	13	0.7	0.9	0.7	0.3	1	28	0	23	0	36	0.6
Honey-Yogurt Dressing	14	0.6	3	0.2	0.1	0.7	8	0	22	0	9	0.9
Italian Dressing	8	0	0.7	0.6	0.1	0	43	0	4	0.1	60	2
Orange-Basil Vinaigrette	15	0.1	2	0.7	0.1	0	19	0	6	0.1	49	8
Spicy French Dressing	25	0.1	4	0.9	0.1	0	100	0.1	3	0.1	39	0.7
MEATS												
Chayote with Spiced Lamb Filling (page 93)	199	19	23	5	1	50	281	2*	61	3	796	33
Chile Beef Stir-fry (page 82)	262	25	12	13	4	68	226	1	68	3	2,256	29
Cool Pork with Zucchini & Wheat Berries (page 90)	408	35	42	12	3	72	531	0.9*	53	5	1,009	36
Curry Beef in Lettuce (page 82)	197	22	17	4	1	49	118	3	27	4	508	17

Recipe	Calories	Protein (g)	Carbs. (g)	Total Fat (g)	Sat. Fat (g)	Chol. (mg)	Sodium (mg)	Fiber (g)	Calcium (mg)	Iron (mg)	Vit. A (IU)	Vit. C (mg)
Dilled Lamb Stew (page 92)	306	29	32	7	2	75	149	7	131	4	42,914	41
Grilled Orange-Coriander Steak (page 87)	190	28	6	6	2	71	53	0.4	24	3	50	16
Italian Pork Stew with Polenta (page 87)	399	31	49	8	2	77	321	5	71	5	1,288	30
Lamb Chops with Papaya Chutney (page 92)	338	21	47	9	3	51	98	3	192	3	1,996	65
Mediterranean Veal Ragout (page 95)	203	28	14	4	1	89	236	5	54	3	1,300	26
New Pot Roast (page 24)	351	38	25	11	4	94	290	4	37	5	17,532	25
Oregon Spring Stew (page 93)	298	28	24	10	3	71	120	6	59	4	16,268	26
Souvlaki in Pitas (page 85)	560	42	82	8	2	70	831	10	172	7	2,082	30
Spicy Pork Tenderloins (page 90)	201	26	12	5	2	84	283	0	18	2	42	0.6
Sweet & Sour Flank Steak (page 85)	254	22	14	12	5	58	473	0	9	2	0	0.3
Veal Curry with Fruit (page 95)	495	30	70	12	3	93	217	6	107	3	10,546	14
LEAN MARINADES & SAUCES (pages 88–89)												
Barbecue Stir-fry Sauce	46	0.6	11	0.3	0	0	86	0	10	0.3	0.2	0.5
Fajita Marinade	4	0.1	0.9	0.1	0	0	2	0	6	0.2	4	1
Ginger-Sherry Stir-fry Sauce	31	0.9	6	0.2	0.1	0	310	0	7	0.4	68	0.6
Lemon-Soy Marinade	14	0.9	3	0.1	0	0	454	0	7	0.3	2	4
Mustard-Tarragon Sauce	9	0.1	2	0.3	0	0	76	0	2	0.1	8	0
Orange-Anise Marinade	17	0.3	4	0.1	0	0	1	0.1	6	0.2	24	12
Rosemary-Pear Stir-fry Sauce	43	0.1	11	0	0	0	3	0.5	8	0.3	10	0.8
Thyme Sauce	8	0.4	1	0.3	0.1	0	9	0	7	0.6	14	0
Wine–Blue Cheese Sauce	24	1	2	1	0.8	3	67	0	23	0.1	30	0
POULTRY												
Apricot-Mustard Chicken (page 104)	380	41	46	3	0.7	86	352	0.4*	29	3	892	36
Baked Chicken with Pears (page 103)	259	34	25	2	0.5	86	97	2	25	1	46	6
Chicken Enchilada Bake (page 105)	254	19	28	8	2	39	293	4	186	3	1,752	29
Chicken in a Squash Shell (page 103)	282	29	30	6	0.9	66	396	7	88	3	2,074	58
Chicken-on-a-Stick with Couscous (page 101)	595	50	65	14	3	91	200	0.3*	211	3	749	12
Chicken Yakitori (page 98)	295	39	16	9	1	86	332	3	95	4	111	8
Chili-Citrus Rabbit (page 110)	417	35	41	12	3	90	185	4	75	3	300	63

Some fiber data not available; actual fiber content may be higher.
**Sodium data doesn't account for draining beans; actual sodium content may be lower.

Recipe	Calories	Protein (g)	Carbs. (g)	Total Fat (g)	Sat. Fat (g)	Chol. (mg)	Sodium (mg)	Fiber (g)	Calcium (mg)	Iron (mg)	Vit. A (IU)	Vit. C (mg)
Cool Spiced Chicken (page 105)	191	28	8	4	1	89	102	0.6	46	2	267	29
Grilled Turkey with Peaches (page 106)	310	42	28	3	0.9	108	180	2	47	3	1,385	15
Honeyed Chicken (page 101)	229	35	12	4	0.7	86	398	0	47	2	32	2
Oven-fried Chicken (page 98)	204	35	8	2	0.5	86	404	0.7	39	2	429	3
Raspberry-glazed Turkey Tenderloins (page 106)	241	34	18	3	0.7	90	358	0	25	2	7	4
Sake-steamed Chicken (page 104)	312	39	31	3	0.5	86	726	3	103	3	2,245	23
Summer Turkey Stir-fry (page 108)	384	33	49	6	1	70	416	11	71	4	24,024	19
Turkey & Corn Chili (page 108)	375	37	39	9	2	64	794**	8	117	6	2,554	76
Turkey & Eggplant Parmigiana (page 110)	242	19	17	11	4	43	239	4	246	2	1,545	21
Turkey Burgers with Tomato Salad (page 109)	512	36	59	15	4	60	545	7	326	5	1,183	34
White Wine Turkey Loaf (page 109)	207	19	10	10	3	46	134	2	40	3	1,064	40
SEAFOOD												
Ahi Steaks with Bacon (page 120)	248	41	1	8	2	82	453	0	32	2	179	1
Baked Sole & Ratatouille (page 117)	238	31	12	8	2	75	176	3	144	3	3,393	155
Chinese-style Steamed Fish (page 121)	170	32	2	3	0.6	60	254	0.3	24	1	1,070	6
Clam Paella for Two (page 127)	450	29	61	9	1	61	312	2	135	29	2,021	24
Cool Salmon with Radish Tartar (page 118)	515	49	48	14	3	113	274	7	184	5	2,531	72
Curried Fish & Rice (page 118)	459	41	44	13	3	75	185	5	241	3	6,496	121
Dilled Roughy in Parchment (page 123)	283	21	19	14	0.6	28	97	0.1	14	0.8	1,190	25
Fish Pot-au-Feu (page 114)	324	37	35	4	0.8	73	216	5	117	5	24,116	30
Greek-style Shrimp on Zucchini (page 129)	209	23	16	6	2	148	442	3	186	4	11,300	36
Halibut with Tomatoes & Dill (page 114)	236	37	7	6	0.9	54	103	2	101	2	2,150	28
Mussels Provençal (page 128)	159	13	15	5	0.8	26	569	3	101	6	1,370	36
Oyster Jambalaya (page 127)	388	20	59	8	2	66	573	5	104	12	2,919	127
San Francisco-style Cioppino (page 128)	296	38	18	8	1	167	664	3	156	8	2,204	77

Recipe	Calories	Protein (g)	Carbs. (g)	Total Fat (g)	Sat. Fat (g)	Chol. (mg)	Sodium (mg)	Fiber (g)	Calcium (mg)	Iron (mg)	Vit. A (IU)	Vit. C (mg)
Shellfish Couscous (page 123)	484	30	66	10	2	94	477	2*	98	3	791	49
Shrimp Fajitas (page 131)	220	17	28	4	0.6	94	285	2	120	3	416	83
Simmered Cod & Vegetables (page 117)	276	26	38	2	0.1	49	672	3*	56	2	867	65
Soft-shell Crab with Ginger (page 131)	122	22	3	2	0.2	108	306	0.1	115	1	208	2
Steeped Shrimp with Artichokes (page 201)	202	22	25	3	0.4	140	247	7	124	5	434	16
Stir-fried Scallops & Asparagus (page 129)	378	19	55	9	1	19	149	2	44	2	540	20
Stuffed Trout (page 121)	363	38	18	14	2	100	279	1	96	4	1,985	52
Swordfish with Mushrooms (page 120)	210	31	4	7	2	59	332	1	43	2	1,407	18

MICROWAVED SEAFOOD (page 124)

Recipe	Calories	Protein (g)	Carbs. (g)	Total Fat (g)	Sat. Fat (g)	Chol. (mg)	Sodium (mg)	Fiber (g)	Calcium (mg)	Iron (mg)	Vit. A (IU)	Vit. C (mg)
Fennel-seasoned Salmon with Vegetables	388	43	23	13	2	109	97	3	40	3	629	38
Sea Bass with Ginger	181	32	3	3	0.9	70	517	0	22	0.8	330	8
Sole Fillets with Capers	105	21	0.3	1	0.3	54	111	0	23	0.4	180	3

PASTA

Recipe	Calories	Protein (g)	Carbs. (g)	Total Fat (g)	Sat. Fat (g)	Chol. (mg)	Sodium (mg)	Fiber (g)	Calcium (mg)	Iron (mg)	Vit. A (IU)	Vit. C (mg)
Chilled Oriental Pasta with Shrimp (page 147)	487	35	59	14	2	168	647	9	166	6	2,921	31
Cool Pasta Shells with Scallops (page 147)	402	26	47	13	2	30	182	2*	170	5	3,162	91
Farfalle with Fresh Tomatoes & Basil (page 134)	382	13	72	5	0.7	0	16	3	151	6	1,727	22
Noodles with Cabbage & Gruyère (page 144)	446	25	72	9	4	32	696	13	249	5	347	71
Orecchiette with Spinach & Garlic (page 141)	434	14	68	12	2	0	78	4	108	6	5,808	25
Pasta with Beans (page 141)	523	21	98	6	0.8	0	1,069**	15	170	7	13,520	46
Pasta with Parsley-Lemon Pesto (page 138)	487	18	71	14	4	12	289	3	255	5	1,432	25
Penne with Broccoli & Ricotta (page 134)	539	25	75	16	6	29	147	2*	322	5	2,980	83
Perciatelli with Turkey Marinara (page 144)	497	25	73	13	3	33	809	7	129	7	9,635	86
Seafood Linguine (page 145)	342	25	35	11	2	147	410	0.5*	78	6	1,198	11
Spinach & Tofu Manicotti (page 142)	293	14	43	9	2	5	672	5	184	4	5,710	64
Summertime Pasta Alfresco (page 140)	283	11	56	2	0.7	2	97	4	142	5	2,649	64
Tortellini & Peas in Creamy Lemon Sauce (page 145)	333	18	46	9	2	45	424	1*	314	3	700	26
Vegetable Lasagne (page 142)	458	31	53	16	6	28	505	8	558	12	24,036	57

*Some fiber data not available; actual fiber content may be higher.
**Sodium data doesn't account for draining beans; actual sodium content may be lower.

Recipe	Calories	Protein (g)	Carbs. (g)	Total Fat (g)	Sat. Fat (g)	Chol. (mg)	Sodium (mg)	Fiber (g)	Calcium (mg)	Iron (mg)	Vit. A (IU)	Vit. C (mg)
Vermicelli with Vegetable Sauce (page 138)	466	15	83	9	1	0	355	6	76	6	2,494	71
Winter Garden Pasta (page 140)	455	16	82	8	1	0	171	5*	72	7	3,646	47
GRAINS & LEGUMES												
Baked Lemon Rice (page 155)	213	5	39	4	0.7	0	64	0.6	20	3	431	6
Barley-Onion Pilaf (page 157)	194	5	33	5	0.9	0	60	6	22	1	125	3
Black Bean Tacos (page 162)	484	19	80	10	2	6	858	9	285	5	5,085	92
Brown Rice & Beans (page 161)	227	11	42	3	0.5	0.6	269**	7	135	4	1,049	19
California Hoppin' John (page 162)	292	13	45	8	1	0	293	12	64	5	1,731	69
Cannellini with Kale (page 158)	207	12	32	5	1	5	601**	14	146	3	6,196	91
Confetti Wild Rice (page 156)	205	8	38	3	0.4	0	28	3	45	2	3,991	114
Fruited Rice Pilaf (page 150)	260	6	47	6	1	0	37	3	18	2	507	0.4
Grits Cake with Corn & Asparagus (page 158)	200	9	28	6	3	17	121	2	137	1	624	15
Kasha with Fruit (page 155)	318	6	50	13	2	0	18	3*	34	2	1,290	15
Lebanese Lentils with Bulgur (page 161)	318	15	47	10	2	53	310	11	80	5	341	66
Quinoa with Mushrooms & Broccoli (page 157)	218	9	33	7	1	0	95	1*	55	5	1,174	49
Saffron Risotto (page 150)	296	8	43	10	2	5	195	0.3*	92	3	160	2
Spiced Bulgur with Apple (page 156)	201	5	34	6	0.9	0	22	6	22	1	20	4
VEGETABLES												
Burgundy-braised Cabbage (page 171)	202	3	41	4	0.7	0	72	4	102	2	199	72
Gingered Asparagus (page 172)	37	2	3	2	0.4	0	4	0.6	15	0.4	541	23
Green Bean & Tomato Casserole (page 171)	95	4	15	3	0.7	1	87	4	82	2	1,508	30
Lemon-Garlic Swiss Chard (page 172)	55	3	7	3	0.3	0	334	0*	82	3	5,172	54
Mashed Potatoes & Broccoli (page 173)	258	7	42	8	1	1	127	6	61	2	1,706	116
Oven Ratatouille (page 166)	100	4	18	3	0.4	0	17	4	104	3	5,232	148
Potato & Carrot Oven-fries (page 175)	341	7	64	8	0.9	0	97	11	61	3	63,853	56
Roasted Red & Yellow Potatoes (page 175)	315	5	58	7	1	0	27	7	35	2	22,772	52

Recipe	Calories	Protein (g)	Carbs. (g)	Total Fat (g)	Sat. Fat (g)	Chol. (mg)	Sodium (mg)	Fiber (g)	Calcium (mg)	Iron (mg)	Vit. A (IU)	Vit. C (mg)
Stuffed Micro Potato (page 207)	364	33	51	3	1	9	960	5	175	3	4,845	60
Sweet & Bitter Mustard Greens (page 173)	99	2	19	3	0.4	0	19	2	73	1	2,823	40
Vegetable Curry Stir-fry (page 166)	280	9	48	7	0.8	0	300**	8	84	4	10,524	60
SEASONINGS & VINEGARS (pages 168–169)												
Barbecue Seasoning Mix	13	0.3	3	0.4	0	0	1	0	71	2	238	1
Italian Seasoning Mix	14	0.5	3	0.3	0	0	1	0	71	2	275	1
Mexican Seasoning Mix	15	0.6	3	0.6	0	0	21	0.6	40	2	801	2
Scandinavian Seasoning Mix	10	0.4	2	0.1	0	0	3	0	29	0.6	1	3
Basil-Oregano-Peppercorn Vinegar	2	0	0.5	0	0	0	0	0	0.6	0	2	0
Garlic–Green Onion Vinegar	2	0	0.5	0	0	0	0	0	0.4	0	13	0.2
Herb Vinegar	2	0	0.5	0	0	0	0	0	0.1	0	0.1	0
Rose Petal Vinegar	2	0	0.5	0	0	0	0	0	0.2	0	5	0.1
Spicy Chile Vinegar	3	0	0.6	0	0	0	0	0	0.6	0	29	0.1
BREADS												
Applesauce Raisin Bread (page 181)	234	4	43	6	0.8	18	115	2	59	2	44	8
Apricot–Oat Bran Scones (page 182)	121	3	20	3	2	19	187	2	66	2	672	0.2
Bulgur Wheat Rolls (page 178)	215	6	40	3	0.9	21	131	2	36	2	130	0.2
Cornmeal-Oat Muffins (page 180)	207	5	34	6	0.9	19	283	1	150	2	87	0.3
Dilled Bread (page 178)	180	6	36	1	0.5	3	130	3	61	2	75	0.3
Herb-Cheese Muffins (page 181)	145	5	22	4	1	22	157	2	100	1	224	21
Irish Soda Bread (page 182)	263	8	52	4	2	10	452	5	84	2	138	1
Mini-Calzones (page 180)	38	2	6	1	0.2	1	88	0.8	14	0.5	477	2
DESSERTS												
Angel Food Cake (page 192)	128	4	27	0.1	0	0	146	0	4	0.6	0	0
Baked Apples & Figs with Cassis (page 195)	172	0.9	40	3	0.4	0	24	2*	38	0.5	202	9
Crazy Cocoa Cake (page 193)	264	3	44	9	1	0	240	1	7	1	0.4	0
Creamy Peach Yogurt Pie (page 191)	255	7	43	7	5	24	166	1	113	0.3	815	6
Lowfat Cheesecake (page 26)	211	8	31	6	0.9	23	292	2	114	0.8	216	7
Minted Poached Pears (page 186)	229	1	53	0.8	0	0	2	4	49	0.9	41	26
Oatie Peach Crumble (page 192)	314	3	59	8	1	0	93	4	25	1	1,229	12

*Some fiber data not available; actual fiber content may be higher.

**Sodium data doesn't account for draining beans; actual sodium content may be lower.

Recipe	Calories	Protein (g)	Carbs. (g)	Total Fat (g)	Sat. Fat (g)	Chol. (mg)	Sodium (mg)	Fiber (g)	Calcium (mg)	Iron (mg)	Vit. A (IU)	Vit. C (mg)
Oatmeal Raisin Cookies (page 199)	79	2	13	3	0.3	0.1	23	0.9	12	0.6	11	0.1
Old-fashioned Apple Cake (page 193)	279	4	52	7	0.9	14	190	2	72	1	52	3
Quick Macaroons (page 199)	67	1	12	2	2	0	30	0.4	1	0.1	0.1	0.1
Sherry-Plum Crisp (page 191)	333	4	63	9	1	0	122	5	30	2	1,182	16
Spiced Pumpkin Roll (page 195)	177	4	37	2	0.4	48	123	0.4	88	0.8	2,645	0.6
Wine & Berry Compote (page 186)	134	0.8	34	0.4	0	0	7	3	18	0.5	85	34
FRESH FRUIT FINALES (pages 188–189)												
Cantaloupe in Raspberry Purée	131	2	28	0.6	0	0	14	3	27	0.6	4,634	71
Frosted Corinth Grapes	247	2	64	0.5	0.2	0	17	0*	22	0.5	157	6
Island Fruit Platter	161	2	41	0.8	0.1	0	12	3	37	0.6	3,402	106
Oranges in Ginger Champagne	188	0.7	33	0.2	0	0	7	2	54	1	172	39
Papaya Snow	40	0.6	10	0.1	0	0	3	0.9	26	0.1	1,921	61
Ricotta-Pear Parfaits	283	13	38	9	5	34	144	4	337	0.9	544	12
Strawberries with Gingered Vanilla Yogurt	121	5	23	2	0.7	4	58	4	168	0.7	89	91
BEVERAGES (pages 196–197)												
Banana-Citrus Coolers	102	0.3	26	0.2	0.1	0	6	0.5	19	0.4	106	51
Chilled Apple-Ginger Spritzers	177	0.3	14	0.1	0	0	16	0.1	32	1	2	26
Citrus Spritzers	72	0.4	18	0.1	0	0	7	0.1	6	0.1	100	37
Frozen Cappuccino	68	4	7	2	1	10	68	0	156	2	250	1
Fruit Smoothies	121	8	20	1	0.6	5	102	0.4*	271	0.5	110	19
Fruit Sorbet Sodas	110	0.5	28	0.1	0	0	11	0	8	0.5	6	4
Ginger-Peach Smoothies	106	4	21	1	0.7	5	131	0.6	151	0.7	235	5
Steaming Honey-spiced Milk	200	10	28	6	4	23	148	0	365	0.4	603	3
Warm Apricot Jewel	155	1	40	0.3	0	0	9	2	22	1	3,592	123

*Some fiber data not available; actual fiber content may be higher.

**Sodium data doesn't account for draining beans; actual sodium content may be lower.

■ INDEX

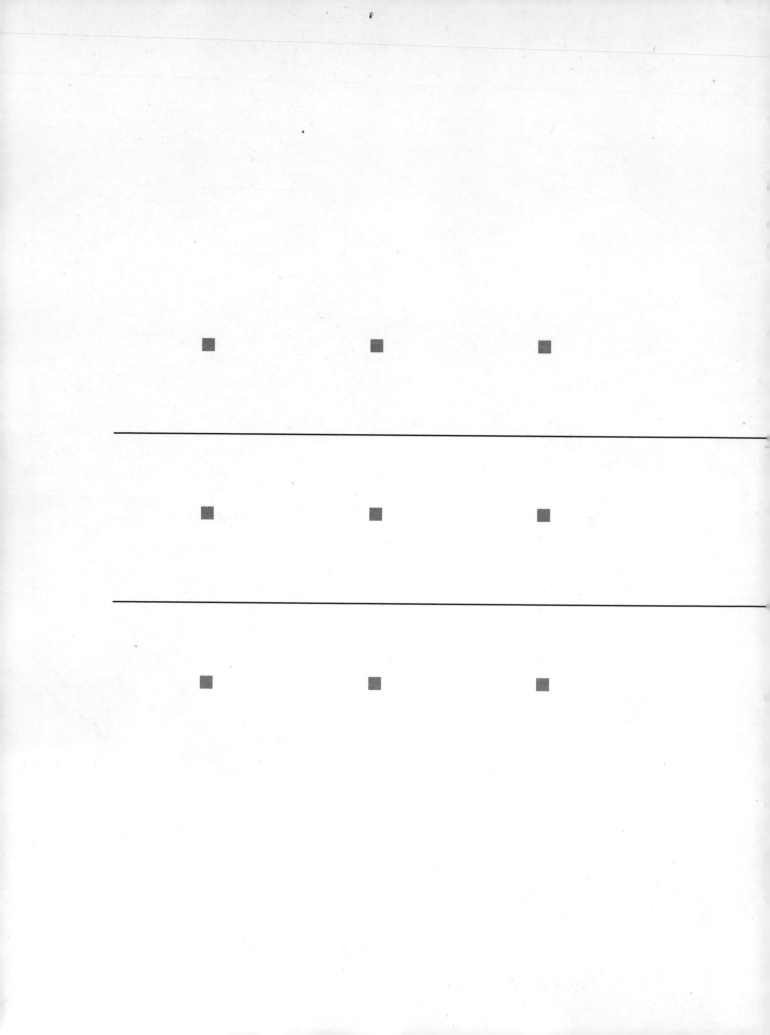